The SPIRITUAL EVOLUTION *of* NATIONS

Astrology Eclipses, Stars & Planet Transits.

Leoni Hodgson

About the Author

Leoni Hodgson works professionally as a practitioner and teacher in several specialist areas in the esoteric arts - Astrology (DMNZAS - Diploma Member of the NZ Astrological Society 1982, and the PMAFA - Professional Member of the American Federation of Astrologers 1983), Esoteric Psychology (MA in Esoteric Psychology and Ph.D. in Esoteric Philosophy), Raja Yoga and Esoteric Healing (INEH Certificate).

About this Book

The book was inspired by information that came to light when Covid-19 was researched and possible charts related to its origins. Eclipses were studied, for the year before the disease was publicised on December 2019. Of these, the last eclipse before the reporting - a partial lunar eclipse on 16 July 2019, seemed the most significant and powerful. It "told" the story of the origins of the disease and its lethal effect.

This led to an investigation of the Spanish Flu and the Bubonic Plague that decimated millions in the Middle Ages. Eclipses for these pandemics were studied. The investigation extended out into other natural disasters in the past and also the Great Wars of the 20th Century.

A common theme emerged.

> Firstly, preceding the event, at least two of the outer planets (Saturn, Uranus, Neptune or Pluto), by transit; were forming a "hard" aspect with each other. Of these, the conjunctions, squares or oppositions between Saturn and Pluto were most significant and most numerous.

> Secondly, an eclipse preceding the event "hit" these transiting outer planets. The eclipse Sun and Moon positions often connected into the planets by conjunction, square or opposition.

In the book I call these configurations - transit outer planets in aspect to each other, and a connecting eclipse - "evolutionary patterns." The impact of the forces released by the planets at the time of an eclipse, and the catastrophes they caused; these changed the course of history, of evolution.

This is what I have attempted to demonstrate in this book.

Leoni Hodgson

Acknowledgments

This book is dedicated to the world service work of the Tibetan Master Djwhal Khul; particularly in the field of Esoteric Astrology.

Loving thanks to my husband Jim Hodgson who supports me so generously in all my endeavours. Many thanks also to my friends Jeanni Monks and Marion Child for their ongoing support and assistance.

Other Books Written by the Author

Journey of the Soul.
A Handbook for Esoteric Psychology and Astrology.
Published 2018.

Medical Astrology.
Discover the Psychology of Disease using Triangles.
Published February 2018.

Astrology of Spirit, Soul and Body.
A Handbook for Esoteric Astrology.
Published November 2018.

Learn Astrology.
A Guide for Absolute Beginners.
Published February 2020.

Foreword

It is wonderful to have this opportunity to write this foreword to Leoni Hodgson's excellent and ground-breaking new book on 30 of the world nations, "The SPIRITUAL EVOLUTION of NATIONS." The analysis of national or Mundane Astrology is not as popular or widespread as some of the other fields in this great science, however, Leoni Hodgson's book goes a long way to fill that void.

This book is pioneering in that it brings in the spiritual element and makes a comparison between the manner in which individual souls evolve and that of nations. Just as each individual soul is on a journey from ignorance to enlightenment, so are nations evolving along this same process.

As all astrologers know, the future we are evolving into is the Great Age of Aquarius. Current evolution is forcing us to move on from the "I am first and best" attitudes of lower Leo consciousness, to the group-sharing humanitarian principles of the Aquarian Age. In Leoni's analysis and examination of the nations of the world, an enlightening discovery is made of how these nations are all moving away from the "me first and best approach", to "how can we all work together to make the world a better place?" It is exciting to witness that the world en masse is taking on an Aquarian influence.

In these modern times, the advanced nations in the world may appear to be somewhat more "refined", "cultured" and Aquarian in their dealings with other nations of the world. However, if we go back 100 years or so we will find that things were very different. Individual standards have certainly changed/ evolved which are reflected in the national development of countries today. These evolving changes are carefully explored and scrutinised in this book, creating much hope for the future of our planet.

Another pioneering aspect of this book, is that it gives the "permanent" astrology signs for the soul and personality aspects of a nation. So even when a nation goes through a change or rebirth and acquires a new national chart; these signs remain constant. This information is obtained from the work of the eastern Master Djwhal Khul, in Alice Bailey's book "The Destiny of the Nations." Khul had access to ancient writings archived in Buddhist and Vedic spiritual temples. For those who work with the rays, he also gave the rays that rule 11 nations. This information is merged seamlessly into this book so that it will be easy for readers to understand.

A unique aspect of the "The Spiritual Evolution of Nations," which is at the core of the way the progression of nations has been followed, is how Leoni has linked together PLANET TRANSITS, ECLIPSES and STARS. Leoni calls these combined forces 'CHANGE AGENTS of EVOLUTION'. Eclipse charts for catastrophic events on earth have been compared to national charts and the results are presented in the book for readers to ponder over.

What I found fascinating in this book, is Leoni's analysis and description of how fixed stars and the eclipse charts around each nation evoked a cocktail of forces which changed the direction in which nations were travelling, especially with regard to how they behaved and how they evolved!

If you, the reader, are interested in developing your competency to investigate any major event that occurs in the world, then "The Spiritual Evolution of Nations," is for you 'a must read' – and more than that, a definite 'must study'! It will help all astrologers grasp more easily, the philosophy and principles that underlie the progress of nations in the world today; and how to apply them in research.

I believe this book will serve to expand astrological understanding and skills by encouraging the reader to conduct further independent examination into the field of each nation's soul and spiritual evolvement into the Age of Aquarius.

How grateful I am to Leoni for her incredible research and writing of this book. Bless you Leoni! This book is an amazing gift to humanity at this historical time of great change on our planet earth. To you reading this book, greetings and heart-felt blessings for the illuminating journey that lies ahead of you.

Namaste & Blessings, Jeanni Monks

Active committee member of QFA (Queensland Federation of Astrologers); APA (Association of Professional Astrologers) and an examiner on the FAA Examination Board. BA Psych.; Master of Science in Esoteric Psych.; Post Grad. Education/Counselling Dip; FAA Practitioner's Diploma.

The SPIRITUAL EVOLUTION *of* NATIONS

Astrology Eclipses, Stars & Planet Transits.

The world is based on the emergence of ideas, their acceptance, their transformation into ideals, and their eventual superseding by the next imposition of ideas. The major ideas in the world today fall into 5 categories:

1. The ancient and inherited ideas which have controlled the racial life for centuries — aggression for the sake of possession.

2. Those ideas (from the early 20th Century) such as Nazism, Fascism, and Communism. They are alike on one point - The State counts as of importance whilst the individual does not; he can be sacrificed at any time for the good of the State.

3. The idea of democracy in which (supposedly but as yet never factually) the people govern and the government represents the will of the people.

4. The idea of a world state, divided into various great sections. This is the dream of the inclusively-minded few.

5. The idea of a spiritual Hierarchy which will govern the people throughout the world and will embody in itself the best elements of the monarchial, the democratic, the totalitarian and the communistic regimes. The Aquarian Age will see the restitution of this inner and spiritual guidance.

Bailey, Alice A. The Destiny of the Nations, page 8 and 9.

Contents

Chapter 1.
Introduction

It is of major interest for us to know something about the energies and forces which are producing the present international situation and presenting the complex problems with which the United Nations are confronted. In the last analysis, all history is the record of the effects of these energies or radiations as they play upon humanity in its many varying stages of evolutionary development. These stages extend all the way from those of primeval humanity to our modern civilisation; all that has happened is the result of these energies, pouring cyclically through nature and through that part of nature which we call the human kingdom.

Bailey, Alice A. The Destiny of the Nations, page 3.

A. Souls and Personalities

The signs, planets and stars are the agents of evolution. Because our Sun, in its greater 30,000-year cycle, is currently moving into the sign Aquarius; the consciousness of the human race is transitioning from the mass ignorance and materialism of the Piscean Age - to the enlightened wisdom of an Aquarian Age soul or consciousness. Evolution is the force in nature that drives the unfoldment of human consciousness. All human souls in all nations are in this process and this is the reason for the turmoil and trouble on earth. Some retrogressive people want to stay in the past. Others are progressing forwards rapidly. The signs, planets and stars are simply the agents of nature that force us to keep moving forwards.

Men have souls and so do nations.

Man's nature is dual. His higher nature is the soul, the force of love, wisdom and intelligent action that is continually trying to make its presence felt through the personality or lower self. The soul of a nation is formed by the individuals in the nation who are operating at this higher level, who are demonstrating the altruistic and inclusive qualities of the Aquarian Age.

Likewise, men have selfish egos or personalities - and so do nations.

A nation's personality is formed by those who are still Piscean in consciousness - the mass ignorant, average, selfish and greedy people operating as a collective. A nation's personality dominates the national consciousness for as long as the representatives of these people control the avenues of power. When people start fighting against their dictators or oppressive governments, they are being driven by the power of the nation's soul, which always cries out for freedom.

A battle is continually being waged between a nation's soul and personality.

When the soul is more dominant, those who represent its interests - the more spiritually advanced souls in the nation; they dominate the nation's narrative for that world period. They inspire the masses to rise up and "be their better self," to merge their efforts to help move the nation to a better and higher place. Abraham Lincoln was such a man - he was our prototype for the Aquarian Age man.

> Abraham Lincoln, coming forth from the very soul of a people, and introducing and transmitting racial (Aquarian) quality. [1]

Lincoln urged the people to repudiate the evil of slavery, most followed and they did. Another example is Winston Churchill. He urged the people of the United Kingdom to stand up to the evil of the Nazis. They did and with the help of the Allied nations, WWII was won.

However, when the personality of a nation is more dominant, dictators, autocrats and plutocrats assume leadership; powerful individuals who convince those susceptible to their messages that they care about them (in words) when they clearly do not (in their actions).

> The soul and those who are soul-expressive are always inclusive. The personality and those who are driven by greed and self-interest, are always in it for themselves.

---

1 Bailey, Alice A. *Externalisation of the Hierarchy*, 298.

They give themselves permission to harm or use others to promote their own interests.

For example, Adolf Hitler. He convinced many Germans that because they were a "Master Race" and had been unjustly treated in WWI, they had a right to kill, maim and take what belonged to others to assume their rightful dominance in the world.

Through history, sometimes the soul of a nation will be stronger, but in most cases, the personality aspect continues to dominate. But as we move deeper into the Aquarian Age the periods when a nation's soul dominates the national consciousness will gradually get longer and longer.

The forces of planet transits, eclipses and stars drive evolution.

The forces of Nature - of God if you will, are carried to earth and into humanity, by the planets and stars. All planets and stars carry higher spiritual forces that are designed to drive man along the Path of Evolution and to his higher destiny.

When the outer planets - Saturn, Uranus, Neptune and Pluto team up together by conjunction, square or opposition; they are change-agents of evolution. They bring challenging events that are designed to test the moral character of the nation and to break up and remove decaying structures that are impeding the evolution of its soul.

When eclipses coincide with these major transits, upheavals happen on earth. When stars add their power, major disasters, pandemics and wars are triggered. *These are the catalysts that drive evolutionary progress and change.*

Whatever is going on in humanity at any point in history, whenever there are blocks and obstacles to the higher and refreshing energies of freedom and fairness; the planets mirror these then set about destroying them. In this manner, the souls of individuals and nations, are continuously being refreshed and energised with the healing and inspirational forces of Deity; while simultaneously, the ego is continually being checked and rebuked and taught a lesson by the teachers and monitors of the solar system.

In the aftermath of catastrophes, there is always a reassessment period, an opportunity is provided to do a reset and adjustment in an attempt to make sense of the carnage that has occurred and to avoid a similar occurrence in the future. In such periods, decisions are made for future actions. Depending upon the leaders of the nation and where they are on the Path of Evolution, such decisions will either promote the soul advancement of the nation because they focus on the well-being of the whole community - or selfish decisions will be made to benefit a privileged few.

In summary.

All nations are evolving, are moving away from being closed and selfish communities, to those that are more inclusive and open and that honour human rights for all. The spiritual maturity of each nation can be gauged by assessing where it generally stands in this process.

Are dictators and autocrats controlling the nation's interests through repression and denial of human rights? Or, is the nation's soul assuming control, through the wiser members in its community? If this is the case, the Aquarian Age civil liberties and opportunities for all are being instituted and not just to benefit the privileged few.

B. The Soul and Personality Rays of Nations.

This book follows the progress of 30 nations that are covered in 'The Destiny of the Nations'. The name on the book is Alice Bailey, but the true author is an eastern Master - Djwhal Khul. This book is highly recommended for all who are interested in this topic.

> For thirteen "major" countries, Khul gave the signs and rays ruling the soul and personality aspects of the nation. [1] For seventeen other nations, he gave the signs only. Khul did not divulge the source of this information. But he had access to ancient writings archived in Eastern Buddhist and Vedic Temples.

Khul analysed how these different forces helped to shape and colour the evolutionary progression of the nations, the ideals they aspired towards and the problems they encountered.

The Seven Rays [2]

The rays are the basic building forces of the universe. They give colour, shape and quality, to every living thing - in all kingdoms, on all levels. *The rays travel across the universe, through the signs and planets, to reach man on earth.* The number, name and colour of each ray gives the clue to each ray force.

The three major rays:

Ray 1 of Will and Power (the red ray).
Ray 2 of Love and Wisdom (the indigo blue ray).
Ray 3 of Active Intelligence (the green ray).

The rays of attribute (derivatives of the major rays) :

Ray 4 of Harmony through Conflict (the yellow ray); a derivative of Ray 2.
Ray 5 of Concrete Science (the orange ray); a derivative of Ray 3.
Ray 6 of Devotion and Idealism (the pale blue ray); a derivative of Ray 2.
Ray 7 of Ceremony, Order and Magic (the violet ray); a derivative of Ray 1.

1. The Soul and Personality Rays of Nations.

Each nation is conditioned and influenced by a Soul Ray and a Personality Ray.

> All of the great nations are controlled by two rays, a personality ray, which is the dominant potent and main controlling factor at this time, and by a soul ray which is sensed only by the disciples and the aspirants of any nation. [3]

The Soul Ray: it determines the manner in which the nation will spontaneously serve and contribute to the greater world good. Citizens who are consciously in touch with their own souls are channels through which the nation's soul can express itself. They promote the greater good of the nation and of the world. The nature of the soul is always inclusive.

---

1 Note that these are not related to the natal charts that we usually work with for each nation.
2 All astrologers should note - the traditional meanings of the signs and planets do not change when the rays are added. Traditional astrology is founded upon the rays, which simply add a deeper level of understanding.
3 Bailey, Alice A. The Destiny of the Nations, 49.

The Personality Ray: it determines the manner in which materialistic and greedy people in the nation will try to seize power and control in the community and in the wider world.

We can gauge how soul-aligned a nation is or is not, by how it treats its citizens and neighbours. Warlike, abusive and aggressive nations are still dominated by the lower traits of the Personality Ray (and their astrology). Such nations also misuse the energies of the soul, twisting these higher forces to evil use.

Chart: the Rays, and the Signs and Planets they express through: [1]

	Rays	Signs	Planets
1	Will and Power	Aries, Leo, Capricorn	Pluto, Vulcan
2	Love and Wisdom	Gemini, Virgo, Pisces	Sun, Jupiter
3	Intelligent Activity	Cancer, Libra, Capricorn	Earth, Saturn
4	Harmony through Conflict	Taurus, Scorpio, Sagittarius	Moon, Mercury
5	Concrete Mind	Leo, Sagittarius, Aquarius	Venus
6	Devotion and Idealism	Virgo, Sagittarius, Pisces	Mars, Neptune
7	Ceremony, Order & Magic	Aries, Cancer, Capricorn	Uranus

Ray 1, Will and Power (the ray of leadership)

Nations with this ray expressive in their natures have the responsibility to bring about the greater good for all nations in the world, and to provide leaders to ensure this is achieved. They think in terms of the whole and not in terms of the part. Abraham Lincoln, Winston Churchill and Franklin D. Roosevelt are human examples of this higher type.

But when the 1st ray is used selfishly, unscrupulous leaders use its power aggressively, through war, to intimidate citizens and other nations. Adolf Hitler and Joseph Stalin are examples of this type. China has a 1st Ray Soul, the forces of which are currently (2021) being misused by its leaders.

The 1st Ray flows through Pluto, Aries, Leo and Capricorn; so, nations with that planet and those signs prominent, also carry the power ray.

- 1st Ray Souls: China and India; also, Geneva, the capital of Switzerland.
- 1st Ray Personalities: Germany and the United Kingdom.

Ray 2, Love and Wisdom (the ray of teachers and healers).

Ray 2 is the ray of the World Teacher, the Christ and also of the Buddha. Consequently, nations expressive of this ray have the task of becoming centres of wisdom and inclusiveness. Their job is to teach the world to live together in peace and harmony. Albert Schweitzer, Carl Jung and Mother Teresa are human examples of this higher type.

The UK has a Ray 2 Soul and it has given wise judicial and political systems to the world. The USA also has a 2nd Ray Soul, and it will carry the baton of peace into the future when its current problems with greed are sorted out. This unpleasant trait (greed) is a consequence of lower Ray 2. Fear is another trait. However, Ray 2 people are very magnetic and these nations can turn on the charm when it suits them to gain benefits and advantages.

---

1 Vulcan is a planet included in the list although it has not yet been discovered by scientists. Djwhal Khul places its orbit between the Sun and Mercury.

The 2nd Ray flows through Jupiter and Gemini, Virgo and Pisces; so nations with that planet and those signs prominent, carry this ray.

- 2nd Ray Souls: the United Kingdom and the United States of America.
- 2nd Ray Personalities: Brazil.

Ray 3, Intelligence - (the ray of thinkers, philosophers).

Nations expressing this ray produce brilliant intellects, people who think intelligently and reason carefully about important matters so that the best solutions to problems can be found. When higher Ray 3 is in expression, advanced thinkers will use their talents to help solve important world problems and to help lift the minds of the race to a more philosophical level. Aristotle, St. Thomas Aquinas, Albert Einstein and Bertrand Russel expressed higher Ray 3.

However, when the Ray 3 Personality dominates, this talent is used in devious and manipulative ways to promote selfish interests. Niccolo Machiavelli's book, 'The Prince', explains how this force can be used to acquire and maintain political power.

The 3rd Ray flows through Saturn, Cancer, Libra and Capricorn; so, nations with that planet and those signs prominent, also carry the intelligence ray.

- 3rd Ray Souls: none given.
- 3rd Ray Personalities: China and France. New York has a 3rd Ray Personality.

Ray 4, Harmony, Conflict and Beauty - (the ray of harmonisers and artists).

This is the ray of conflict, and nations that have it in their makeup seem to grow through constant conflict and war. Look at the histories of the nations listed below.

But the 4th Ray is also the ray of beauty and it produces the most brilliant artists. Germany may have initiated two World Wars, but it also produced classical music giants such as Wagner, Bach, Beethoven and Brahms to name a few; evidence that the soul of the nation did manage to express itself through the arts if not through politics.

The 4th Ray flows through the Moon and Mercury, and Taurus, Scorpio and Sagittarius. So, nations with those planets and signs prominent, also carry the 4th ray.

- 4th Ray Souls: Austria, Brazil and Germany.
- 4th Ray Personalities: India and Italy. Tokyo has a 4th Ray Personality.

Ray 5, Concrete Mind and Science - (the ray of scientists).

Nations with this ray expressive have the task of producing brilliant scientists to help solve the world's problems and factually accurate thinkers to help the race deal with realities in a practical and scientific way. The Renaissance for example produced rational thinkers who helped rid the world of religious superstition, which unscrupulous churches used to control the masses. Galileo, Charles Darwin, Isaac Newton, Louis Pasteur and Madame Curie are examples of this ray.

But when this force is controlled by the lower elements in a nation, thinkers are produced who have no heart, who will use science for atrocious ends. For example, Nazi doctor Josef Mengele had this ray is his make-up. He performed inhumane experiments on captives to gain knowledge.

The 5th Ray flows through Venus, Leo, Sagittarius and Aquarius; so, nations with that planet and those signs prominent, also carry the 5th ray.

- 5th Ray Souls: France. London has a 5th Ray Soul.
- 5th Ray Personalities: Austria. Darjeeling also has a 5th Ray Personality.

Ray 6, Devotional and Idealistic - (the ray of devotees, religion).

The masses in nations with this ray prominent are devotional and highly idealistic. They are passionate, feeling people because this is the force that rules the plane of emotions and desire. They love pageantry and colourful displays that evoke patriotic pride and a sense of reverence for their nation, or for the 'tribe' they 'worship', which could be their church, their football team, the local gun-club or the nation's current leader. Higher Ray 6 types are Jesus, Joan of Arc, Florence Nightingale and Reverend Martin Luther King.

The 6th Ray is a dangerous force if the wisdom of the soul has not been developed to keep it in check, because this force flows through Mars. Then mob rule can rise and aggressive fanatics who are driven by their narrow beliefs and ideals, which they try to force onto others. The religious zealots of the Spanish Inquisition are examples of this type. When the 6th Ray soul is influential in a nation, it will be devoted to selflessly serving the needs of the citizens of the world.

The 6th Ray flows through Mars and Neptune, and Virgo, Sagittarius and Pisces. So, nations with those planets and signs prominent, also carry the idealistic, emotional ray.

- 6th Ray Souls: Italy and Spain. Tokyo also has a 6th Ray Soul.
- 6th Ray Personalities: Russia and the United States of America.

Ray 7, Ceremony, Order and Magic - (the ray of harmony and rhythm through order).

7th Ray nations are showy and ceremonial in a grand and structured way. Spain for example, with its regal and colourful cultural displays such as flamenco dancing and the ritual of bull-fighting. It has a 7th Ray Soul. The hallmark of the 7th Ray is a need for order. But before soul dominance, when egotistical leaders rule a country, then order upon the people is enforced rigorously to make people do what they are told. Russia has a 7th Ray Soul and is still at this early stage.

As the soul becomes influential, then a new and higher rhythm to national life will follow. At this level, all citizens willingly contribute to the orderly progression of the nation - in a way that suits their individual style. The 7th Ray is the ray of "magic," simply, the revelation of nature's hidden mysteries through science. In the future, nations ruled by Ray 7 will contribute to world good in ways that seem magical.

The 7th Ray flows through Uranus, Aries, Cancer and Capricorn; so, nations with that planet and those signs prominent, also carry the magical ray.

- 7th Ray Souls: Russia.
- 7th Ray Personalities: Spain. London has a 7th Ray Personality.

> On the next page, the "Nations and Cities" chart summarises the information given by Djwhal Khul in Alice Bailey's book 'The Destiny of the Nations'.
>
> Note that, Iceland, Sweden, Norway and Denmark are grouped under "Scandinavia."

Chart: Nations and Cities, their governing Rays and Astrology

Country	Soul ray	Ruling sign	Person. ray	Ruling sign	Spiritual Motto
Argentina	Not given	Cancer	Not given	Libra	Not given
Australia	Not given	Virgo	Not given	Capricorn	Not given
Austria	4	Libra	5	Capricorn	I serve the lighted Way
Belgium Brussels	Not given	Sagittarius Gemini	Not given	Gemini Capricorn	Not given
Brazil	4	Leo	2	Virgo	I hide the seed
Canada	Not given	Taurus	Not given	Libra	Not given
China	1	Taurus	3	Libra	I indicate the Way
Denmark	Not given	Libra	Not given	Cancer	Not given
Finland	Not given	Capricorn	Not given	Aries	Not given
France Paris	5	Pisces Virgo	3	Leo Capricorn	I release the Light
Germany Berlin	4	Aries Scorpio	1	Pisces Leo	I preserve
Great Britain London	2 5	Gemini Not given	1 7	Taurus Gemini	I Serve Not given
Greece	Not given	Virgo	Not given	Capricorn	Not given
Holland	Not given	Aquarius	Not given	Cancer	Not given
India Darjeeling	1 2	Aries Not given	4 5	Capricorn Scorpio	I hide the Light
Iceland	Not given	Libra	Not given	Cancer	Not given
Ireland	Not given	Virgo	Not given	Pisces	Not given
Italy Rome	6	Leo Taurus	4	Sagittarius Leo	I carve the Paths
Japan Tokyo	Not given 6	Scorpio Not given	Not given 4	Capricorn Cancer	Not given Not given
New Zealand	Not given	Gemini	Not given	Virgo	Not given
Norway	Not given	Libra	Not given	Cancer	Not given
Poland Warsaw	Not given	Taurus Capricorn	Not given	Gemini Pisces	Not given
Romania	Not given	Leo	Not given	Aries	Not given
Russia Moscow	7	Aquarius Taurus	6	Leo Aquarius	I link two Ways
South Africa	Not given	Aries	Not given	Sagittarius	Not given
Spain	6	Sagittarius	7	Capricorn	I disperse the Clouds
Sweden	Not given	Libra	Not given	Cancer	Not given
Switzerland Geneva	Not given 1	Aries Not given	Not given 2	Aquarius Leo	Not given
Turkey	Not given	Cancer	Not given	Scorpio	Not given
USA New York Washington	2 2	Aquarius Not given Cancer	6 3 Not given	Gemini Cancer Sagittarius	I light the Way

C. Signs and Planets in Esoteric Astrology.

The twelve signs are an evolutionary, educational system. They teach us to grow in consciousness and progress spiritually. Each sign can be viewed as a class, with three levels to help develop the three levels of consciousness we commonly call "Body, Soul, and Spirit." These levels can be related to junior school, high school and university.

- The 1st *exoteric* level develops *personality* (ego) consciousness.
- The 2nd *esoteric* level develops *soul* (community) consciousness.
- The 3rd *hierarchy* level develops *spiritual* (global) awareness.

Consequently, there may be up to three planet rulers or "teachers" for each sign. However, in this book, the global level will not be investigated. The world is still struggling to develop the soul aspect - individually and nationally. The following chart - 'Astrology Signs and Planet Rulers', gives the exoteric and esoteric rulerships.

Astrology Signs and Planet Rulers

Signs	Exoteric Ruler	Esoteric Ruler
	Personality ruler	*Soul purpose ruler*
Aries	Mars	Mercury
Taurus	Venus	Vulcan
Gemini	Mercury	Venus
Cancer	Moon	Neptune
Leo	Sun	Sun v. Neptune
Virgo	Mercury	Moon v. Vulcan
Libra	Venus	Uranus
Scorpio	Mars, Pluto	Mars
Sagittarius	Jupiter	Earth
Aquarius	Uranus, Saturn	Jupiter
Capricorn	Saturn	Saturn
Pisces	Jupiter, Neptune	Pluto

"v" = veiling. The Sun and Moon block higher-vibe forces (the second planet), until they can be safely received by a recipient.

1. The Ego or Personality of a nation, works through the Sun sign.

The Sun represents the "personality." Nations that are mature and stable generally express the positives of the Sun sign and of all planets. Nations who react without thought, emotionally, who attack and take from those around them - they are not mature personalities. They are still at the adolescent stage of development and generally express the negatives of the Sun sign and of all planets.

Forces that rule the personality of a nation can be 3-fold.

a. The Ray that rules the personality of a nation - given by Djwhal Khul.

b. The Sign that rules the personality of a nation - given by Djwhal Khul.

c. The Sun Sign in the latest natal chart for the nation and its aspects.

> **The Personality Ray of a nation - and the personality sign (given by DK); these work through the Sun sign in a nation's current natal chart. When this ray and personality sign information is not known (all nations not included in this book), the Sun sign is the primary representative.**

Example: Djwhal Khul gives Ray 6 and Gemini as the personality rulers of the USA. It currently has a Cancer Sun in its natal chart. Putting these forces together negatively, the USA can be fanatical in expression of its ideals (R6), superficial (Gemini) in its adhering to its Democratic principles, and very tribal (Cancer) in its attitude to other nations. Positively, the USA communicates (Gemini) its highest ideals to the world and is devotional (R6) in its efforts to see all nations in the world's family (Cancer). Depending upon who the current President is and whether he or she is soul aligned, either the higher or lower route will be followed.

2. The soul works through the ascendant sign.

A smaller number of people in all nations are tuning into their own souls. They will also therefore, be responding to the nation's soul. The ascendant sign represents the purpose of the soul in the current chart incarnation

> **The Soul Ray of a nation, and the Soul Sign (given by DK); these work through the ascendant sign in the current natal chart for the nation. When this soul-ray and soul-sign information is not available, the natal chart ascendant sign is the primary representative of the soul-purpose of the nation - and the esoteric planet ruler of that sign.**

Example: Djwhal Khul gives Ray 2 and Aquarius as the soul rulers of the United States. It currently has a Sagittarius ascendant in its natal chart. Putting these forces together negatively, the United States can be fear-filled (R2), isolating itself in its ivory tower of wealth and privilege (Aquarius), and not assisting needy nations, instead preaching (Sagittarius). But used positively, the United States is on a path to become a World Teacher of love and wisdom - and this is its actual destiny.

3. The Moon Sign represents the "Prison of the Soul."

The Moon represents psychological, pre-patterned habits and impulses that reside in the unconscious mind. Psychology calls these "negative core beliefs." They galvanise the lower self, to think, feel and react in a pre-patterned, unconscious way. For nations, the Moon sign generally represents "the people". Negatively expressed - the habits and patterns embedded in the nation's psyche that cause it to act in defensive and self-defeating ways.

For positive growth, the Sun and ascendant sign qualities should be emphasised rather than the Moon Sign. Likewise, the affairs of the house the Sun is in and the ruler of the ascendant sign, these should be emphasised. Positively expressed, the Moon Sign indicates how the nation's people contribute positively to the national good.

Chapter 2. Transits, Eclipses & Stars in Mundane Astrology.

Mundane Astrology - also known as Political Astrology, is the application of astrology to world affairs and events.

Disasters, pandemics and wars, these are the catalysts that drive evolutionary progress and change. They force kingdoms in nature - including the Human Kingdom, to adapt to prevailing circumstances or face extinction. Whether natural or manmade, these eventful catastrophes alter the course of history.

Astrologers map these critical periods in history, noting that they occur - firstly, when the outer planets form hard aspects to each other (conjunctions, squares and oppositions); and secondly, when solar and lunar eclipses occur.

This book maps critical periods for the 30 nations in this book.

A. Planets and Houses.

A1. The Personal Planets.

The inner, "personal" planets represent different aspects of the nation. Generally, the way the nation expresses its personality and power (Sun), how the people express themselves (Moon), how the nation communicates (Mercury), the values of the nation (Venus), and how the nation will fight to get what it wants or to defend itself (Mars).

1. The Sun.

The status of the Sun - the sign and house it is in, its aspects and whether it is afflicted or positively placed (this applies to all planet statements); represents the personality of the nation, the collective, "I-am-I, and I want to dominate my environment." The Sun also represents the aristocracy, the king or queen, a nation's rulers, eminent people in the nation, the government and those with authority. The Sun carries the 2nd Ray of Love and Wisdom.

2. The Moon.

The status of the Moon, represents the masses of people that embody the nation, the public, the nation's women, the common people or working classes, the domestic affairs of the nation and living habits. The Moon also represents fear-based emotional patterns that constitute the defensive reactions of a nation. In transformational eclipses, the Moon represents decaying structures imprisoning the nation's soul and that impede freedoms and rights. The Moon carries the 4th Ray of Harmony through Conflict.

3. Mercury.

Mercury rules the intellectual life of a nation, communication and the literary world. Its status represents how a nation educates it citizens and communicates within itself and with the other nations of the world. It governs transport - short distance travel by road, rail and air. It governs the commercial life of the nation, its tradesmen and markets. With Uranus, it rules the internet. Mercury carries the 4th Ray of Harmony through Conflict.

4. Venus.

The status of Venus, represents the values of a nation and refinements made to improve life for its citizens. Ruling the 2H of money, it also represents finance, the economy and banking. It indicates how easy or hard it will be for a nation's people to express love and affection. Younger women and woman's activism is indicated by Venus. It carries the 5th Ray of Concrete Mind and Science. At its highest, Venus represents love-wisdom in the nation.

5. Mars.

The status of warrior Mars, represents the passions of the people, a nation's selfishness and jealousies and how its citizens will react when they are angry. It shows how a country will defend itself if it should come under attack and whether it will be aggressive to other nations. It governs war, the nation's military, blue-collar workers and pioneering explorers. Mars carries the 6th Ray of Devotion and Idealism.

A2. The Maturing, Synthesising and Transformational Planets.

• The "maturing" planets are Jupiter and Saturn. They develop the character of the people and help them grow into a responsible, productive and civil nation.

• Saturn, Uranus and Neptune are "synthesising" planets. They blend and synthesise the various disparate elements in society into a more harmonious, multi-cultural whole. Often this work is achieved through hardship and pain.

• Uranus, Neptune and Pluto are "transformational" planets. When they team up together or with Saturn - by conjunction, square or opposition; they are change-agents for evolution. They bring all manner of challenging events that are designed to test the moral character of the nation and to break up and remove decaying structures that are impeding the evolution of its soul (the collective good). Their combinations are called "transformational patterns" in this book.

1. Jupiter.

Jupiter is a "maturing" planet and aids the evolution of the nation by helping its citizens grow into wise adults who can make a positive contribution to the community. It represents progressive change that unfolds naturally and easily as the nation matures. When it rules a nation, the more advanced of its people will demonstrate an inclusive love and wisdom for all people - as did Christ; while in the masses it tends towards excess, a love of comfort and greed. Jupiter carries the 2nd Ray of Love and Wisdom and helps the integrative, fusing process that binds communities together. It represents a nation's higher education, the high court and court systems, formal religion, philosophy and the nation's prevailing morals and beliefs.

When Jupiter teams up with the transformational planets, it expands and accentuates the power for change that the other planet represents, and can direct this force into the areas that it rules. Although it is usually a benevolent influence, when major change is underway, it can enhance the difficulties and pain that people are going through.

2. Saturn.

When Saturn rules a nation, it gifts its people with an astute and insightful life-perspective. It also carries the 1st Ray of Will and Power via its sign Capricorn - representing the crystallising, atrophying effect of this force. Saturn carries the 3rd Ray of Intelligence.

It represents a nation's principles and structures, law and order, administrative government, large corporations and the executives and bodies that run these organisations.

Saturn is also a "maturing" planet and aids the evolution of the nation through the retributive force of karma. One of its names is the Lord of Karma. It brings adverse conditions to teach both individuals and the collective to be responsible for their actions. In an eclipse or major event charts, Saturn represents crystallisations in society and the structures upon which the nation is founded, which have become old and rigid and that need to be discarded. Then, from the chaos that massive change causes, it consolidates anew, building healthier foundations.

When Saturn teams up with the outer planets, the rigidities it represents are destroyed according to the nature of the other planet - shattering quickly with Uranus, slowly dissolving with Neptune, and totally destroyed with Pluto.

3. Uranus.

Uranus is a transformational planet. It is an agent of evolution and its job is to keep humanity progressing forwards in its psychological and spiritual growth. It achieves this with the 7th Ray of Ceremony-Order-Magic, a force that carries the electric fire of spirit, and whose action "relates spirit and matter." [1] This accounts for Uranus' shattering effect upon obstinate energy blockages - in nature or in humanity.

When higher Uranus rules a nation, it brings in a sense of shared communal living, awareness of the need for social integration and the observance of human rights issues and progressive values. Uranus gifts its people with a clear intelligence. It awakens them to a greater awareness of themselves, to what is going on around them and instils a vision of how things could be and should be better. When there are human-rights issues, it instigates insurrection and presides over the revolution and mass upheavals in society that follow. Mundanely it represents new technology (the internet with Mercury), and advanced and radical scientific discoveries.

Quick, radical change is the manner in which Uranus aids the evolution of the nation. It rapidly shatters crystallisations in the nation's psyche and removes obstacles to forward momentum so that necessary progressive changes can take place. The means may be chaotic, it may result in a mess. But in the long term, the changes it presides over are necessary and will work out positively. An example is the French Revolution - that brutal and bloodthirsty insurrection. But it helped to free the masses from arrogant aristocratic privilege and selfishness.

When Uranus teams up with the outer planets, it increases that other planet's effect, making it more wide-spread, and faster-acting. It shatters and renews - crystallised governments and ruling styles (with Saturn), beliefs, ideals and religions (Neptune), and is more volatile and destructive with Pluto.

4. Neptune.

Neptune is also a transformational planet, an agent of evolution. It carries the 6th ray of Devotion and Idealism, which rules the emotional plane. Its evolutionary task is to refine the emotional life of humanity and to reorient men and women to the mystical and contemplative way of life. Neptune inspires a search for spiritual understanding and fulfillment.

In nations it represents beliefs and ideals that dominate the national consciousness, and Piscean Age religions - Christianity and Islam. This includes fundamentalist, war-like branches of these religions (ruled by Mars). At the lower level, Neptune represents superstitious and delusory beliefs, and the tendency to be deluded or glamoured; fraud, covert actions and scandals. Mundanely, Neptune rules drugs - legal and illegal, oil, pharmaceuticals, the oceans, weather disasters involving excess water and all events related to shipping.

Neptune's evolutionary action dissolves slowly - left to itself, its results may not be seen for months or years. In this context, it is related to the "gradual disintegration of concrete forms," [2] which is seen when bodies wither away as a result of starvation or lack of adequate nourishment. Consequently, Neptune is often influential in times of crop-failures and famine - not least, because it is also a ruler of the vegetable kingdom. [3]

In relation to disease, Neptune is the primary representative of viruses. The reason why viruses spread so easily is that they are a physical counterpart of toxic emotions, which

1 Bailey, Alice A. Esoteric Astrology, 100.
2 Bailey, Alice A. A Treatise on Cosmic Fire, 596.
3 Bailey, Alice A. A Treatise on Cosmic Fire, 1138.

spread rapidly amongst people. Viruses are of the nature of negative Neptune - stealthy and subtly poisonous, insidious and debilitating. Viruses try to creep unseen into the body to evade detection by the immune system. When successful, they infect cells, rapidly reproduce and spread through the bloodstream like a tidal wave swamping the body.

When Neptune teams up with Uranus or Pluto, change comes faster. Neptune with Saturn indicates that beliefs and religions are crystallised and require change. Sometimes, they represent government manipulation of the beliefs of the nation for nefarious reasons.

5. Pluto.

Pluto is also a transformational planet. Pluto is the Lord of Death - it presides over the death and rebirth cycle. Its force destroys and annihilates, clearing the way for new growth. In human society, it aids evolution by destroying decaying forms, attitudes, conventions and institutions that are retrogressive and are hindering evolutionary momentum. Whichever sign Pluto happens to be in - the part of human life which that sign represents, it is targeted for radical change and transformation followed by renewal. As such, Pluto is also a healing factor. Pluto carries the 1st Ray of Will and Power.

> Pluto, is a deity with the attributes of the serpent. He is a healer, a giver of
> health, spiritual and physical. [1]

Because of its rulership of the masses and death, sometimes mass-deaths and carnage can eventuate when Pluto is involved in eclipses. In this regard, Pluto is a ruler of plagues.

When it rules a nation (through Scorpio), Pluto gifts its people with a powerful will and the ability to endure under extreme circumstances. Lower type rulers would have an obsessive need for power and control and will use bullying tactics, war and terrorism to get what they want. In spiritually advanced leaders, Pluto demonstrates as the wise use of power and the ability to bring transformational change through peaceful means.

Mundanely, Pluto rules those who have mega-power in the state - financially such as plutocrats, politically such as dictators and political power-factions and crime-bosses in the underworld. When Pluto teams up with the other planets, it destroys crystallisations (with Saturn), it destroys through rebels and revolution (with Uranus), it eliminates delusion and predatory behaviours (with Neptune).

The Pluto-Saturn cycle - destruction and reconstruction.

Of all the planet combinations, Saturn and Pluto bring about the most far-reaching changes. Negative Saturn represents rigid and oppressive laws, leaders and governments that are repressing the freedoms of people, while Pluto represents the gathering mega-dangerous forces that will destroy these rigidities. These destructive forces could come from nature or from the masses, to which Pluto is also related.

The conjunction is the most powerful. This is because the forces of the two planets combine, bringing double trouble! However, the more important reason, is because the conjunction starts a developmental period in history that will play until the next conjunction, and sometimes even into future cycles. During a cycle, the separating and applying squares and the opposition, trigger events that are related to the purpose of the foundational conjunction. The minor hard aspects, semi-square, inconjunct, sesquiquadrate, etc., they also fit into the "hard" category, but have a smaller effect during the cycle. The Saturn - Pluto cycle lasts for approximately 33 years. Here is an example, using the World Wars to clarify:

---

1   Bailey, Alice A. Esoteric Astrology, 667.

- A Saturn-Pluto conjunction occurred in 1913. WWI was declared on 26 July 1914.
- In 1922, the 1/4 square formed. WWI was over and the world was restructuring itself.
- In 1931, the opposition occurred. The Nazi Party has seized power in Germany.
- In 1939, the 3/4 square formed. WWII broke out.
- In 1947, WWII was over and the world was again restructuring itself.

In the current period, an eclipse that hit the recent Saturn-Pluto conjunction in 2019, is behind the Covid-19 outbreak. Pluto rules plagues and other massive disasters that cause mass deaths. The ramifications of the eclipse and other events unfolding currently in 2020 and 2021, will influence the destinies of nations until 2053. That is when the next conjunction occurs.

A3. Signs and Houses in Mundane Astrology and Eclipses.

When an angle (cusp of houses 1, 4, 7 and 10), is crossed by an outer planet, or is hit by an eclipse, there will be major national developments. An eclipse that falls in a house, adversely affects the affairs of that house. Not all affairs pertaining to that house could manifest - that depends upon the chart as a whole and where the nation is in its growth.

Aries and the 1H. The 1H represents the nation as a whole, the collective, national characteristic, self-interests, the nation's self-image and appearance as seen by others. *Eclipses*: trouble in the nation, national anxiety. Aries carries rays 1 and 7: it represents leaders, pioneering ventures, war and trouble-makers.

Taurus and the 2H. The nation's values. Its wealth, assets, resources, the gross domestic product, the economy and trade, the money market, banks, financial institutions and the stock exchange. *Eclipses*: national anxiety over money, a stock-market crash, trouble in the business community and with banks, a national crisis over values and principles. Taurus carries ray 4.

Gemini and the 3H. Language, education, freedom of speech. Internal travel, transport, rail, road, domestic air-flight. Communications, the internet, postal service, mass media, authors and literature. Trade, commerce. *Eclipses*: accidents in travel, trouble in communications, in schools, very bad news, trouble with neighbouring countries. Gemini carries ray 2.

Cancer and the 4H. Domestic issues, the common people, the foundations of society, cultural norms, ancestry, traditions; a nation's history, roots and heritage. Tribal attitudes, nationalism and mass ideologies. The land, houses, agriculture, farming, crops and the weather. *Eclipses*: the health of the people could suffer according to the sign of the eclipse, bad for agriculture and the land, trouble at home and opposition to the government or the nation's ruler. Cancer carries rays 3 and 7.

Leo and the 5H. Speculative interests, the stock exchange and share market. Society, social interests, the culture, customs and social behaviours. The creative activities of a society - the arts and pleasure activities. The affairs of the nation's children. *Eclipses*: adverse effects to social affairs, to the nation's children, a setback for the arts. Leo carries rays 1 and 5.

Virgo and the 6H. The working classes. National service, the army, the navy, police service, civil service, trade unions and national defence. The nation's health and health services, health workers, sanitation (6-12), the psychological health of the people. *Eclipses*: a national health crisis according to the sign of the eclipse, an epidemic. Employment crises, discontent in workers and national strikes. Virgo carries rays 2 and 6.

Libra and the 7H. Alliances, international relations, foreign relations, treaties and diplomats. Legal matters and justice. Open enemies of the nation. *Eclipses*: trouble in foreign affairs, changing international relations, war and conflict. Libra carries ray 3.

Scorpio and the 8H. The national debt, foreign investments, taxes, major losses, international finance and multinational corporations. Major separations, mass deaths, death of an eminent person and national mourning. Regeneration of the nation after loss of life or a major catastrophe. *Eclipses*: bad for international finance, bad for the health of the nation, an epidemic, mass deaths and an increase in mass crime. Scorpio carries ray 4.

Sagittarius and the 9H. Foreign lands, foreigners, long distance air travel, the high seas, "overseas", shipping, water routes and maritime law. Legal professions, justice, lawyers, legal matters, the court system, national and international law. Religious affairs, the church and society's morals. Higher education, universities and publishing. *Eclipses*: trouble in the churches, sectarian violence, major changes in law that are controversial, accidents concerning long distance sea and air travel, trouble coming from foreign countries or from foreign nationals. Sagittarius carries rays 4, 5 and 6.

Capricorn and the 10H. The government, those in power, the ruling class, the aristocracy, the king or prime minister, the executive branch of government (the White House, the House of Lords), and the prestige of the country, how the government is seen. *Eclipses*: bad for the ruler or government, loss of international prestige and opposition from the people. Capricorn carries rays 1, 3 and 7.

Aquarius and the 11H. Politics, political ideologies. Institutions that govern, the legislative branch of government - Parliament, Congress, House of Representatives, House of Commons and local government. Collective aspirations, hopes and wishes of the people. Social affairs. Friendly nations. *Eclipses*: unfortunate for government, political dissension and revolutions. Aquarius carries ray 5.

Pisces and the 12H. Anything hidden, enemies hidden within the nation, spies, conspiracies, subversion, secret or underground societies and secret organizations such as White Supremacist groups. A nations self-undoing. Hospitals, prisons, institutions and any place of confinement or detention. Psychological health of the people, mass health. Charities. *Eclipses*: misfortune or sorrow to the country, mass health crisis involving many hospitalisations, increase in crime, hidden or unseen troubles, internal troubles in the nation due to self-undoing by influential groups or subterranean groups. Pisces carries rays 2 and 6.

B. About Eclipses

B1. Technical aspects of Lunar eclipses.

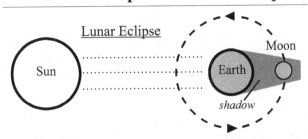

Lunar eclipses occur at some full Moons, when the earth moves directly between the Sun and Moon, blocking the sunlight that normally falls on the Moon. Instead, earth's shadow falls on the Moon, darkening its face.

There are three types of lunar eclipses — total, partial and penumbral. According to experts, about 35% of all eclipses are penumbral, 30% are partial and 35% are total.

    i. *Total lunar eclipse.* The inner part of earth's shadow (umbra), falls on the Moon. At mid-eclipse, the entire Moon is in shadow, which, if atmospheric conditions are right may appear blood red. This is called a Blood Moon. It is an eerie effect and the ancients thought it prophesied doom. For example, here are two quotes from the Bible.

> The sun will turn into darkness, and the Moon into blood, before the great and terrible day of the Lord comes. Joel 2:31.

> And I beheld when he had opened the sixth seal, and, lo, there was a great earthquake; and the sun became black as sackcloth of hair, and the Moon became as blood. Revelations 6:11-13.

    ii. *Partial lunar eclipse.* The umbra takes a bite out of only a fraction of the Moon. The dark bite grows larger, and then recedes, never reaching the total phase.

    iii. *Penumbral lunar eclipse.* Only the more diffuse outer shadow of earth – the penumbra, falls on the Moon. This eclipse is more subtle and difficult to observe.

a. Moonlight and health.

Esoterically, the effects of an afflicted Moon are thought to be detrimental to physical and psychological health. Given the right circumstances - unhygienic conditions, poverty, poor food quality, humans squashed together in squalor. An afflicted Moon can indicate disease.

> The emanation coming from the Moon has in it the seeds of death and disease, because it is a "dead planet." [1]

> When the builders are the lunar lords and those who work under the control of the moon and at the behest of the lower Personal self, then you have disease, ill health and death. [2]

---

1   Bailey, Alice A. Esoteric Healing, 608.
2   Bailey, Alice A. Esoteric Healing, 191.

Moonlight during eclipses or the full moon can have a detrimental effect on health. This quote is from Helena Blavatsky.

> In the year 1693, on January 21, during the eclipse of the Moon, thrice as many sick people died on that day than on the preceding and following days. Lord Bacon used to fall down senseless at the beginning of every lunar eclipse and returned to consciousness when it was over. [1]

Here is a second quote:

> No experienced captain will allow his men to sleep on deck during the full-moon, no person even one with remarkably strong nerves - could sit, lie or sleep for any length of time, in a room lit by moonlight without injury to his health. [2]

Moonlight also spoils food.

> Every observing housekeeper knows that provisions of any nature will decay and spoil far more rapidly in moonlight than they would in entire darkness. [3]

b. Lunar eclipses and psychology

Traditionally, lunar eclipses are said to be more concerned with our inner emotional world and expression of feelings. This quote from Bailey supports this view.

> The Moon's influence is more potent at the time of the full-moon upon all who are (emotionally) unbalanced. [4]

Bailey gave the cause:

> This lack of equilibrium exists between the astral body, the etheric body and the physical mechanism. Those who are unbalanced, emotional, and frequently swept by uncontrolled desire, are hindered, overstimulated, and psychically upset by these cycles. [5]

c. Solar and Lunar eclipse effects

Research has shown, that when bad things happen in the human kingdom, when there are wars, massacres and people doing bad things to other people; it usually happens under a lunar eclipse. Of these the full or Blood Moon eclipse is the worst indicator.

> The decay of a moon has as great an evil effect upon all that contacts it as a decaying body on earth has upon its surroundings. It is occultly "offensive."

As for natural disasters in nature: very often a solar eclipse portends events such as earthquakes and volcanic explosions, while lunar eclipses foretell watery events such as cyclones that cause flooding.

---

1 Blavatsky, Helena. Collected Writings, Volume IV, 396-397.
2 Blavatsky, Helena. Collected Writings, Volume IV, 396-397.
3 Blavatsky, Helena. Collected Writings, Volume IV, 396-397.
4 Bailey, Alice A. Esoteric Healing, 341.
5 Bailey, Alice A. Esoteric Healing, 341.

B2. Technical aspects of Solar eclipses.

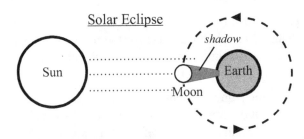

Solar Eclipse

When the Sun and Moon come together in the same part of the sky as they do once a month, a solar eclipse occurs when the Moon is so uniquely aligned between the Sun and earth; its bulk covers the Sun's face, blocking its light when viewed from earth. Consequently, the Moon's shadow is then thrown over earth.

A solar eclipse viewed from the right angle is very dramatic. Daylight Sun is totally obscured, excepting for a corona of its light, which streams out around the lunar orb.

There are 4 types of solar eclipses.

i. Total solar eclipses. When the Moon totally covers the Sun. They are dramatic. The Bible Gospel of Luke, indicates there was a solar eclipse when Christ was crucified - "and the Sun was darkened."

ii. Annular solar eclipses. The Moon covers the Sun's centre, leaving the Sun's visible outer edges to form a "ring of fire" or annulus around the Moon.

iii. Hybrid solar eclipses. At certain points from earth the eclipse appears total, but at other points it appears annular.

iv. Partial solar eclipses. The Moon partially blocks the face of the Sun.

B3. General points.

Most years have four eclipses, the minimum number possible in a year. Two of these four eclipses are always solar eclipses. While rare, the maximum number of eclipses in a calendar year is seven. A lunar eclipse can only occur whenever a solar eclipse happens. If one does take place, it is usually within two weeks before or after the solar eclipse.

a. When eclipses hit vital points in a natal or progressed chart, they bring unforeseen events in the life that can set those affected on a totally new path.

b. Impactful eclipses are fast and shattering in action and profoundly important in the changes they bring to the structures of life (Saturn). They are of the nature of Uranus; in that they bring sudden changes and force people into a new and often unexpected direction. Major, transformational eclipses that affect the lives of millions change the course of nations and history. In a sense you could say these are karmic forces, shunting mankind into closer alignment with the natural flow and harmony of the universe.

c. An eclipse describes the nature of event that is approaching. From this angle, the eclipse date can be viewed as a true natal chart of the event. Energies that cause a physical event to manifest, gather prior to the event. These gathered forces represented by the eclipse chart, are released later when an inner, fast-moving planet triggers the pattern.

d. The eclipse chart assessed against the natal or progressed chart of a nation, shows how the eclipse will impact that nation.

e. Ancient astrologers believed that eclipses were only effective in regions where an eclipse casts its shadow. That is not correct for the modern, global-brain age. Research has shown that an eclipse that hits vital points in a natal chart for a person, city or nation anywhere on earth has a potent effect.

f. In a lunar eclipse, the Sun sign represents progressive qualities to be built into the fabric of society (Sun sign) - and where (Sun's house). [1] The Moon sign represents decaying traits that need to be eliminated (Moon sign), and from where (Moon's house).

1. The Lord of an Eclipse.

The lord of the eclipse is the planet that rules the sign in which an eclipse occurs. Its sign, aspects and location in the houses, will also indicate areas in the national life that will be impacted.

For example, if a solar eclipse (Sun and Moon conjunct), occurs in Aries; the lord of the eclipse is Mars. If Mars was in the 8H of death - because Aries is a military sign, a brutal war could break out with many deaths.

If a lunar eclipse (Sun and Moon opposite), occurs in Aries and Libra; Mars and Venus are the Lords of the Eclipse. If Mars was in the 2H of values and Venus in the 4H of the people; there could be a dispute over values or money.

2. Transits, Progressions and Eclipses on the Angles.

The angles are the 1st (Asc), 4th (IC), 7th (DC) and 10 (MC) house cusps. They are the most sensitive points in the chart to the effects of transits, progressions, eclipses and stars. Whenever an outer planet or star hits an angle in an eclipse or event chart, major national developments and changes will follow in line with the nature of the planet, star and angle.

The Angles also indicate timing

Whenever an outer planet or star is located on an angle in an eclipse or event chart, their influences will tend to dominate the event.

• Outer planets and stars on the Asc: influence both the start point of an event and the event in its entirety.

• On the MC: influence the early stages of the event, will have a major impact upon the entire event, and will shape the event's important goals.

• On the DC: influence the middle (age) part of the event.

• On the IC: influence the outcome of the event and the legacy that follows.

3. Eclipses in the Elements.

• Eclipses in fire signs portend excess heat, drought so crops fail and there is famine. Volcano eruptions, disastrous wild-fires.

• Eclipses in earth signs. Excess earth activity such as earthquakes, also volcanic eruptions. Scarcity of products of the earth - crops, impaired agriculture so there is famine. Mining disasters.

---

1 Bailey, Alice A. The Light of the Soul, 302. The sun in its aspect of light is the symbol of the soul.

- Eclipses in air signs. Excess and violent atmospheric conditions, high winds, cyclones, tornados, destructive storms.
- Eclipses in watery signs. Excess water, rain, floods, tsunamis, drowning, turbulent rivers, lakes and oceans. Crops are flooded so there is famine. Destruction of fish, animal and bird life living on or in the sea or close to water. Shipping disasters.

4. The use of "undiscovered planets" in historical eclipses.

In relation to the outer planets Uranus, Neptune and Pluto; some astrologers believe they do not affect events on earth before the date of their discovery. For events in nature, this is not correct. "Undiscovered" planets have always been present, orbiting and casting their energies over the earth and causing interferences in the patterns of nature or to the forces of the planet. Use them in relation to the natural processes of nature, for natural disasters and for mass events that affect human life. For instance, Pluto has always been involved in major catastrophes causing mass deaths.

Regarding the evolution of consciousness in man, traditional thought is that when a new development occurs, a planet is discovered. For example, Uranus was discovered at the time of the Renaissance and rise of science. Consequently, some astrologers believe that the outer planets should not be used in charts for people born before the date of their discovery. But this is incorrect for advanced men and women. Unique individuals who are "giants" in humanity, those who make their mark on history, they are consciously receptive to these higher forces before the "common" folk. Use the outer planets in the charts of historical figures who appeared to be ahead of their time. They can also be used in a general sense. For example, Neptune, discovered in 1846, has been drawing people into the mystical/ religious life since the dawn of time. Uranus, discovered in 1781, has always presided over progressive change.

5. The timing of eclipse effects.

A question often asked is, "How long does the influence and effect of an eclipse last?" The tradition is that a lunar eclipse is more immediate in its effects and its period of influence is determined by the length of time of the eclipse - one month in time for every minute of the eclipse. Solar eclipses may not be so immediate and their effects can last for as long as the period of an eclipse - a year in time for every minute of the eclipse.

However, research shows that when a solar or lunar eclipse is accompanied by, and makes contact with, major transformational transits of outer planets (especially if that contact is a conjunction, square or opposition); the effect can extend for years.

The eclipse is like a fuse, igniting the evolutionary work of the outer planets, which have their own agendas and cycles. The eclipse accentuates the potency of the planets involved, power-boosting their effect. It sets the timing for the start of critical events and adds greater detail about how they will unfold and where. The eclipse potency is carried forwards by the outer planets as they continue their cycles of growth and unfoldment.

When Saturn and the outer planets form hard aspects with each other, the intensity of the "evolutionary patterns" they form bring major changes to the foundations of society. When an eclipse hits the pattern, the transformational effect is lifted to a new level. The eclipse triggers events to help the evolutionary goals of the planets that are working in tandem together to be achieved.

B4. Eclipses used in this book

Historical natural disasters are included in the book. But the main body of work focuses on critical periods in recent history that radically shaped the whole of humanity and changed the course of history - World War I (WWI) and the Spanish Flu pandemic, World War II (WWII) and the Covid-19 pandemic of the 21st Century. Here is an overview of topics covered:

1. Natural and man-made disasters.

- Eclipse charts for major floods that caused catastrophic damage are studied. Included are floods in Belgium, Denmark, Germany, the Netherlands, Norway and Poland. The effects of two tsunamis are studied. The 2004 tsunami in South East Asia, in relation to the effect it had on Swedish people; and the Japan tsunami in 2011.
- Fires and volcanic eruptions are studied. Fires for Australia and London; and volcanic eruptions in Iceland, Italy and Indonesia.
- Earthquakes are studied in Greece and Romania.
- Finally, catastrophic famines are studied for China, Finland, France, Greece, Ireland, Japan, Russia and Turkey.

2. The Bubonic Plague

The bubonic plague is the most virulent pandemic recorded in human history. It is a bacterial infection that is spread by fleas living on rats. The disease often killed within days of people developing a high fever. It attacked the lymphatic system, which was followed by a rash. Then buboes or swellings in the armpits and groin appeared, which turned black and exploded, expelling pus and bacteria. The affected person usually died.

Experts claim the plague first originated in China over 2000 years ago. Several virulent waves swept the world in the Middle Ages.

Blood Moon eclipse, Bubonic Plague 18 Mar 1345, 21:45, Paris, France.

Here is a chart for the virulent European outbreak that lasted from 1346 to 1353. It caused about 75 to 200 million deaths. Astrologers in France set up a chart for this epidemic, blaming "a conjunction of three planets in 1345 that caused the great pestilence." [1]

- Since Uranus, Neptune and Pluto had not been discovered, the conjunction refers to Mars, Jupiter and Saturn that were conjunct in early 1345. Those astrologers did not know it, but there was another conjunction of three planets: Jupiter (that multiplies), Uranus (bacterial infections) and Pluto (powerful and virulent toxicity and mass deaths). Ominously, they connected into a Blood Moon eclipse!

- Note that the evolutionary pattern is a Uranus-Pluto conjunction; which the eclipse hits.

1 Horrox, Rosemary. Black Death, 159.

3. Spanish Flu, the 1918-1920 Influenza Pandemic.

The Spanish Flu did not originate in Spain. It was called that because Spanish newspapers were the first in Europe to start reporting it. WWI was raging and combatant countries did not want to alert their opponents that their fighting forces were being weakened by a new and very virulent disease.

According to British researchers, the virus first appeared in late 1916.

Research published in 1999 by a British team led by virologist John Oxford, [1] stated that the virus first appeared in a noticeable way during WWI, in Étaples, France, a United Kingdom army and hospital camp. It was near farms with pigs [2] and the cross-over effect may have given rise to the outbreak - between December 1916 and March 1917. This is much earlier than is commonly thought.

From its first outbreaks in Europe, the virus mutated and gained a marked ability to spread in 1918. And spread it did, amongst soldiers weakened by fighting on the Western Front. The danger of new and highly virulent viruses, is that the human immune system does not have anti-bodies to fight the new disease. In such circumstances, a pandemic is created. The virus travelled with military personnel from camp to camp. United States reports state that:

At the height of the American military involvement in the war, September through November 1918, influenza and pneumonia sickened 20% to 40% of U.S. Army and Navy personnel. [3]

When soldiers went home after the war, the virus went with them, spreading the infection globally. During the three major waves between 1918 and 1920, the number of deaths is estimated to be around 50 million.

The root cause of influenza, is emotionalism (the 6th Ray).

In the book 'Esoteric Healing', by Bailey - on page 70, the Master Djwhal Khul gives the esoteric cause of influenza.

Worry and irritation are dangerous because they lower vitality to such a point that [people] become susceptible to disease. The scourge of influenza has its roots in fear and worry, and once the world settles down to freedom from the present "fearful" condition, we shall see the disease die out. [People become] so highly infectious from the astral point of view they lower the astral atmosphere, and thus make it hard for people - in the astral sense [emotionally], to breathe freely. Because the astral conditions of fear, worry and irritation are so widespread today, they might be regarded as epidemic, in a planetary sense.

Virulent mass fear and worry are directly linked to the emergence of this virulent strain of the virus during WWI. It it likely - because conflict is ever-present on earth, that the world has never been free of anxiety since the transport and communication systems of the Industrial Age (18th Century), began to knit humanity into a global community. Fear and worry remain present in the 21st Century and is behind the 2019, Covid-19 outbreak. Consequently, it seems we are stuck with viral pandemics for a long while yet.

---

1 Prof. John S. Oxford (UK's top expert on influenza), Douglas Gill (a military historian). A possible European origin of the Spanish influenza and the first attempts to reduce mortality to combat superinfecting bacteria: an opinion from a virologist and a military historian. Human Vaccines & Immunotherapeutics, 2019

2 Scientists speculate that the virus originated from pigs. Martha Nelson, Michael Worobey; American Journal of Epidemiology, 26 Jul 2018, Origins of the 1918 Pandemic: Revisiting the Swine "Mixing Vessel" Hypothesis

3 https://www.ncbi.nlm.nih.gov/pmc/articles/PMC2862337/

Spanish Flu, partial lunar eclipse 15 Jul 1916, 05:40 BST, Etaples, France.

Lunar rather than solar eclipses are usually at the centre of pandemics because germs breed in damp and dark conditions, which the shadowed Moon represents. Further, the Moon represents all human living conditions including those toxic, unhygienic and squalid living conditions that many are forced to live in because of need, war and poverty.

• This eclipse is perfect for the influenza outbreak because of the stellium of forces in Cancer. Ruled by the Moon, it is a sign that is related to the emotions and "The scourge of influenza has its roots in fear and worry."

• Although Saturn is separating from its conjunction with Pluto, the transformative power of the union extends into this pandemic, because they are connected via the Cancer stellium. The disease continued the evolutionary work of WWI.

• The stellium is in the 12H of "self-undoing." The eclipse struck at the mid-point of the war. Fear and worry were rampant, debilitating nations and rendering people susceptible to viruses. The 12th also governs hospitalisation, which is where millions of people ended up.

• Opposite the Cancer stellium, is the Moon, afflicted in Capricorn, in the 6H of health. Esoterically, the emanation coming from the moon has in it the seeds of death and disease, because the moon is a "dead planet." [1]

• Of the outer planets, Neptune is the most prominent planet in the chart, because it is rising and on the Asc angle. Any planet or star on an angle, in an eclipse event chart, tends to dominate the event and Neptune did in this case.

Neptune is the planet that represents viruses. Viruses are of the nature of negative Neptune - stealthy and subtly poisonous. Viruses try to creep unseen into the body to evade detection by the immune system. If successful, they infect cells, rapidly reproduce and spread through the bloodstream like a Neptune-driven tidal wave swamping the body.

Neptune is on 2-degrees Leo. In Sabian Symbols, [2] this is the epidemic degree in the zodiac that represents pandemics. Here is Dane Rudhyar's interpretation of this 2nd degree.

> *The school closed by an epidemic, children play together.* Constructive result of inconveniences of life in developing communal values. [3]

In his interpretation, Rudhyar gives insight into the evolutionary purpose of epidemics - to teach the race to be more sensitive to the other people we share this world with, for the greater communal good. Nature wants us to learn to accept with good grace ("children playing"), the personal inconveniences that epidemics bring - such as social distancing and wearing masks.

---

1   Bailey, Alice A. Esoteric Healing, 665.
2   The Sabian Symbols were created in 1925 by clairvoyant Elsie Wheeler, who "saw" them when she meditated on the degrees of the zodiac. Astrologer Dr. Marc Edmund Jones, recorded these symbols in his book, 'Sabian Symbols'.
3   Rudhyar, Dane. The Astrology of Personality, 285.

4a. World War I, 1914-1918.

The eclipse chart selected to represent WWI is 10 months before the assassination of the Austrian Duke and Duchess that triggered the war. It is set up in Sarajevo, where the assassination, took place. The Blood Moon eclipse is an appropriate symbol for the carnage that was to follow. Another reason that justifies the early date, is because conflict was already underway in the Balkans - in 1912 and 1913. Skirmishes between Serbia and Austria led directly to the Great War. The World Wars are considered by scholars to be one war. [1] The interval between them gave time for a new generation of soldiers to grow up and to continue in 1939, where battle proceedings paused in 1918.

<u>Blood Moon eclipse for WWI: 15 Sep 1913, 13:45, Sarajevo, Bosnia.</u>

a. Evolutionary pattern.

• The evolutionary pattern shaping events is Saturn conjunct Pluto, still forming at this stage. They are always present when decay and crystallisations in society need breaking down and rebuilding.

b. Mars, God of War.

• When war is unleashed, its violence becomes an unstoppable force of nature. The assassination was carried out by Serbian ideological and political fanatics (Mars the fanatic, in ideas Gemini).

It triggered a world-wide conflagration - Mars conjunct Pluto, in a grand-cross with the eclipse and the Asc/DC. The scope of the hardship to come would extend to the four corners of the earth.

c. The constellation Auriga - the Charioteer.

A constellation primary to the conflict was Auriga. Mars was on the star *Menkalinan* (29 Gemini) in Auriga, and Saturn was *Hoedus I* and *II* (17-18 Gemini), also in Auriga.

> In Roman mythology, Auriga is often identified with the crippled son of the blacksmith Vulcan. He was credited with inventing the four-horse chariot, which he modelled in the image of the Sun's chariot. The chariot was used in battle and it was described as being as swift as the wind.

Here is a descriptive quote from Marcus Manilius.

> The Charioteer lifts his team from the ocean (where icy Boreas lashes with his bitter blasts), holding in check the 4 mouths curbed with foam-flecked bits the spirited steeds outstrip the winds. [2]

The four horses in Auriga, can be related the Biblical 'Four Horsemen of the Apocalypse', in the Book of Revelations. It prophesied a coming apocalypse, which would be triggered by a "Lamb." [3] When the Lamb broke certain "seals", the Four Horsemen rode out.

---

1 Encyclopaedia Britannica.
2 Manilius, Marcus; Astronomica, 305-309. Manilius was a Roman poet, astrologer and author of Astronomica
3 Bible: Revelations 5-6.

Interpreting the Bible story from an astrological perspective - Mars represents the Lamb (Mars rules Aries, the Ram). The prophecy is about a holocaust, which Mars, the God of War, presides over. When civil discourse breaks down and men decide to go to war, Mars' force is unleashed,

In this context, the assassination of the Duke and Duchess (Mars) ripped open the seals (started the war), which let loose the Four Horsemen and events of the apocalypse. The relevant passages in Revelations, chapter, are paraphrased here:

(2-3) The 1st seal revealed "A white horse. Its rider had a bow. He went out as a conqueror and to conquer."

(4) The 2nd seal revealed, "A fiery red horse. Its rider was permitted to take peace from the earth so that people would slaughter one another. He was given a great sword."

(5-6) The 3rd seal revealed, "A black horse. Its rider held a scale in his hand."

(7-8) The 4th seal revealed, "A horse, pale greenish grey. Its rider was named Death and Hades accompanied him. They were given authority over a quarter of the earth, to kill with sword, famine, and plague."

(9) The 5th seal revealed the souls of those slaughtered.

(12) The 6th seal revealed a great earthquake, the sun turned as black as dark sackcloth and the whole Moon became like blood."

The last part of the quote "and the whole Moon became like blood," refers to a total lunar eclipse, in which - if atmospheric conditions are right, the Moon turns a ruddy reddish brown (a Blood Moon). Perhaps these passages in Revelations are really meant for astrologers. The word "seal" that hides the prophecies, could be a metaphor for the esoteric arts, of which astrology is one. Then, whenever Mars is in aspect to Pluto (Hades), in a Blood Moon eclipse; it is a warning of a potential world-wide catastrophic war.

d. Stars on the angles.

• The ascendant in a mundane chart represents the start point of the event - the war in this case; and its prevailing influence. On the ascendant, influencing affairs was *Markeb* (28 Sagittarius), a star in the sail of great ship Argo. War involves many "voyages" as armies and their support camps are sent to the fields of battle and manoeuvre to outflank and best each other. In this case, armies crossed seas and flew through the skies until the war's end.

• The MC of the chart represents the early stages of the war and prominent events. Close to the MC, is *Nekkar* (23 Libra). Arab astrologers called *Nekkar* and *Seginus* (a star close by), the "Female Wolves or Hyenas, lying in wait for their prey." This refers to military strategy that deals with the planning and conduct of campaigns, the movement of forces to deceive the enemy.

• The descendant of the chart represents the middle and main part of the war. With Mars, Pluto and Menkalinan (ruin and violent death) located there; the war was a brutal and bloody slaughter that ruined nations.

• The IC represents the legacy of the event. *Vertex* (26 Aries 39), a star in the thigh of Andromeda, the Chained Woman is there. It is a spiral galaxy with millions of stars. It was a warning - as long as man is chained to greed and avarice, there will be future apocalypses. The warning was not heeded. WWII was only 21 years away.

4b. World War II.

Berlin is set as the location of this war eclipse, because Germany planned it and started it.

Blood Moon eclipse for WWII: 3 May 1939,16:16, Berlin

The war was fated (angles in the 29th degree). WWII was a continuation of WWI. The seeds of this conflagration were sown aeons past. Djwhal Khul (the true author of Alice Bailey books) said that World Wars I and II were the continuation of a World War from ancient times. Here is the quote:

> That great struggle [in] the Atlantean civilization, culminated in the destruction called the flood. [1] The forces of light, and of darkness, were arrayed against each other. The struggle still persists, and the World War through which we have just passed was a recrudescence of it. On every side in that World War two groups were to be found, those who fought for an ideal as they saw it, for the highest that they knew, and those who fought for material and selfish advantage. [2]

a. The Eclipse, Saturn and Pluto

The eclipse supported the evolutionary work of Saturn square Pluto. These planets were at the 3/4 phase of their conjunction, which happened in 1914 when WWI started. Both planets carry the 1st ray of power, whose physical destruction is seen in volcano eruptions and nuclear explosions. In humanity, they destroy crystallised and decaying social attitudes and political structures, which bind the soul of humanity in servitude.

b. Mars, God of War

Aggressive Mars is powerful - exalted in Capricorn and in a t-square with Saturn and Pluto. It is on *Sulaphat* (21 Capricorn), a bright-yellow star in the Lyra constellation. It is said to represent a "Swooping Vulture or Eagle," with a "musical instrument hanging from the claws." [3] It can also be used to represent Hitler and the Nazis; whose symbol is the eagle carrying the swastika.

c. The Myth of the Cetus, the Beast.

Another important part of the chart that was descriptive of what was to come, is based upon the stars and constellations that the planets on the right-hand side of the chart are aligned with. They connect us with the myth of Andromeda, the chained woman.

> Andromeda was the beautiful daughter of Cepheus and Cassiopeia, the King and Queen of Ethiopia. They sacrificed her to save their kingdom, had her chained to a rock and left prey for the sea monster *Cetus*, who had been sent by Poseidon. But the hero Perseus intervened. He rescued Andromeda and married her.

---

1   This "flood" is the one in the Bible, in Noah's time.
2   Bailey, Alice A. Initiation, Human and Solar, 35.
3   Hinckley Allen, Richard; Star Names, 281.

Two stars are in the constellation Cepheus - *Erakis* and *Kurdah* (10 and 23 Aries). *Rucha* (17 Taurus) is in Cassiopeia. *Almach* (13 Taurus) is in Andromeda, and *Menkar* (13 Taurus) is in *Cetus*. *Menkar* is a bright orange star that "marks the Monster's open jaws. It portends danger from great beasts." [1] Finally, *Scheat* (29 Pisces), is in Pegasus, the winged horse that Perseus flew.

Here is how the myth could be interpreted for WWII:

> The sea monster *Cetus*, is Nazi Germany. The sacrifice of Andromeda generally represents the peoples of the world; specifically, the European nations that were drastically affected by the war and European Jews and other groups persecuted by the Nazis. Perseus, the rescuer represents generally the United Kingdom who first stood up to the monster. There is a connection between this myth and the English legend of Saint George, who slew the dragon (*Cetus*) about to devour a princess. [2]

d. Stars on the angles.

• On the ascendant, the primary influence in the war, is *Vindemiatrix* (9 Libra), a bright yellow star in the right arm of the Virgin. It has been called the "Gatherer of the Grapes" and the "Widow Maker." An interpretation is - you reap what you sow. Because of the aggression and violence, nation at war with nation, many wives would become widows.

• The MC: *Sirius*, the Dog Star, is located here (13 Cancer). One of its associations is with flooding - in ancient Egypt, the annual helical rising of Sirius marked the annual flooding of the Nile. In this case, in the early stages of the war, Germany was unstoppable. It was like a tsunami, destroying all in its path. Then, in the later stages of the war when the Allies gained the upper hand; Germany was swept with a river of retributive fire. A karmic backlash for the previous misdeeds.

• The descendant: *Erakis* in Cepheus (9 Aries), is there. It represents earthquakes and major events that affect large swathes of people. Millions were killed, maimed, injured and displaced by the war.

• The IC, the legacy of the war: *Nunki/ Pelagus* is located here (12 Capricorn), a star on the vane of the arrow in the Archer's hand.

Of the nature of Jupiter and Mercury, *Nunki* positively expressed, bodes well for the future - giving a blessing of good-fortune and improved international relations and communications. In the war's aftermath, America became the world super-power, the west opposed the Soviet Union Republic and its efforts to spread Communism, colonialism began its demise, women's liberation from traditional female roles began, and western alliances laid the foundations for international law.

But *Nunki* negatively expressed - with militant Mars in a wide conjunction to the IC; carries a warning. The world could not be complacent, or the drums of war would sound again. The reality is, there has continued to be conflict somewhere in the world ever since. But fortunately, not a world war - so far.

---

1   Hinckley Allen, Richard; Star Names, 162.
2   St. George and the Dragon: Introduction in: E. Gordon Whatley, Anne B. Thompson, Robert Upchurch, Saints' Lives in Middle Spanish Collections (2004).

5. The Covid-19 Pandemic. [1]

The partial lunar eclipse on 17 July 2019, was the last eclipse before the outbreak. The potential virulence of this disease and its mass-spread, was indicated by the eclipse falling on the very powerful, crystallising and destroying conjunction of transit Saturn and Pluto. These forces created a "once is a century" event - Covid-19. Because it is a conjunction, the impact of Covid-19, the changes that occur in humanity as a consequence of the pandemic; these will not reach a definite completion until the next time these two meet - in 2053.

It is the most devastating disease to afflict humanity since the 1918 influenza outbreak. From the point of view of esoteric healing, physical epidemics are triggered by widespread fear and worry. These are so infectious astrally, they can trigger the physical condition.

In 2019, there were three major world worries that contributed to the pandemic: (1) Greedy and corrupt autocrats, politics and politicians, governments and big business. Greed in action has resulted in the rich getting richer and the masses poorer. (2) Concerns over climate change and the health of the planet. (3) The flood of refugees fleeing to the west because of war, corrupt leaders, poverty and hunger.

<u>Lunar eclipse for Covid-19: July 17, 2019, 05:39, Wuhan, China.</u>

The eclipse location is set at Wuhan, China, where the outbreak allegedly occurred.

• Saturn and Pluto are shaping events. When they come together, government structures and ruling dynasties that are crystallised and no longer serve the common good are targeted for destruction.

• The Moon is conjunct Saturn-Pluto. As well as representing the masses, it symbolises "the past," and the nature of the problem to be dealt with. Moon in Capricorn points to greedy ambition and unbridled ambition as the illness in the world that has given rise to the physical pandemic (Moon 6H).

• Mother Earth is ill (fear and worry in humanity; Moon 6H), and the pandemic is Nature's attempt to heal.

• With the vitalising Sun in Cancer and on the ascendant, the goal of the eclipse is to revitalise life conditions for the masses - through a purging illness (the lords of the eclipse - Moon and Saturn, are in the 6H, with Pluto). Esoterically, disease is purificatory, a means to remove obstacles to the flow of life-giving energies, so that health can be restored.

• The virus was born (Sun rising on ascendant), in unsanitary conditions and food preparation habits (opposite Moon-Saturn in the 6H of health and nutrition), pregnant with toxicity (Moon-Saturn-Pluto).

• Airborne and easily spread by coughing, talking or by physical contact, the virus will become a pandemic (Sun conjunct Mercury, at 2 Leo, the Sabian Symbol epidemic degree in the zodiac). Also, on the ascendant, is *Pollux* (24 Cancer) in the Gemini constellation. This <u>star portends virulent</u> diseases, extreme sickness and fevers.

1   This book was written during the Covid-19 outbreak.

• Governments were being forced to be more Aquarian-Age like, in handling the pandemic (Uranus in the 10H, dominating the chart). Radical, socialist methods were used - the giving away of millions of dollars to people who had lost their jobs or businesses; to help avoid economies going into recession.

• The world was being taught to relate in new ways (Venus disposits Uranus), to be more community-spirited (Venus' sign Taurus is on the 11H), to be mindful of one's effect on others, and to care for the most vulnerable in the community (eclipse in Cancer).

• Overall, the race is being taught to develop higher spiritual values to live by (Neptune in Pisces, 9H), to be more sensitive and compassionate for those most at risk and also to be mindful for the well-being of the community. Such changes will help humanity become a "Lighted House" (Cancer ascendant).

• The effects of the pandemic will radically change the world's perspective of what is important. The Sabian Symbol for 7 Taurus, Uranus' degree is: *"Woman of Samaria comes to draw water from the well. The gaining of perspective by a return to ancient sources of being."* We are being taught to reconnect with simpler and healthier ways of being and living.

• As a consequence of the entire event, deep cleansing and healing will take place. Post-pandemic, humanity will be slimmer and more highly energised to make changes that result in improvements in the quality of life for all.

From a spiritual perspective, a major crisis like Covid-19 is an attempt by the universe, by Nature, to balance human and environmental affairs, to reset world values, direction and policies. Covid revealed the truth about our world. It brought to our attention the deprivation, inequalities and political unrest that exist. Covid revealed the calibre of political leaders and their humanitarianism (or lack of) in their handling of the pandemic. When faced with a choice between saving lives or the economy, humanitarian leaders chose people first. Materialists chose the economy or put their own interests first. Pragmatists tried to balance the two interests.

The result in countries ruled by pragmatists and materialists is that the virus ravaged the masses and there will be consequences. People do not forget and many governments and leaders will fall because people believed their leaders did not look out for them or put them before other selfish interests.

In the following sections, the eclipses for the World Wars, for the Spanish Flu and Covid-19; these are compared to national natal charts to see how the nation was affected, how the people coped and how the nation changed as a consequence of the crises.

In the future, whenever Saturn and Pluto in particular are forming hard aspects to each other, all eclipses that occur in that time frame should be studied in relation to the national natal chart. Finding those periods when an eclipse makes a powerful impact on the natal chart will help prepare leaders for coming conflicts or catastrophes.

C. The Evolutionary Function
of Fixed Stars.

When viewed from earth, the fixed stars do not appear to move when compared to the moving planets and objects in our solar system. They do move, but so slowly (about 50.333 seconds a year), this change is nearly imperceptible on our time scale.

The stars are suns, vastly more powerful than planets in terms of light and energy. Although all stars excepting for our sun lie outside the solar system (which relates moreso to our own human development), they still affect all life on earth.

This, because the universe is an integrated organism. Our solar system is part of the universal whole and we are connected to the cosmos by an interlinking web of fire through which the universal forces flow. Here is a relevant quote:

> The field of space is etheric in nature and its vital body is composed of the totality of etheric bodies of all constellations, solar systems and planets which are found therein. Throughout this cosmic golden web there is a constant circulation of energies and forces and this constitutes the scientific basis of the astrological theories. [1]

1. The effects of stars.

Roman astronomer and astrologer Claudius Ptolemy, born about 90 AD, studied the fixed-stars. Much of the fixed-star information used in this book originates from his work, interpreted and compiled by Vivian Robson (1890 -1942) in his book, 'The Fixed Stars & Constellations in Astrology'. According to Robson, the influences of fixed-stars are more dramatic and violent than planets.

> The influence of the fixed-stars [are] much more dramatic, sudden and violent. The stars appear to exercise most of their influence in sudden, hard, vehement bursts, producing tremendous effects for short periods and bringing a series of dramatic and unexpected disasters. [2]

This is one way to view the effect of stars. But from the spiritual perspective, the stars represent the evolutionary forces of nature, just as the signs and planets do. Their effects are determined by the quality of the form upon which they are impacting - whether this is a man or a nation. If the form is decaying and crystallised, and is inhibiting the flow of life through it; these high vibrational forces can shatter the form. This may come in the form of a serious illness in man, a war in a nation and death in both - psychological or physical.

The point is, star forces do not control men's actions. If men do evil things, it is due to their deficiencies and not the stars. If evil things happen on earth, it is because there are crystallisations that need shifting so that the healing energies of the universe can flow in.

2. Issues arising when stars are way north or south of the celestial equator.

Stars do not orbit around our Sun, but instead, circumscribe their own destinies in other parts of the universe. Consequently, they do not travel tidily along the ecliptic like the planets do. There are several problems this raises for some astrologers.

---

1   Bailey, Alice A. Esoteric Astrology, 11.
2   Robson, Vivian; Fixed Stars & Constellations in Astrology, 92.

Problem 1: Stars that cannot be sighted at birth, have no effect.

Due to their location in relation to our solar system, the orbits of some stars remain only in the northern or in the southern hemispheres. Based on this, some astrologers believe that only those stars that can be seen from a location on earth, will have any effect on that location; and "unsighted" stars should not be used. However, Karen Rosenberg, author of 'Secrets of the Ancient Skies, vols.1 and 2, disagrees:

> I strongly take issue with the idea that if a star cannot rise (and therefore will never be visible) at a particular location or birthplace it should not be used in the birth chart. All of the sky belongs to all of humanity, without strictures or curtailments relating to birth latitudes, longitudes or visual passages. The universe is not 'out there' - it is within and a part of all of us, our co-creation with God; each of us resides at the focal centre of our personal universe, and the entire cosmos is both within and without each of us. Every member of the human race, whatever his or her latitude of birth, is heir to, and part of, the entirety of the cosmos. [1]

Rosenberg's opinion aligns with the esoteric principles of human spirituality and man's connection with the universe/ the Divine, upon which this book is based.

Problem 2: Dimmer stars have less effect on earth.

Astrologers who hold this view believe that 1st magnitude, brighter stars have a more powerful effect on earth events than dimmer stars do. But Diana K. Rosenberg said:

> Size, magnitude, had apparently no connection with a star's importance. Some very dim stars pack quite a wallop! [2]

Rosenberg came to this conclusion as a result of her very extensive research on the stars and their effects on major earth-events.

Problem 3: Remoteness of a star by latitude, diminishes its effect on earth.

Astrologers who hold this view believe that, even if a star is conjunct a planet by longitude, it may be way north or south of the planet by latitude. This remoteness by latitude weakens its effect. But Rosenberg also disagreed with this notion. She said in an interview:

> Nearness to the ecliptic had apparently no connection with a star's importance. [3]

Alan Oken in his "Complete Astrology" also disagreed with the notion:

> [He placed] a far greater importance on an exact longitudinal position in order to establish the relative strength of a star rather that judging it by its proximity (either north or south) to the celestial equator. [4]

Oken was referring only to the conjunction and opposition. Vivian Robson also disagreed:

> It is usual to take the conjunction in exactly the same way as a planetary conjunction in a horoscope, by the degree of ecliptic longitude. [5]

1   Rosenberg, Diana. Secrets of the Ancient Skies, vol.1. xxviii.
2   Interview with Edith Hathaway, 2010. http://edithhathaway.com/pdf/DianaKRosenbergInterview.pdf
3   Ibid
4   Oken, Alan. Complete Astrology, 572-574.
5   Robson, Vivian; Fixed Stars & Constellations in Astrology, 95.

Problem 4: "Stars cast no rays".

Ptolemy wrote "fixed stars cast no rays." Some astrologers say this means only the *conjunction* is valid to use when working with stars, because traditional calculations to find all other aspects do not work. Alan Oken disagreed for the opposition aspect:

> Due to the laws of polarity, "For every action there is an equal and opposite reaction", the opposition must exert some influence. [1]

Vivian Robson also disagreed. With the conjunction he used the opposition, square and parallel aspects.

> It is usual to take the conjunction (with a star) in exactly the same way as a planetary conjunction in a horoscope, by the degree of ecliptic longitude affected by the star, and the parallel by its declination, and these positions are the only orthodox ones to use. It will be found however, that the opposition is almost as powerful as the conjunction and that the square has an undeniable influence. [2]

In summary, it is accurate to use conjunction and opposition aspects. For other aspects, Robson gave a special calculation in his book on page 253. However, it is important to remember that once a planet receives a star's power, it can then distribute this power to any planet or point it is in aspect to.

3. Tight orbs are recommended.

Stars are graded by their brightness as seen from earth on a magnitude scale from -1 to 6. The brightest star, Sirius, has a magnitude of -1.4. The faintest star visible to the naked eye has a magnitude of +6.0.

Orbs advocated by Vivian Robson. [3]

- 1st magnitude star - 7° 30'
- 2nd magnitude star - 5° 30'
- 3rd magnitude star - 3° 40'
- 4th magnitude star - 1° 30'
- 5 onwards and clusters - 1°

Oken:

- 1st magnitude star - 2°,
- 2nd magnitude star - 1° to 1 and 1/2°

Rosenberg and the author of this book:

- 1° on either side [of all stars].

4. Stars on Angles and the timing of their influence.

- On the Asc: the star's energy manifests quickly and endures throughout the life of the event or nation. This is the strongest position for a star.
- On the MC. The star's effect manifests quite early, with a pronounced effect.
- On the DC. The star manifests more potently in the middle part of an event.
- On the IC. The effect will manifest in "old age," will colour the legacy of the event.

---

1 Oken, Alan. Alan Oken's Complete Astrology, 574.
2 Robson, Vivian; Fixed Stars & Constellations in Astrology, 95.
3 Robson, Vivian; Fixed Stars & Constellations in Astrology, 103.

5. Overview of some stars used in this book.

All the star quotes in this book that do not have reference information come from Vivian Robson's 'Fixed Stars & Constellations in Astrology' book. Readers interested in the stars should purchase that book.

A few stars seem to come up constantly when disasters or catastrophes occur and a few are included here. Longitude locations are for 1 January 2020. Minutes have been rounded out to the closest degree.

Achernar (16 Pisces) in Eridanus, magnitude .445, of the nature of Jupiter. "The End of the River" because of its location. *Negatives*: "Natural disasters, fires and floods". [1] *Positives:* a beneficial (Jupiter) effect.

Aldebaran (10 Gemini) in Taurus, a magnitude -2.1 star of the nature of Mars. It is one of the four Royal stars or Watchers of the Heavens. *Negatives*: A very violent and evil martial star, loss through fire, war and bloodshed. Sickness fevers, infectious diseases, lingering death (starvation). *Positives:* honour, intelligence, eloquence, steadfastness, integrity, courage, public honours. Directly across in the zodiac is its opposite, the star - Antares (10 Sagittarius 03).

Algol (26 Taurus) in Perseus, magnitude 2.12, of the nature of Pluto. [2] It is called "the most evil star in the heavens, representing the Medusa's head, the Gorgon. The Chinese called it "Tseih She," Piled-up Corpses. *Negatives*: misfortune, violence and violent deaths. Death by water or poison. *Positives*: "purging of poison, healing at a deep level". [3]

Antares (10 Sagittarius) in Scorpius, magnitude 1.09, of the nature of Mars and Jupiter. Also called the Scorpion's Heart, it is one of the four Royal stars or Watchers of the Heavens. *Negatives*: martial, malefic, destructive, evil, brings calamities. Sickness, pestilent disease, danger of death and drowning. *Positives:* honour, promotion and good fortune - especially in the military or in politics.

Aselli, two stars in Cancer, of the nature of the Sun and Mars. North Asellus (8 Leo), magnitude 3.94. South Asellus (9 Leo), magnitude 4.65. *Shared negatives:* sickness, fevers, serious accidents and burns, danger of fire. *Shared positives:* care and responsibility, a charitable and fostering nature.

Baten Kaitos (22 Aries) in *Cetus*, magnitude 3.7, of the nature of Saturn. The Whale's Belly. *Negative:* compulsory transportation, misfortune, shipwreck. "A stormy star, known for shipwrecks and drowning." [4] *Positive:* change, emigration, rescue at sea.

Bellatrix (21 Gemini) in Orion, magnitude 1.64, of the nature of Mars and Mercury. The Female Warrior, Swiftly Destroying. *Negatives*: disease, extreme sickness, fevers and violent death. *Positives:* civil or military honour.

Betelgeuse (29 Gemini) in Orion, magnitude .58, of the nature of Mars and Mercury. The Coming of the Branch, *Negatives*: acute diseases, fevers. *Positives:* martial honour, promotion and wealth.

Castor (21 Cancer) in Gemini, magnitude 1.58, of the nature of Mercury. It represents Castor, the mortal twin. A Ruler yet to Come. *Negatives*: if actions are not honourable -

---

1 Brady, Bernadette. Fixed Stars, 142.
2 Allocation by Leoni Hodgson.
3 Allocation by Leoni Hodgson.
4 Rosenberg, Diana. Interview with Edith Hathaway, 22 July 2010.

disgrace, trouble, great affliction. Sickness, violent fevers, serious accidents. *Positives:* it gives "distinction, a keen intellect, success in law, many travels, fame and honour but also disgrace." In esoteric astrology, Castor represents the personality, whose light is waning, and the other Twin, Pollux, represents the soul whose light or power is waxing.

Deneb Kaitos - "Difda" (3 Aries) in *Cetus*, magnitude 2.02, of the nature of Saturn. *Negatives*: misfortune, sickness, destruction, forced change, treachery from secret enemies, domestic disagreements, death by fire. "Harsh, cruel, vindictive treatment. Brute force, ruination, losses." [1] A stormy star, known for shipwrecks, drowning. The stars of *Cetus* portend earthquakes and tsunamis. *Positive:* seeks to enact laws of benefit to the community.

Denebola (22 Virgo) in Leo, magnitude 2.113, of the nature of Saturn and Venus. Known as the Judge, or Lord who Cometh. *Negatives*: swift judgement, despair, dangers, anxieties, misfortune from the elements of nature. Sickness, malignant contagious diseases and death. *Positives:* nobility, generosity and promotion.

Dschubba (Isidis) (3 Sagittarius) in Scorpius, near the right claw, magnitude 2.32, of the nature of Mars and Saturn. *Negatives*: it creates an evil environment, brings malevolence and domestic disharmony. Malignant disease, sudden or violent death, accidents from fire, water and electricity. *Positives:* "courageous and intelligent." [2]

Dubhe (15 Leo), in Ursa Major, magnitude 1.79. "The great Mother. *Negatives*: the harshness of Mother Nature. *Positives*: nurturing and protective." [3]

Fomalhaut (4 Pisces) in Piscis Austrinus (the Southern Fish), magnitude 1.16, of the nature of Venus and Mercury. Located in the Fish's Mouth, it is one of the four Royal stars or Watchers of the Heavens. *Negatives*: malevolence of a sublime scope. *Positives:* very fortunate and powerful.

Grafias (18 Sagittarius) in Scorpius, magnitude 5.07, of the nature of Mars and Saturn. It is situated on the head of the Scorpion. *Negatives*: extreme malevolence, mercilessness, fiendishness, repulsiveness, malice and crime. Pestilence contagious diseases and death after a lingering illness. *Positives:* promotion, great power and honour.

Menkar (15 Taurus) in *Cetus*, magnitude 2.53, of the nature of Saturn. *Negatives*: ruin, great trouble, violent death, failure of crops, loss through fire. Disease, sickness. *Positives:* legacies and inheritances.

Pleiades (0 Gemini) in Taurus, a magnitude 1.6 cluster, of the nature of the Moon and Mars. The Seven Sisters. Alcyone is the principal star, situated on the shoulder of the bull. All are within about one degree of longitude. *Negatives*: an evil influence, loss and suffering through fires. Sickness, violent fevers, death by pestilence. *Positives:* ambitious, optimistic, peaceful, many journeys and success in agriculture

Polaris (29 Gemini), in Ursa Minor, magnitude 1.97, of the nature of Saturn and Venus. The Pole Star. Esoterically, Polaris is called the "Star of Re-orientation, of Direction," that brings man back to his originating (spiritual) source. [4] The entire north sky wheels around Polaris. *Negatives*: sickness, trouble, great affliction. *Positives*: legacies and inheritances.

Pollux (23 Cancer) in Gemini, magnitude 1.14 of the nature of Mars. Called Hercules, A Heartless Judge. *Negatives*: malevolence [sadism], rape and calamity. Extreme sickness,

1   Rigor, Joseph. The Power of Fixed Stars, 47.
2   Allocation by Leoni Hodgson.
3   Brady, Bernadette. Solar Fire astrology software.
4   Bailey, Alice A. Esoteric Astrology, 196.

disease, fever, a virulent disease, suffocation, drowning or assassination, a violent death. *Positives*: honour and promotion.

Praesepe (8 Leo) a nebulous cluster, magnitude 3.5, in the constellation Cancer, of the nature of Mars and the Moon. The Beehive, called by the Chinese "Tseih She Ke" - Piled-up Corpses. *Negatives:* causes brutal acts. Disease, sickness, violent fevers; danger of death from fire, iron or stones. *Positives*: industry, order and fecundity.

Regulus (0 Virgo) in Leo, magnitude 1.3, of the nature of Mars and Jupiter. The Lion's Heart, the Crushing Foot. It is one of the four Royal stars or Watchers of the Heavens. *Negatives*: violence, destructiveness, trouble. A violent death, fevers, acute diseases. *Positives*: military honour, success, high ideals, strength of spirit, magnanimity, generosity and independence.

Scheat (0 Aries) in Pegasus, magnitude 2.42, of the nature of Mars and Mercury. *Negatives*: bad for domestic affairs, extreme misfortune, danger. Bad for health, sickness, death/ accidents through water (drowning), from engines, from fiery cutting weapons (modern weapons today). *Positives*: many voyages.

Sirius (14 Cancer) in Canis Major, magnitude -1.4, of the nature of Mars and Jupiter. Sparkling or Scorching, the Chieftain's Star. Chinese called it the "Heavenly Wolf." To esotericists it is known as The Star of Sensitivity and is connected with spiritual growth. *Negatives*: attacks from thieves. Sudden death, dog bites. *Positives*: it gives honour, wealth, faithfulness, and makes its people custodians and guardians.

Spica (24 Libra). The brightest star in Virgo, magnitude 1.04. Marks the Ear of Wheat shown in the Virgin's left hand. *Negatives*: "crop failures that lead to famine." *Positives*: fertility, agriculture, "gifted with nature's bounties." [1]

Sulaphat (22 Capricorn), in Lyra, magnitude 3.3. The "Swooping Vulture (or Eagle) with a lyre hanging from its claws." [2] *Negatives:* "being preyed upon." [3] *Positives:* the lyre made by Mercury, its music enchanted the beasts, birds and rocks.

Toliman - Bungula, (1 Sagittarius), in Centaurus, magnitude -0.1, of the nature of Venus and Jupiter. *Negatives*: trouble in domestic affairs. Death through a virulent disease. *Positives*: has a beneficial effect, friends, refinement and a position of honour.

Vega or Wega (16 Capricorn) in Lyra, magnitude .03, of the nature of Venus and Mercury. The Descending or Falling Vulture. *Negatives*: hard-heartedness, a cold, miserly attitude, domestic sorrow, ugliness. Ill-health, deformity, a violent death. *Positives*: beneficence, hopefulness and refinement.

Zuben Elgenubi - "Scale, South" (15 Scorpio) in Libra, magnitude 2.9, of the nature of Mars and Saturn. The southern Claw, The Insufficient Price. *Negatives*: malevolence, violence, treachery and bloodshed. Disease. *Positives*: Robson gives no positives, these being reserved for its twin, North Scale.

---

1   Allocation by Leoni Hodgson.
2   Hinckley Allen, Richard; Star Names, 281-283.
3   Allocation by Leoni Hodgson.

Chapter 3. Evolution of the Nations.

The nations are in alphabetical order. Most national charts selected have come from Nicholas Campion's "The Book of World Horoscopes."

**Abbreviations used
in this book**

Asc Ascendant, the 1st house cusp

DC Descendant, the 7th house cusp

IC Imum Coeli, the 4th house cusp, angle at the bottom of the chart

MC Midheaven or Medium Coeli, 10th house cusp, angle at the top of the chart

H House

R Ray/ rays

Argentina

Argentina's personality is ruled by Libra, its soul by Cancer. [1]

Argentina has a nurturing and family-building Cancer soul and a vacillating Libra personality. Both these signs carry the 3rd Ray of intelligence, which enables the nation to produce leaders who have an enterprising intelligence and an ability to find ingenious ways to guide the nation and solve its problems. Theoretically! In the hands of materialistic-minded ambitious egos, intelligence has been used for personal profit, power and control. When utilised by enlightened leaders, ingenious ways will be found to nurture and protect the people and guide the nation to its higher good. Raul Alfonsin, president in 1983, appeared to be such a man.

1. Spanish Conquistadors establish the first colony in 1536.

Spanish nobleman, explorer and Conquistador, Pedro de Mendoza established the first colony in Argentina, on 2 February 1536, where Buenos Aires now stands. Then, intentional or not, a systematic genocide of indigenous people followed.

Total Solar eclipse for the Spanish arrival: 24 Dec 1535, 10:03, Buenos Aires.

The evolutionary pattern shaping events is Saturn opposite Pluto. They were in the process of separating - the Spanish were on their way.

• The eclipse was in the 10H. The arrival of the all-powerful invading conquistadors was the beginning of the end for the indigenous people. They were to be eclipsed by their oppressors, represented by the lord of the eclipse - Saturn. It is on the star *Regulus* (23 Leo), also known as the 'Crushing Foot', a very descriptive term for what was to follow.

• Saturn is in the 6H of acute illnesses. Many natives died from diseases such as typhoid, influenza and smallpox, introduced by the Europeans. They had no immunity (Saturn inconjunct retrograde Mercury, ruler of the 4H of the people).

This health crises is shown again by the star *Bellatrix* (14 Gemini), on the IC. It highlighted the legacy left by the Spanish colonists - swift and violent destruction and extreme sickness and death. Historians say that "Indigenous people barely survived after Argentina became independent from Spanish colonial rule". [2]

For 200 years, the Spanish ruled Argentina, under the Spanish Viceroyalty of the Río de la Plata. But, by the 19th Century, resentment was brewing among local born Argentinian's, because plum jobs in government were being taken by Spanish elite sent out from Europe. This bred rebellion.

---

1 Bailey, Alice A. The Destiny of the Nations, 67.
2 Crooker, Richard. Argentina, 33.

2. The Argentine Revolution, 1810.

Solar eclipse for the Argentine Revolution: 3 Apr 1810, 21:47, Buenos Aires.

• The soul of the nation, which always fights for the freedom of its people, made its presence felt through the Argentine independence movement. When King Ferdinand of Spain was overthrown by Napoleon, on 25th May 1810, the locals established an autonomous viceroyalty in Ferdinand's name. This date is now celebrated as the day of the revolution and it produced the first national chart for Argentina.

• It was time to let go of and eliminate, ties to the old structures, to Spain. The evolutionary pattern shaping events was Saturn conjunct Neptune, square Pluto. The revolutionaries acted.

• Warlike *Acumen* (26 Sagittarius), a star north of the stinger of the Scorpion, was on the ascendant, inciting action.

• The eclipse was in fiery, independent Aries and revolutionary Uranus was in the 11H of politics, widely opposing military Mars.

• The locals were clever (3rd Ray). Establishing a "viceroyalty in Ferdinand's name" was a blind for their true intentions. The locals wanted to create their own uniquely Argentinian culture (5H emphasis), and they used trickery to get it. The ploy was successful.

3. Birth of Independent Argentina (1): 25 May 1810, 12:00, Buenos Aires

----

• The chart is set for the date the Spanish Viceroy was deposed in Argentina and a patriotic junta was installed - on the 25 May 1810. In the absence of a known time, 12-noon is used. It gave Argentina its first, "modern", natal chart.

• The Sun and three other "personal" planets are in Gemini. This is a transit sign and the people were still in the planning stage for full independence. This came a few years later, in 1816.

• The martial star *Aldebaran* (7 Gemini), lay between warlike Mars, the MC and the Sun; fuelling the people's aspirations for autonomy and self-determination.

• The Saturn-Neptune conjunction, is on the IC, and so is the powerful military star *Antares* (7 Sagittarius). The people would have to fight to achieve their ideals for independence, and they were ready to do so. However, it took 6 more years.

4. Birth of Independent Argentina (2): 9 Jul 1816, 14:00, Tucuman.

On 9 July 1816, full Argentine independence was declared. Nicholas Campion in his book World Horoscopes, said there is documented evidence for a
14:00 time. [1]

• The 14:00 time places travelling Sagittarius
on the ascendant rather than Libra, which some
astrologers use.

Sagittarius rules horses, which fits the gau-
cho, horse-loving image the nation portrays. Argentina is universally recognized as polo's mecca
and has won gold medals at the Olympic Games. The
2 pm time also places Mars on the 10H arm of government, apt for a nation that has been subject to military domi-
nance, revolutions and wars. In the 20th Century alone, there were 6 military coups, the
most infamous was the "Dirty War" in the 70s.

5. Argentina in the World Wars and Spanish Flu.

These events, which had such a catastrophic effect in Europe and other participating nations, seemed to pass Argentine by with minimal effect.

<u>Blood Moon eclipse for WWI: 15 Sep 1913, 08:29,</u>
<u>Buenos Aires; around Argentina 1816 natal.</u>

• Argentine leaders kept the nation neutral during
WWI. This was a wise decision, with the eclipse
Mars-Pluto conjunction falling in Argentine's
8H of death. It could have been much worse.

• However, the transforming effect of WWI
did bring important changes to the nation.
Until 1912, the nation's presidents came
from the aristocracy. A change in electoral
laws allowed military leader Hipolito Yrigoyen, to assume power in 1916.

(a). Eclipse Moon and north-node in the
5H of elections, conjunct natal Pluto.

(b). Venus that rules the nation's personality -
via Libra; was conjunct the MC, sextile Saturn
in the 7H of foreign relations.

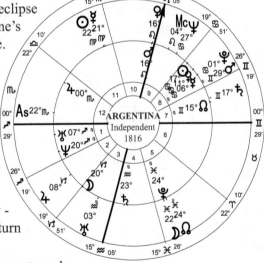

• The local economy benefitted by selling meat prod-
ucts to both warring sides (eclipse Jupiter in the 2H of the economy, opposite Argentine's
Cancer stellium in the 8H of international business).

---

1   Campion, Nicholas. The Book of World Horoscopes, 14:00 time, 39-40.

Lunar eclipse for Spanish Flu: 15 Jul 1916, 00:24, Buenos Aires; around Argentina 1816 natal.

Spanish Flu appeared to have only a minimal impact on Argentina. The most fortunate aspect of its non-participation in the war, was that it did not have returning soldiers bringing the virus back home with them. This was its greatest protection.

• Eclipse Neptune, which represents the virus, forms a t-square with eclipse and natal Jupiter. This indicated that if this foreign infection (Neptune in Argentina's 9H), had gained a foot-hold in the nation, the infection rate would have been enormous (eclipse and natal Jupiter, span the 6th - 12th health houses). So would the death toll have been (eclipse Pluto in the 8H of death, conjunct natal Mercury, ruler of the 8H of death).

• Reports indicate that Yrigoyen did introduce protective precautions. However, news coverage of the pandemic was sparse. This is an indication that the virus did not cut a swathe through the population.

Blood Moon eclipse for WWII: 3 May 1939, 11:16, Buenos Aires; around Argentina 1816 natal.

Popular support at home favoured the Axis nations. This was because most Argentines were of Spanish, Italian, or German descent and had close cultural ties with those nations.

• Argentina remained neutral until a month before the war ended. Then, under intense pressure from the Allies, it declared war on the Axis powers. This non-participation is shown by the eclipse planets not hitting any angles of Argentina's chart and their falling mainly in Argentina's cadent houses (3, 6, 9, 12). This indicated the war would have a more subtle and mental effect on the nation, rather than physical.

• Sceptics write that Argentine's leaders only declared war on the Axis powers so it could send its agents to Europe to help the Nazis and their collaborators escape to Argentina after the war. Thousands did, bringing their looted fortunes with them - a factor that probably helped shape Argentina's decision. War criminals from abroad (eclipse Pluto in the 9H), bringing their wealth and culture to the nation (Pluto trine Jupiter in the 5H).

6. The Dirty War: 1976 to 1983.

The Dirty War, from 1976 to 1983, was a seven-year campaign by the Argentine military government waged on the nation. Many people, both opponents of the government as well as innocent people, disappeared in the middle of the night. It is reported they were taken to secret government detention centres where they were tortured and eventually killed. These unfortunate people are known as "the disappeared."

Blood Moon eclipse for the Dirty War: 18 Nov 1975, 19:27, Buenos Aires; around Argentina 1816 natal.

• The war was a battle over the soul and direction of the nation (eclipse Sun on Argentina's Asc, the soul-purpose point of the chart). The junta leaders wanted to repeal liberal gains and reassert the autocratic controls which they used to have over the people (eclipse Sun square natal Saturn in the 4H).

• On 29 March 1976, a military junta deposed Argentine President Isabel Peron (the eclipse Sun and Mercury, in Scorpio, square natal Mars and the MC).

• The event had a devastating effect (the eclipse Sun and Moon straddle the Asc/ DC axis and formed a grand-cross with the MC/ IC). Thus, all the angles in the nation's chart, its foundational institutions; were impacted.

Ominously, the eclipse Moon was conjunct *Algol* (26 Taurus) "the most evil star in the heavens." The men of the military junta had evil intentions. Although the junta said its objective was to eradicate guerrilla activity, its true agenda was to destroy all political opposition - trade unionists, students, intellectuals, rights activists. Estimates are they killed between 10,000 to 30,000 people.

• The evolutionary pattern shaping events is Uranus square Saturn - the shattering (Uranus), of crystallisations (Saturn), binding the soul. It was a shameful period in Argentine's history, but it brought to the surface corruption and viciousness embedded in a section of the community - in the military government.

In 1983, the junta tried to regain favour with the people by seizing the Falkland Islands. But a humiliating defeat led to its final downfall.

• In the war's aftermath, the new democratically elected government created a National Commission to investigate the disappearances, and to collect evidence about the "Dirty War." As a consequence, most of the perpetrators faced justice. The evil men behind the atrocities were weighed, judged and punished. Eclipse Mercury is on *Zuben Elschemali* (19 Scorpio), "The Full Price." It is a star in the northern scale in Libra, that inspires the weighing of the deeds of men. Though some of these men were later pardoned, their evil deeds were exposed and steps were taken to prevent such evil practices being used again in the future.

7. The Falkland's War - 2 April 1982 to 14 June 1982.

The Falkland Islands lie 300k off the coast of south Argentina. By 1885, British settlers had established a community there and ever since, both Argentina and Britain have laid claim to the islands. Then, on 2 April 1982, the "Dirty War" military junta invaded the islands. Britain sent a naval task and it regained control after the 10-week Falkland's War.

Blood Moon eclipse for the War: 9 Jan 1982, 16:53, Buenos Aires: around Argentina 1816 natal.

• The Saturn-Pluto conjunction squares the Sun, which rules the 10H. Rigid government structures would be destroyed so a rebirth could take place.

• The eclipse Sun hit the natal Moon-*Sulaphat* conjunction, at 19-20 Capricorn. The star *Sulaphat* is called the "swooping vulture." In this case, Britain was the vulture and Argentina the prey. The military government was seen to be incompetent and this debacle led to its eventual demise.

• Interestingly, the Sun-Moon opposition in the eclipse, is the reverse of that in the natal chart. This could be interpreted as the people regaining control over the government (eclipse Moon conjunct natal Sun), and the fall of the junta (eclipse Sun at the bottom of the chart). In a March 2013 referendum, Falkland islanders voted almost unanimously to remain a British overseas territory.

8. Birth of Democratic Argentina: 10 Dec 1983, 12:00, Buenos Aires.

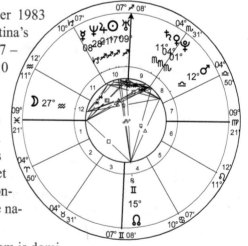

The Argentine general election on 30 October 1983 marked the return of constitutional rule. Argentina's rebirth stems from the day Raul Alfonsin (1927 – 2009), was inaugurated as President. This was 10 December 1983. The chart is set for 12-noon.

• Alfonsin's presidency came to symbolise the return of democracy across Latin America after an era of military dictatorships. This is clearly symbolised by Uranus, the ruling planet of Aquarius, the sign of universal freedoms, conjunct the noon MC. This was a high point in the nation's evolutionary progression.

• Sagittarius, another sign that represents freedom is dominant in the chart, with 4 planets and the MC in that sign.

Raul Alfonsin: 12 March 1927, 14:15, Buenos Aires.

• Alfonsín is considered to be the "father of modern democracy in Argentina." During his first month in office, he introduced measures to purge the military and to prosecute high-ranking officers for human rights' abuses (Jupiter, natural ruler of the 9H, square Mars).

• His downfall was primarily caused because he was unable to control the nation's spiralling inflation. But he had done the important job of instituting democratic reforms. His situation was similar to that of Mikhail Gorbachev, who was forced out of power in 1991 after bringing in reforms that destroyed the Soviet Union.

• Notably, Alfonsin's ascendant was in Cancer, the sign that rules Argentina's soul. His personal soul purpose aligned with that of the nation's - to nurture and protect the people. This he attempted to do. Though imperfect, he was a champion of the nation's masses (Sun in Pisces, trine natal Moon and Pluto, in Cancer in the 1H).

9. Argentina and Covid-19.

Lunar eclipse for Covid-19: 16 Jul 2019, 18:39, Buenos Aires; around Argentina 1983 natal.

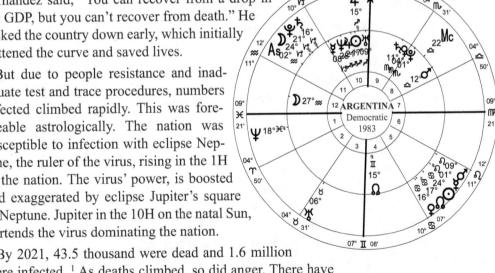

• When Covid reached Argentina, President Alberto Fernandez said, "You can recover from a drop in the GDP, but you can't recover from death." He locked the country down early, which initially flattened the curve and saved lives.

• But due to people resistance and inadequate test and trace procedures, numbers infected climbed rapidly. This was foreseeable astrologically. The nation was susceptible to infection with eclipse Neptune, the ruler of the virus, rising in the 1H of the nation. The virus' power, is boosted and exaggerated by eclipse Jupiter's square to Neptune. Jupiter in the 10H on the natal Sun, portends the virus dominating the nation.

• By 2021, 43.5 thousand were dead and 1.6 million were infected. [1] As deaths climbed, so did anger. There have been demonstrations against the government's handling of the crisis.

• The eclipse falls across the 5th cultural and 11th political houses; indicating transformations in these areas over the next 33 years as a consequence of the diseases effect.

---

1   13 Jan 2021: the 18th ranked nation in the world for deaths per capita.

10. Argentina's Spiritual Progress.

The personality of Argentina is ruled by Libra.

• Argentina's Aquarius Moon (in the 12H, sesquiquadrate Mars in Libra), indicated that prior to the restoration of democracy in 1983, the nation's limiting obstacle to spiritual growth were elites, including the military, who tried to wall themselves off from the masses so they could retain their privileged positions.

• Since democracy returned, Argentina has been grappling with human rights problems. There is still a long way to go, but the fact that this fight is ongoing, is evidence of the presence of the soul actively working in the nation. Libra rules legislation and there have been important legal gains that are liberalising.

Argentine 1983 natal

• The north-node's solitary position at the bottom of the chart in the 4H, is a plea for more attention to be given to the rights and living conditions of the people.

The soul of Argentina is ruled by Cancer.

The family is the centre of Argentine life. The head of family is respected and he or she carries the responsibility to look after the well-being of the family unit (the Cancer influence).

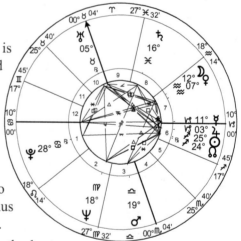

Pope Francis natal chart:
17 December 1936, 21:00, Buenos Aires.

A son of the nation who is fulfilling this duty is Jorge Mario Bergoglio. When he was elected Pope Francis I in 2013, he became the nurturer and protector of the Catholic family. With Cancer rising in his chart, it was his destiny to play such a role. As we know, his "family" is world-wide (Moon in Aquarius, 7H).

As head of the church, Francis is a refreshing "new-broom" who has been trying to eradicate corruption from the Church (Uranus conjunct the MC, square Pluto 1H in Cancer).

• Because Argentina's soul is ruled by Cancer, the best contribution that it can make to the spiritual health and well-being of humanity, is to firstly, build a lighted house within its own country by attending to the spiritual health and well-being of its people. If it does this, it will set a shining example to the world and be in an excellent position to help all other nations do the same.

> The objective of the Cancer experience is: "To build a lighted house and therein dwell." [1] This is Argentina's spiritual keynote.

1   Bailey, Alice A. Esoteric Astrology, 343.

Australia

Australia's personality is ruled by Capricorn, its soul by Virgo. [1]

With two earth signs ruling its destiny, Australia will always take a pragmatic and practical approach to its internal and external affairs. Additionally, the economic well-being of the nation will always be a prime consideration - earth-nations are custodians of the material plane. Historically, Australia has been traditional and conservative in its politics and economics (Capricorn); which means that the wealth of the nation has remained firmly in the hands of the wealthy. But as the Virgo soul begins to influence affairs, a more caring concern for the health and well-being of all people will start to colour the government's approach.

Because it shares a Virgo connection with New Zealand, the two nations will always have very close ties. Australia is also drawn by resonance to Greece, which has the same ruling signs. After WWII, over 250,000 Greek migrants came to the country.

1. Arrival of the First Fleet/ Aboriginal Invasion Day.

The First Fleet, commandeered by Captain Arthur Phillip, sailed into Botany Bay (Sydney), on 24 January 1788. The event marked the start of British settlement. Around 800 convicts were in the fleet. Indigenous Australians call it 'Invasion Day', because it started a long and sad journey of dispossession of their lands and brutalising of its people.

<u>Total Solar eclipse for the First Fleet: 16 Jun 1787, 01:55, Sydney.</u>

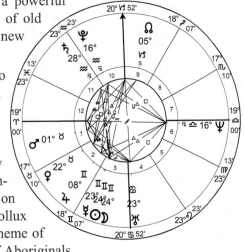

• The evolutionary pattern shaping events is a powerful Saturn-Pluto conjunction, indicating the death of old structures - for the Aborigines, and the birth of a new nation - for the English.

• Life for the indigenous people was about to radically change forever (Uranus on IC). From their point of view, the arrival of these violent people brought extreme hardship (Mars rising square Uranus 4H). They had no defence against the militant English invasion. The legacy they inherited was sickness, calamity, imprisonment and violent death (star *Pollux*, 22 Cancer on the IC, conjunct Uranus). Another name for Pollux is the 'Heartless Judge'. Violence has been a theme of government and law-enforcement treatment of Aboriginals ever since.

• The eclipse was in the 3H. New settlements with new neighbours were established (Moon rules 4H). There were bustling markets, a strange language and people travelling about.

• The settlers/ British, did not recognise Aborigine ownership of the land and set about forcibly taking it. Killing Aborigines was the norm - and with disease and dispossession, within a hundred years Aborigine numbers were reduced from 300,000 to 60,000. Those who survived had their traditional ways destroyed and their culture suppressed.

---

1 Bailey, Alice A. The Destiny of the Nations, 68.

2. Birth of the Australian Federation: 1 Jan 1901, 13:25, Melbourne.

On 1 January 1901, a ceremonial proclamation of the federation was made at 13:25 in Melbourne. The Commonwealth of Australia was born, and the natal chart from that birth is still current today.

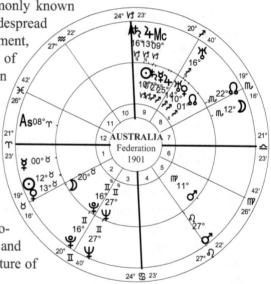

• Aries rising is ideal for this progressive and pioneering nation. Mars rules the military and via Scorpio, criminals. These groups were the original white immigrants to Australia and they established the cultural tone to the nation in those early years (Mars in the 5H).

• The 1901 Sun in Capricorn represented the penal state of the colony. This great sign has gifted the people with fortitude and endurance to persevere in the hard Australian land and climate.

3. The White Australia Policy, 1901.

Lunar eclipse, White Australia: 4 May 1901, 04:17, Melbourne; around Australia natal.

• The Immigration Restriction Bill (commonly known as the "White Australia policy"), had widespread support when it was introduced into parliament, just a couple of weeks after the new nation of Australia was born (Mercury and Saturn in the 9H of major legislations).

• A belief in white genetic and cultural superiority was revealed during the debates. For example:

Let us keep before us the noble idea of a white Australia—snow-white Australia if you will. Let it be pure and spotless. [1]

Restricting the immigration of non-Europeans was considered 'a matter of life and death to the purity of our race and the future of our nation'. [2]

• In 1973, the Whitlam Labor government renounced the White Australia policy, replacing it with a policy of multiculturalism. Many in Australia have forgotten this part of the nation's history, but seeds of this divisive evil live on. Racism is still entrenched in the race and police in particular, brutalise Aborigines taken into custody. Anecdotal information given by Aborigines is that they experience racism every day - in the 21st Century.

1   James Black Ronald, 'Immigration Restriction Bill', House of Representatives, Debates, 11 September 1901, p. 4666.
2   William McMillan, 'Immigration Restriction Bill', House of Representatives, Debates, 6 September 1901, p. 4629.

4. World War I and the Spanish Flu.

Blood Moon eclipse for WWI: 15 Sep 1913, 22:45, Canberra;
around Australia natal.

The United Kingdom entered WWI on 4 August 1914, and so did Australia. The nation was just 13 and still hugely attached to England. When "mother" went to war (Moon in the political 11H), there was a rush to defend her. Many thought it was a duty to fight (eclipse Sun in dutiful Virgo). For others, it was an adventure (Mars 5H). 416,809 men enlisted from a population of less than five million.

• Eclipse Uranus was in the 10H and on stars in the constellation Capricornus - in a lunar eclipse, it brings major storms. WWI was a hurricane that swept Australia up in its wake. The effects were shattering on the people. Over 61 thousand enlisted persons died and 156,000 were wounded or taken prisoner. Mars and Pluto are the war planets and rule Australia's 8H of death. In the eclipse chart, they are in a t-square with the Sun and Moon.

• The campaign that is deeply etched in the Australian psyche is the Gallipoli campaign in Turkey. Of the 60,000 troops who fought there, about a 7th were killed or died of disease, with no significant impact on the war. Australians are highly competitive fighters who like to win (Aries rising). If the campaign had been successful, perhaps the pilgrimage of mourning that thousands of Australians make each year to Gallipoli would not take place.

Lunar eclipse for Spanish Flu: 15 Jul 1916, 14:40, Sydney:
around Australia natal.

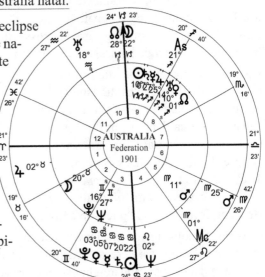

• Returning soldiers brought the flu home (eclipse Moon-Sun in the 3-9 travel houses and on the nation's MC/IC). It wreaked havoc. Reports state that a third of Australians were infected and 13,000 died. The Aboriginal mortality rate approached 50 per cent in some communities [1] (eclipse Venus, ruler 6H of health, conjunct Pluto)

• Neptune is the primary representative of viral infections and the epidemic was portended by eclipse Neptune's location on 2 degrees Leo (Sabian Symbol epidemic degree) and in the 4H of the people, square Jupiter in the 1H of the nation.

---

1   Cleland Burton J. Disease among the Australian Aborigines. J Trop Med Hyg1928

5. Australia in World War II.

Blood Moon eclipse, WWII: 4 May 1939, 01:16, Canberra; around Australia natal.

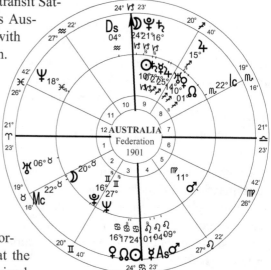

• Australia made an important new friend in the war - the USA. When Japan bombed Darwin in February 1942, the USA became Australia's major ally, stationing thousands of troops in the country. This explains Australia's enduring affectionate alliance with America into the 21st Century (Sun-Uranus eclipse in 1H of the nation, trine natal Sun-Saturn, 9H).

• But Australia's sacrifice was heavy (Pluto, ruler of natal 8H, on the 4H cusp). From a population of 7.5 million in 1939, "almost a million men and women served," [1] and approximately 27-30,000 died.

Australia changed after the war. Became more independent from the UK (Aries Asc, Mars on MC), more multicultural at home, and forged greater links with the rest of the world (Sun in the international 9H).

6. Black Summer bushfires, 2019-2020; and Covid-19, 2020.

After a prolonged drought, in 2019-2020 holocaust-like fires broke out. Fire-fronts were up to 100 kilometres wide. 72,000 square miles of land were burnt, 34 people and an estimated 1 billion animals were killed. This fire season was named "Black Summer." The 16 July 2019 eclipse that portended the bush fires in Australia and throughout the world, also portended the Covid-19 outbreak.

Lunar eclipse, Black Summer: 17 July 2019, 07:39, Sydney; around Australia natal.

• This powerful eclipse connected into the transit Saturn-Pluto conjunction. When it fell across Australia's MC/IC axis, forming a grand-cross with the angles, it portended massive devastation.

• Mars and malevolent stars were clustered in the 4H that rules the land and environment. Volatile Mars is in fiery Leo, square electrical Uranus, in the 1H. This cocktail of incendiary forces - with the eclipse, fuelled the Black Summer fires. The malevolent stars *Praesepe* and the *Aselli* (7-9 Leo), warn of death and destruction from fire and "piled-up corpses."

• World famous historian, David Attenborough said these fires were an example that the predicted dangers of climate-change had arrived.

1   https://www.awm.gov.au/articles/second-world-war

• The Sabian Symbol on the eclipse IC (23 Scorpio), represents the legacy of the devastation: "A bunny metamorphosed into a fairy." A more relevant symbol that conveys the same meaning is "The phoenix, rising from the ashes of its funeral pyre with renewed youth." From the ashes of the fires will come renewed energy to transform and rebuild in a manner that will better serve the people, the land and wildlife in the future. (Hopefully).

7. Australia and Covid-19.

Lunar eclipse for Covid-19: 17 Jul 2019, 07:39, Canberra; around Australia natal.

The same eclipse for Black Summer also brought Covid.

• Guarding the borders to ensure infected foreign travellers did not enter Australia would be its greatest protection (eclipse across 3-9 travel houses).

AUSTRALIA Federation 1901

The state of New South Wales made a disastrous start. In March 2020, the cruise ship Ruby Princess discharged its passengers without officials ensuring they were Covid free. They were not and the virus spread through the country. But other state leaders shut their borders, applied lockdowns and contact-tracing; and the virus was eventually brought under control. Further outbreaks due to breaches of quarantine rules were similarly handled and by 2021, the toll was relatively modest - 900 dead from 28.5 thousand people infected. This in a nation of 25 million. [1]

• *Changes indicated by the Covid eclipse:* Although the popularity of most state and federal leaders rose during the crisis, there will be casualties, directly attributable to how the public perceive some mishandled matters (the eclipse forming a grand-cross with the angles).

8. The Spiritual Destiny of Australia.

The personality of Australia is ruled by Capricorn.

• Due to its ruling signs, Australians are realists who do not waste time chasing frivolous dreams. They have to be, with the harsh climate. The Australian psyche is stern and can be rigid and hard - this was especially so in its founding stage (a Capricorn personality, expressing through a Capricorn Sun, conjunct Saturn). But the combination has also gifted the people with deep reserves of inner strength to draw on. When times get tough, when there are catastrophes, they pull together in "mate-ship" to see the nation through. It is a most positive part of the nation's psyche.

• Australia's limiting pattern in 1901, was the devalued status it gave to the indigenous Australians (Moon in 2H, ruler of 4H), and the cruel way they were treated (Moon sesquiquadrate Saturn). Its current task is to move away from its patriarchal Capricorn past and to heal (Virgo) the troubles left in its wake - especially racism towards Aborigines that still lingers.

---

1   13 Jan 2021: the 99th ranked nation in the world for deaths per capita.

One way this is being done is through sport and the creative arts (Asc ruler Mars, in Virgo, 5H). Australia celebrates its sports champions and talented artists, many of whom have been Aboriginal. Through sport, the soul is attempting to improve the culture of the nation. An example is Adam Goodes, an Aboriginal who played football for the Sydney Swans. He was racially vilified and this inspired football clubs to put in educational interventions and rules to try to eliminate racism in their teams and from amongst spectators.

The soul of Australia is ruled by Virgo.

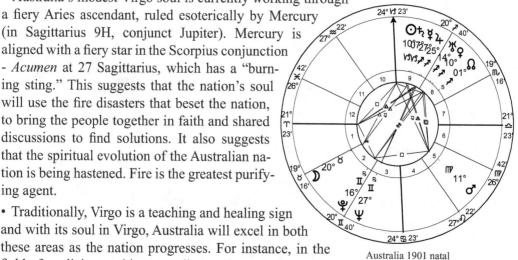

Australia 1901 natal

• Australia's modest Virgo soul is currently working through a fiery Aries ascendant, ruled esoterically by Mercury (in Sagittarius 9H, conjunct Jupiter). Mercury is aligned with a fiery star in the Scorpius conjunction - *Acumen* at 27 Sagittarius, which has a "burning sting." This suggests that the nation's soul will use the fire disasters that beset the nation, to bring the people together in faith and shared discussions to find solutions. It also suggests that the spiritual evolution of the Australian nation is being hastened. Fire is the greatest purifying agent.

• Traditionally, Virgo is a teaching and healing sign and with its soul in Virgo, Australia will excel in both these areas as the nation progresses. For instance, in the field of medicine, making new discoveries and pioneering new and advanced methods of treatment.

• Virgo is also the sign of service. One way Australia is currently serving the world is through its universities, which are educating a high number of foreign students from less developed nations. This helps the advancement of the home countries when students go home. However, many students also choose to remain in Australia, adding richness to the nation's multicultural nature.

• Virgo also represents purification and its esoteric task is to awaken or give birth to a "Christ consciousness." This is a perspective of life that is wise, loving and compassionate. In the future, an esoteric school will open in Australia, [1] which trains students to develop such a consciousness. All those who pass through this higher level of training will contribute to Australia's ultimate purpose - to help the world's masses become enlightened. This ideal is captured in the following quote:

> When that spiritual reality, spoken of by St. Paul as "Christ in you, the hope of glory," is released in man and can manifest in full expression. When a sufficient number of people have grasped this ideal, the entire human family can stand for the first time before the portal which leads to the Path of Light, and the life of Christ will flower forth in the human kingdom. [2] Australia's spiritual keynote is: "Christ in you, the hope of glory."

1 Bailey, Alice A. Letters on Occult Meditation, 306-308.
2 Bailey, Alice A. From Bethlehem to Calvary, 16-17.

Austria

Austria's personality is ruled by Capricorn, its soul by Libra.[1]

The Austrian region was settled by Germanic tribes, a warrior people who were fiercely devoted to their leaders. Driven by an urge for power and control (Capricorn), these ambitions came to their fullest expression during the very successful reign of the Habsburg Empire.

Since the World Wars, Austria has been going through a series of inner changes as the nation adapts to the higher influence of its Libra soul. These changes are indicative of a spiritually advanced nation and will allow the organising and executive talents of Capricorn to be used to promote and serve world peace and harmony.

1. The Great Plague of Vienna 1679.

Plagues and pandemics have always been with the human race. Unstoppable, they swept the world and such was their devastating effect, they have been the cause of the fall and rise of kings and dynasties. Some historians argue that the seeds of Capitalism, the Renaissance and the Reformation were all sown with earlier waves of the plague in the 14th and 15th Centuries. The plague of Vienna hit in the early months of 1679. By then, ultra-conservative Vienna was a bastion of the Counter-Reformation and a target for evolutionary forces.

Blood Moon eclipse for the Bubonic Plague: 29 Oct 1678, 21:10, Vienna.

• Lunar eclipses usually trigger pandemics, because they are spread by human interactions that the Moon represents. The plague recurred for over a decade in Vienna, claiming an estimated 76,000 lives.

• The evolutionary pattern shaping events is Uranus square Pluto. They bring shattering and far -reaching changes very quickly - often through brutal (Pluto) revolutions (Uranus). Several rebellions were triggered in Europe and America following this aspect. But - as in this case, major change can also come via a plague or epidemic. This because Uranus also represents bacterial infections such as the bubonic plague and Pluto presides over mass deaths.

• The plague dominated Vienna's affairs (Jupiter, ruler of the 6H of health, conjunct the MC), disrupting social life (Jupiter semi-square Moon, sesquiquadrate Sun, in the 5th-11th social houses), bringing normal life to a halt. To protect themselves, people went into hiding (Jupiter square Saturn 12H).

• Pluto is on *Canopus* (11 Cancer), a star that portends fevers and death through the bite of a serpent. Infected fleas did the biting, but the plague venom was just as lethal as a snake bite and killed almost as quickly. This venom extended to human affairs. Jews were accused to have caused the plague by poisoning wells. All Jews from Cologne to Austria were killed in a series of massacres in 1348 and 1349. [2]

---

1 Bailey, Alice A. The Destiny of the Nations, 67.
2 According to the chronicler Heinrich von Diessenhoven (1342-1362).

2. Birth of the Austrian-Hungary Empire: 8 June 1867, 12:00, Vienna.

The ruling dynasty in Austria - the Habsburg Monarchy, was one of the most influential and distinguished royal houses of Europe. It stretched from the 13th Century until the end of WWI. The throne of the Holy Roman Empire (HRE) was continuously occupied by the Habsburgs and Francis II (a Habsburg) was its last ruler. In 1804, as Napoleon Bonaparte began his rampage across Europe, Francis officially created the Austrian Empire from those parts of the HRE that belonged unofficially to the Habsburgs. Then he dissolved the HRE.

When Prussia-Germany took its territories out of the Habsburg Empire in 1866, Austria morphed into the Austro-Hungarian Empire, formalised at the Coronation of Francis (Franz) Joseph I and Elisabeth Amalie (Queen of Hungary), on 8 June 1867. The natal chart stemming from this date was governing Austria when it entered WWI.

N.B. When the time for a nation's rebirth is unknown, astrologers such as Nicholas Campion use a 12 pm time. This places the Sun on the MC - the 10H cusp. This is a point of governmental power, which fits the occasion.

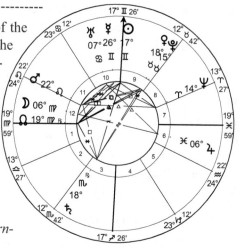

3. Austria in WWI and the end of the Habsburg Empire.

<u>Blood Moon eclipse for WWI: 15 Sep 1913, 13:46, Vienna;
around the Austrian-Hungary natal.</u>

Serbian nationalism and expansionism were at the root of WWI. Serbs had gained independence from the Ottomans in 1815. Now they wanted to unite all Slav-speaking people into a united country, including those living in Austrian-ruled territories.

• When the Serbs assassinated the Archduke and Duchess of Austria on 28 June 1914 (around 10:45), in Sarajevo, Serbia; Austria declared war. (Its Germanic warlike spirit is represented in the chart by Mars in Leo). Germany sided with Austria, other countries piled in and the Great War started.

• The eclipse grand-cross (Sun, Moon, Mars-Pluto, Asc), hit the angles of the Monarchy chart, indicating profound structural changes for the 46-year-old nation. It was about to go through a rebirth, take on a new form.

• WWI was a time of great reckoning for many nations and empires. Saturn, Lord of Karma, was moving through Auriga, the Charioteer constellation whose horses are related to the Four Horsemen of the Apocalypse and to war. Though war is sometimes inevitable, Saturn weighs up the deeds of men's hearts and metes out punishments for those who use such catastrophic means for venal purposes. The forces of war swept over the nation and about a million people died during the hostilities.

The end of the Habsburg Empire

• The eclipse forces and those of the war ended several ruling houses. Pluto-Mars and Saturn in the 10H, indicated this was going to happen to the Habsburgs.

Charles I (1887-1922), was the last reigning Habsburg - the empire ended with him. He became heir presumptive to the Austrian-Hungary throne when his uncle Franz Ferdinand was assassinated in Sarajevo, the event that triggered WWI. He was crowned during the war, in November 1916. Between January and May 1917, Charles met secretly with the Allies, promising to take Austria-Hungary out of WWI if it could be treated kindly in the war's aftermath. These talks failed, largely because he refused to give up Habsburg territories in Italy. In hindsight, a fatal and stupid decision that ended the dynasty. Following the war's end, Charles tried to save his throne but powerful political groups in the nation wanted a republic (and the Habsburg fortunes) and they were successful.

On 3 April 1919, Parliament passed the Habsburg Law, which dethroned the Habsburgs and confiscated their property. Charles was permanently banished into exile (to Madeira), where he lived in impoverishment, dying of pneumonia in 1922. A miserable ending for one of the most glittering periods in royal European history. But he was later beatified by Pope John Paul II in 2004 (as Blessed Karl of Austria), "for putting his Christian faith first in making political decisions, and for his role as a peacemaker during the war."

4. Birth of the Austria Republic: 12 Nov 1918, 16:00, Vienna.

On 12 November 1918, at 16:00 hours, the Austrian Republic was born. This chart is still used today.

• Austria's Capricorn personality was strengthened with that sign ruling the 9th and 10th houses. This drew the Austrian people back into their old Germanic tribal beliefs of racial superiority. In 1939, they enthusiastically supported the rise of Adolf Hitler and the Nazi Party.

• Soul-ruling sign Libra, is intercepted in the 6H (and Venus is afflicted in Scorpio), indicating that in 1918, the influence of the soul was weak. But the values of justice and fairness remained influential in the hearts of ordinary people, in the working classes.

• Uranus, the esoteric ruler of Libra is very strong - in its own sign and house (11). Its conjunction to the Moon indicates that the effects of the war would bring about a radical transformation to the way people lived.

5. Austria in WWII.

<u>Blood Moon eclipse for WWII: 3 May 1939, 16:16, Vienna; around Austria natal.</u>

Austria was largely composed of people with Germanic roots and Adolf Hitler was family - he was born in Austria. With the rise of the Nazis, Austria retreated into its patriarchal past, implementing an authoritarian constitution in 1934 that swept away human-rights. This sealed the fate of Austrian Jews. By 1942 almost all of them (around 220,000) had emigrated, were in concentration camps or they were dead.

• But Austria was punished. Hit by bombing raids, approximately 250,000 were killed or went missing in the war (eclipse Mars on Austria's MC, opposing Pluto 4H).

• It was karmic, a consequence of the decisions made by Austria's leaders (eclipse Saturn in the 12H of self-undoing).

• But the war and Hitler's defeat also provided an opportunity for Austria's renewal and independence, for the nation to develop its own unique self-hood (eclipse Sun and Uranus on the Asc). This Austria has done and in the 21st Century is a progressive and prosperous nation.

6. Austria and Covid-19.

<u>Lunar eclipse for Covid-19: 16 Jul 2019, 23:39, Vienna; around Austria natal.</u>

• Although the Covid eclipse planets made a direct hit on Austria's MC/ IC axis; natal Mercury, the ruler of the 6H of health, is strengthened by the wide conjunct to eclipse Jupiter and trine to Mercury.

• Though Covid was still virulent by January 2021, Austria's statistics were modest in comparison to some other states. The government applied lock-downs quickly to try to control the virus' spread, with relative success. Austria, with its population of almost 9 million, in January 2021 had over 6 thousand dead and 365 thousand infected. [1]

• The nation will change in some way, with the eclipse Sun and Moon on the MC/ IC axis.

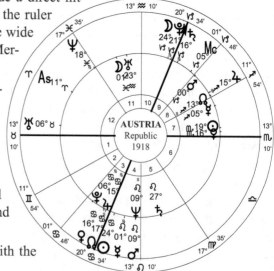

---

1   13 Jan 2021: the 32nd nation in the world for deaths per capita. All stats for this date derived from https://www.statista.com/statistics/1104709/coronavirus-deaths-worldwide-per-million-inhabitants/

7. Austria's Spiritual Destiny.

NB. a. The personality of a nation and negative traits that impede spiritual progress are represented by its personality ray, personality sign and the planet ruler of this sign - for Austria, this is the 5th ray, Capricorn and ruler Saturn.

b. The nation's personality force also works through the Sun in the current rebirth chart. The Sun is in Scorpio, in the 7H.

c. The Moon - its sign and house, represent negative patterns in the nation's psyche that keep it bound to the past. Austria's Moon is in Pisces, 11H.

The personality of Austria is ruled by Capricorn and Ray 5 of Concrete-Mind & Science.

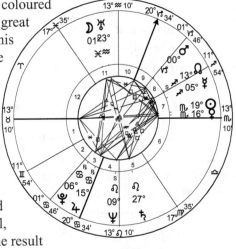

Austria 1918 natal

• The ambitious Capricorn Austrian personality is coloured by the 5th ray of Mind and Science. This gives great scope for intelligent Austrian's to rise to power. This theme is repeated again with Saturn in Leo, trine Mars exalted in Capricorn.

• *Problems*: By the mid-20th Century, Austrians still tended to repress their emotions (Moon in Pisces opposite Saturn). In 1984, Austrian psychiatrist Erwin Ringel described the Austrian psyche this way:

> An Austrian is hampered in his development because of an authoritarian, loveless childhood rearing that connects itself with the ideological, social, and economic faults line of the past. The result is a person crippled in the soul. [1]

Austrian's also fear a loss of freedom (Uranus), being controlled by harsh people or forces (Moon conjunct Uranus, opposite Saturn). These fears are currently (in 2021), being stoked by far-right politics. The fanatical Scorpio Sun (square Saturn in Leo), is adding to the current tension.

The soul of Austria is ruled by Libra and Ray 4 of Harmony & Conflict.

NB. a. The nation's soul is ruled by the soul ray and sign, and the esoteric ruler of that sign. Austria has a Libra soul, ruled by Uranus (the esoteric ruler of Libra).

b. The soul also works through the ascendant sign of the current rebirth chart (which represents the purpose of the soul), and through that sign's esoteric planet ruler. Vulcan [2] is the esoteric ruler of Taurus. [3]

---

1 Ringel Erwin. "The Austrian Soul."
2 Vulcan is generally thought to be conjunct the Sun, on Mercury's side.
3 The soul will also work through the exoteric ruler (Venus for Taurus), or through any planet if the need requires this.

• Uranus - as the esoteric ruler of Libra, represents the force of Austria's Libra soul. The soul wishes to awaken the people to more liberal and inclusive ways of thinking (Uranus in Aquarius 11H). It won't be easy, with Uranus opposed by the lynch-pin of conservatism (Saturn), representing Austria's patriarchal Germanic roots.

Uranus transits over the Asc in 2021, and will remain in the 1H of the nation and its interests; until 2028. It will bring in a new crop of political leaders to implement the soul's interests during this period and the following decades. By that time, Austria will have re-newed its entire "appearance".

Externally, Austria's task is to build bridges to fringe nations so they are integrated into the society of friendly and progressive nations in the world. Austria has been doing this. Located uniquely as it is between western and eastern Europe, it supported the Balkan states entry into the EU and into western alliance's such as NATO. In the future, Austria is poised to play a greater peace-making and nation-building role in the Middle East and Central Asia.

• Another way Austria can contribute to harmonisation in the world is to produce brilliant artists and music that is healing for the human soul (ruling the nation's soul is the 4th ray of art and of beauty).

• The Austrian soul is a combination of harmony and conflict. The 4th ray force rules the warrior caste of souls, who instigate a fight when it is inevitable, but with the goal in mind of bringing about eventual peace (Libra soul). This is Austria's higher task in world affairs.

Austria's spiritual motto is "I serve the Lighted Way." [1]

Austria's mission is to demonstrate steadfast and unwavering service to the greater good of humanity, by becoming a reconciliating force in world affairs.

> The nation's spiritual keynote is: "I choose the way which leads between the two great lines of force." [2]

• The soul of the nation - via Uranus, is aligned with several stars. One of them is called "The Luckiest of the Lucky" - *Sadalsuud* (22 Aquarius). It is a pale-yellow star in the left shoulder of the Water Carrier, and it was considered lucky because when it rose it portended gentle and continuous rain that brought abundant crops and harvests. It is a good luck charm for Austria's spiritual evolution at this stage of its journey.

---

1   Bailey, Alice A. The Destiny of the Nations, 50.
2   Bailey, Alice A. Esoteric Astrology, 251.

Belgium

Belgium's personality is ruled by Gemini, its soul by Sagittarius. [1]

The Gemini - Sagittarius combination gifts Belgium with intelligence and a travelling, philosophical orientation. These are the communicative/ travel signs. Negative Gemini's influence over Belgium's personality suggests a superficial approach to the world, with many voices trying to be heard, with many different opinions that may not necessarily convey the truth. Traditionally, Gemini is "little mind," which chatters.

On the other hand, Sagittarius is "broader or higher mind." As the soul of the nation begins to influence more deeply, as the nation becomes truly integrated as a people, then a more consistent note will emanate from the heart of the nation. The people will begin to speak with one voice and what they truly believe will be consistently conveyed through its messages and actions to the world. With Sagittarius ruling its soul, Belgium is destined to become a centre of wisdom and will communicate this to the world to help other nations find their higher orientation and true calling.

1. Birth of Independent Belgium: 4 October 1830, 12:00, in Brussels.

Belgium's early history is enmeshed with that of its neighbours - the Netherlands, Germany, France and Luxembourg. The region that is now known as Belgium, was either a part of a larger territory, or divided into a number of smaller states. Due to its strategic location between these various nations, Belgium has been called the "crossroads of Europe". Due to the many battles that have been fought on its soil, it has also been called the "battlefield of Europe."

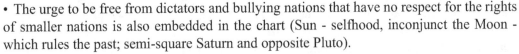

After Napoleon's defeat in 1815, Belgium was annexed by the Netherlands. But on 4 October 1830, Belgium proclaimed its independence. In the absence of a recorded time, the chart is set for 12-noon. The natal chart for this birth is still used today.

Shortly after, the Royal House of Belgium was established and the dynasty continues its popular rule into the 21st Century.

• The urge to be a free and independent nation that forges its own way through life is reflected in the 1830 chart with Uranus strong in its own sign Aquarius; trine the Sun (independent selfhood).

• The urge to be free from dictators and bullying nations that have no respect for the rights of smaller nations is also embedded in the chart (Sun - selfhood, inconjunct the Moon - which rules the past; semi-square Saturn and opposite Pluto).

• With the Sun in Libra, Belgians just want peace. They reject the constant conflict forced on them by their belligerent neighbours (Sun inconjunct Moon in Taurus square Uranus).

---

1   Bailey, Alice A. The Destiny of the Nations, 68.

2. Belgium in World War I and the Spanish Flu.

<u>Blood Moon eclipse for WWI: 15 Sep 1913, 12:46, Brussels;</u>
<u>around Belgium natal.</u>

• As WWI broke - and despite its neutrality, Germany invaded Belgium on 4 August 1914. The eclipse angles were just 2-3 degrees off the natal chart angles. King Albert I was heroic, staying with the Belgian army, which retired to the west of Flanders as the Germans invaded. They held this position until 1918. To the invading Germans, Albert proclaimed, "Belgium is a nation, not a road." The eclipse MC fell on the Sun - the king, whose position and status was strengthened by trines to Uranus and Saturn.

• As long as Belgium retains this chart, it will be assisted by benevolent Jupiter in the 1H of the nation, trine the Moon representing the people of the nation.

• The war brought a total rebirth and change of direction. Belgium evolved into a 20th Century state.

<u>Lunar eclipse for the Spanish Flu: 15 Jul 1916, 06:40, Brussels;</u>
<u>around Belgium natal.</u>

In April-May 1918, Spanish Flu was active in military hospital camps. Belgium Grenadier, Gustave Groleau was seriously wounded and was sent to a hospital camp where patients were dying, quickly. On 1 October 1918, he wrote:

> What's going on in camp! The number of invalids grows each day. Even the doctors would like to know - this illness that doesn't forgive. Death is cutting a swath through the NCOs, and my table has been hit hard. There are eight of us at each table. At ours, five of the lads are ill, four very severely; amongst the latter, two have died. [1]

• The eclipse stellium mostly falls in the 7H of "known enemies." But the driving planet of the stellium (that is, the first planet after going around the chart in an anti-clockwise direction), is Pluto. It rules the 12H of "hidden things". The virus may have been unknown and unseen in Belgium before the war, but by war's end it was recognised

---

1 https://www.rtbf.be/ww1/topics/detail_the-spanish-flu-hits-belgium-1918-1919.

as a major infection. By the end of 1920, the virus was killing more rapidly and effectively than human weapons (Pluto conjunct Venus, ruler of the 6H of health).

• Eclipse Neptune represents the virulence of the virus. It is on the Sabian Symbol degree in the zodiac for epidemics - 2 Leo, and forms a t-square with natal Uranus and the Moon. The virus crept up (Neptune) on the nation unseen and unheralded and began to suddenly (Uranus) kill (Neptune in 8H) masses of people (the Moon).

3. Belgium in World War II.

Blood Moon eclipse for WWII: 3 May 1939, 16:16, Brussels; around Belgium natal.

• Belgium tried again to remain neutral when war broke out in 1939. But the Nazis, no respecter of other nations or people's rights; invaded anyway on 10 May 1940. The militant aggression of the enemy and nationalistic values were abhorrent to peace-loving Belgians (Mercury rules the 7H of open-enemies, with Gemini on the cusp. Eclipse Mercury is in military Aries; square Mars, 2H. Sun in Libra opposite Mercury). Consequently, the government fled to the United Kingdom and formed a government-in-exile.

• King Leopold III remained in Belgium under house arrest. His goal was to try to mitigate damage to the nation, by appealing/ negotiating with Hitler. But you cannot negotiate with a war-monster. Mercury, the ruler of the 7H of "open enemies" with Gemini on the cusp, it is on *Nodus II* (15 Aries), a deep yellow star in the constellation Draco, the "Dragon or Sea-Monster." [1]

• As time went on the occupation grew more repressive. The people suffered greatly (eclipse Saturn in the 4H, in a t-square with Mars and Pluto in the 8H). Jews were persecuted. Of about 75,000 in the country, around 24,000 were murdered. Additionally, Belgian civilians were forcibly deported to work in German factories.

• If Germany had won the war, it is doubtful that Belgian would have survived as an independent entity, with eclipse Mercury (the enemy) on the nation's IC, its foundational roots. As previously stated, Mercury is on *Nodus II*, a star in the 'Dragon or Sea-Monster' constellation. Germany would have gobbled Belgium up without a second thought in order to consolidate its might and to extend its borders.

• Belgium was declared fully liberated in February 1945. It had a remarkable economic resurgence in the early postwar years and has continued its prosperous growth into the 21st Century.

---

1   Hinckley Allen, Richard; Star Names, 203.

4. North Sea Flood, 31 January to 1 February 1953.

Coastal European countries have always been susceptible to flooding and the region that Belgium covers has endured many floods during its history. The "North Sea Floods" in 1953 are covered here, a modern reminder of nature's onslaught on this country and its neighbours since early times.

Blood Moon eclipse for the North Sea Floods: 30 Jan 1953, 00:43, Bruges; around Belgium natal.

A combination of a high spring tide and a severe wind-storm caused a storm tide of more than 5.6 metres above mean sea level in some locations. The floods struck Netherlands, Belgium and the United Kingdom, overwhelming sea defences and causing extensive flooding. 2551 deaths were recorded in the countries affected, including 230 lost on boats and ferries unlucky enough to be out when the storm struck. Tens of thousands of animals died and thousands of buildings were destroyed. Twenty-eight people died in West Flanders, Belgium.

• The trouble began with a very high tide, which occurs at new and full moons. A lunar eclipse is often associated with flooding.

• The eclipse Moon is conjunct the eclipse MC, straddling that malevolent trouble-spot in the Cancer constellation - star cluster *Praesepe* and the *Aselli* stars (7-8 Leo). Ominously for Belgium, this group of forces fell in the 8H of death. The eclipse Sun and Moon formed a t-square with the natal Moon, portending the devastation that was to occur to people and property.

• Neptune, God of the Oceans and Sea-storms, was conjunct the eclipse ascendant - square natal Neptune, afflicted in Capricorn. A dire omen for an impending, lethal storm.

To make matters worse, eclipse Neptune was aligned with the star *Arcturus* (24 Libra), whose influence was always dreaded by seamen because of its stormy reputation. [1] In all, a perfect, classical placement for such a massive flood.

• Eclipse Neptune fell in Belgium's 10H of government and rule, causing them to act in response to the storm and damage it caused. Money was found (Sun in the 2H of money), to upgrade and renew dykes and other storm barriers, vastly improving Belgium's weather defences (Sun conjunct Uranus).

A 2021 report indicated that frequency of floods in Belgium has increased over recent decades, with major floods occurring in 1995, 1998, 2002, 2003 and 2005. Although building practices are a major contributor to this trend, it is thought also that climate change is a factor.

---

1   Hinckley Allen, Richard; Star Names, 99.

5. Belgium and Covid-19.

Lunar eclipse for Covid-19: 16 Jul 2019, 23:39, Brussels; around Belgium natal.

• With expansive Jupiter on the ascendant (the body-part of the Nation), square Neptune (the virus); Belgium was in danger from an explosive outbreak of Covid. This became a fact due to inadequate protective measures being taken in attempt to protect the economy (eclipse Moon in 2H).

In January 2021, he nation had the highest death rate in the world with 1443 cases per 100,000 people. Overall, almost 20 thousand were dead and 650 thousand had been infected (eclipse Sun in 8H of death). These are stark figures in a nation of just 11.5 million people.

• *Changes indicated by the Covid eclipse:* With eclipse Saturn straddling the 2H cusp of values and the Moon and Pluto in that house, the crystallisations that need to be addressed are the nation's values. Nationalist, right-wing politicians have been dividing the nation over issues such as Islam, painting it as a threat to Belgium's very civilisation. Another issue concerns the influx of asylum seekers into the country. Consequently, attitudes have hardened. These values will be debated over the coming decades. Whatever the outcome, Belgium is due for an internal transformation (eclipse Sun 8H; eclipse Saturn, Pluto and the nodes forming a t-square with the MC).

6. The Spiritual Destiny of Belgium.

The personality of Belgium is ruled by Gemini.

• The Gemini influence has caused Belgians to have mixed feelings about their identity as one nation. This is a result of being occupied by many foreign European powers through the centuries and influenced by many cultures.

In the 21st Century, the refugee crisis has exposed a division between the conservative Flemish who want a hard line taken with the newcomers; and left-leaning Walloons who are more tolerant.

• Negative Gemini has also affected Belgium's ability to self-govern. There are too many voices trying to be heard at the same time, with too many competing ideas, all talking over each other. In 2011, Belgium set a Guinness World Record for going through the longest peacetime period without a government.

Belgium 1830 natal

Belgium's Libra Sun and Mercury have not helped. At this stage of the nation's development, they cause people to procrastinate and dither rather than take definite, one-directed action.

• However, the most limiting pattern that Belgium has to contend with is materialism and decisions being made by some in power to profit personally, to the detriment of the nation as a whole (Moon in Taurus inconjunct the Sun; the Sun square Jupiter, afflicted in acquisitive Capricorn).

To emphasise the point, the Sun is aligned with stars in Corvus, the acquisitive Raven. In Greek mythology, Apollo sent the raven to fetch water. But instead, it gorged on figs. Then it picked up a snake and used this and a concocted story to try to escape punishment. There is a message here for Belgium.

There is another pattern that the Moon indicates - a deeply embedded fear that the nation will be overrun again by marauding and butchering savages. The fear that interferes with the leaders' decision-making goes something like: "make the wrong move and someone will beat us up." (Moon square Uranus, semi-square Mars).

The soul of Belgium is ruled by Sagittarius.

• Since 1830, Belgium's Sagittarius soul has had a Sagittarius ascendant to work though. One would think this would make it easier for the nation to swing its direction onto the higher way that Sagittarius represents. And in time that will be correct. But, during the early period of a nation's evolution, when materialistic forces dominate the masses, all energies available are used by the selfish and ambitious people in power. This is true for all nations. Lower Sagittarius gives too many options and a lack of follow-through, which has not helped the nation's Libra insecurity.

• However, in the modern era, Belgium is emerging as a seat of power. Since 1949, it has hosted the North Atlantic Treaty Organisation (NATO), followed by it becoming the unofficial seat of the European Union. When powerful organisations such as these are drawn to a certain location, they do so because of a synchronicity of force - power attracts power.

At first glance, this seems odd, since neither Gemini or Sagittarius - Belgium's ruling signs; are governing signs. However, the personality of Brussels is ruled by Capricorn, [1] and the esoteric ruler of Sagittarius (the Earth - the cross within the circle), is in military Aries, conjunct powerful Pluto. This indicates that the soul of Belgium is becoming influential and this is seen in the important decisions that are being made from Brussels. Many of these decisions are still beneficial only for the few that these organisations represent. But that will change as Belgium's soul becomes more influential. In time, Brussels will be the seat of forward-thinking decisions being made for the good of the world.

• Whether becoming a seat of power is the higher spiritual destiny for Belgium remains to be seen. Sagittarius is the path-finder and is often associated with religion or higher understandings. A new chapter is yet to unfold for this small but influential nation. This chapter will unfold when the nation is more integrated and focused on its collective higher goal.

> On the higher way in Sagittarius, the arrow of the mind is projected unerringly towards the goal. Belgium's spiritual keynote is: "I see the goal. I reach that goal and then I see another." [2]

---

1 Brussels' soul is ruled by Gemini and its personality by Capricorn. Bailey, Alice A. The Destiny of the Nations, 69.
2 Bailey, Alice A. Esoteric Astrology, 193.

Brazil

Brazil's personality is ruled by Virgo, and the soul is ruled by Leo. [1]

Virgo is the serving sign and imbues the nation with modesty, a hard work ethic and a practical attitude to the material world. Brazil is a melting pot. It has absorbed people from all parts of the world, including slaves - around 5 million. Brazil has a great spiritual future and glory ahead of it (Leo soul). So does the United States, which also brought in slaves to work its vast plantations - about 11 million. It seems likely that for both nations to fulfill their higher destinies, they should be composed of people from all nations, ethnic groups and social classes. Brazil is still a developing country and in 2016 about 20% of its citizens were reported to be living below the poverty line.

1. Pedro Alvarez Cabral "discovers" Brazil, 22 April 1500.

At the time of European discovery, there were about 2,000 indigenous tribes living in the region. They were mostly semi-nomadic, subsisting on hunting, fishing, gathering and migrant agriculture. This all changed soon after Portuguese explorer Pedro Cabral arrived. He is generally credited as the first European to reach Brazil, on April 22, 1500, [2] claiming the land for Portugal. Influenced by the wonderful sight of the constellation Crux, (the Southern Cross), he named Brazil the "Land of the Holy Cross" and the constellation has appeared on its postage stamps and flags ever since.

Solar eclipse for Discovery: 2 Dec 1499, 17:36, Bahia, Brazil.

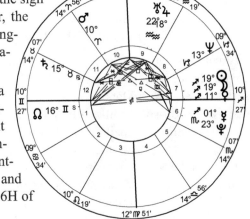

• The travel signs Gemini and Sagittarius are on the eclipse Asc/ DC axis, and the eclipse is in Sagittarius, the sign of long-distance travel and discovery. Further, the ruler of Sagittarius - Jupiter; is in the 9H of long-distance travel to foreign shores, conjunct Uranus.

• On the ascendant is *Rigel* (10 Gemini), a 1st magnitude star in the left foot of the Hunter - Orion. To the Portuguese, the invaders, it brought military preferment, splendour and honours. But to the indigenous people, it represented the boot of servitude, sickness, bloodshed and death (Mercury, ruler 4H of the people, in the 6H of health conjunct Pluto).

• The economy was built by slaves. Initially by Indian slavery, later by millions of slaves imported from Africa. Inter-marriage between all these races - including a flood of immigrants has produced the melting pot that forms the nation today.

• In 1549, Jesuit priests arrived to convert the indigenous people to Christianity (Jupiter in Aquarius 9H). Since then, Catholicism has been Brazil's main religion. Brazilians are united by the Portuguese language and Roman Catholic faith.

---

1 Bailey, Alice A. The Destiny of the Nations, 67.
2 Britannica Encyclopedia.

2. Birth of Independent Brazil: 7 September 1822, 16:47, Ipiranga.

Brazil claimed its independence from Portugal on 7 September 1822. This is when Emperor Dom Pedro I (1798-1834) arrived at the Ipiranga river (sometime between 4 and 5 pm) to preside over the event. Campion said, "Many Brazilian astrologers use a chart set for 16:47." (World Horoscopes, page 63). It gives Brazil a Pisces Asc, which fits the religious, Catholic character of the nation.

• The sign ruling Brazil's personality - Virgo, on the 7H cusp of important relationships, reflects the detailed and intense talks with Portugal as it came of age and negotiated to leave "home." (Mercury opposite Pluto, Mercury also rules the 4H of home).

3. World War I, Spanish Flu, and World War II.

On October 26, 1917, Brazil entered WWI on the side of the Allies, though its contributions were limited to a medical unit and some airmen. Consequently, Brazil fared better with Spanish Flu which was spread by soldiers who picked up the virus on the battle-fields of Europe and then carried it back home at war's end. Brazil's worst outbreak was in Sao Paulo, where 5331 people died.

Blood Moon eclipse for WWII at Rio de Janeiro:
3 May 1939, 12:16, Rio de Janeiro; around Brazil 1822 natal.

• Brazil was the only independent South American country to send troops (about 6,000), to fight overseas in WWII. With Mars in the 9H, it was predisposed to do so. Additionally, the eclipse ascendant falls in Brazil's 6H of national service. Brazil joined the Allied effort, fighting in the Mediterranean. The eclipse Sun and Moon falls across Brazil's travelling houses and is conjunct natal Saturn - Brazil taking a responsible position.

• Brazil modernized as a consequence of its participation (eclipse Sun-Uranus trine natal Sun). Production and exports increased. It supplied technology and equipment to the Allied war effort. (4 eclipse planets including expansive Jupiter fall in the 2H of business, including Mercury that rules the 8H of foreign investments).

4. Rebirth of Brazil: 21 April 1960, 09:30, Brasilia.

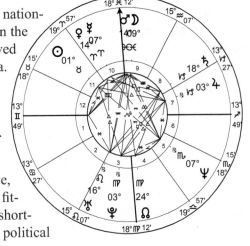

The Astro Databank website gives Brazil a new national chart - for 1960. [1] This rebirth happened when the Brazilian legislature and Supreme Court moved to Brasilia on 21 April 1960, at 09:30, Brasilia. (Source notes: Marcello Borges collection).

• Brazil was a developing country at this stage and personality sign Virgo placed on the 4H of people and land helped this development.

• What confirms this new chart as being effective, is because it places war-like Mars on the MC, fitting in with a military take-over that happened shortly after, in 1964 (Sun in aggressive Taurus in the political 11H, semi-square Mars).

5. Military Coup in Brazil, 31 March 1964.

United States Presidents Kennedy and Johnson were behind the overthrow of Brazil's democratically elected government.[2] Emboldened by this, in early 1964 the generals carried out the coup. The military dictatorship ruled Brazil from April 1964 to March 1985.

Blood Moon eclipse for Coup: 30 Dec 1963,
09:04, Brasilia; around Brazil 1960 natal.

• The evolutionary pattern underlying the coup is the eclipse Pluto-Uranus conjunction on the nation's IC - the legacy point of the chart. This portended major changes to the nation's structures that would affect Brazil way into the future.

• The eclipse Sun and Moon fell across the 2nd-8th house cusps - the coup was about values and wealth. The military made sweeping political changes and set out to purge "corrupt and subversive elements." In practice, this meant the abrogation of political rights and mass incarcerations. Almost 500 people disappeared or were killed, and many more detained and tortured. (eclipse Mars in Capricorn 8H of death, square Venus that is a symbol of justice and fairness).

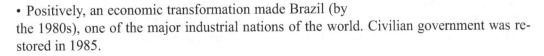

• Positively, an economic transformation made Brazil (by the 1980s), one of the major industrial nations of the world. Civilian government was restored in 1985.

1   https://www.astro.com/astro-databank/Nation:_Brazil
2   https://nsarchive2.gwu.edu/NSAEBB/NSAEBB465/

6. Rebirth of Brazil: 5 Oct 1988, 15:49, Rio de Janeiro.

In October 1988, Brazil adopted a new constitution which represented a significant break from past procedure and practice. The signing of the constitution, which took place at 3:40 pm, was timed from a live television broadcast made by Antonio Harries in Rio de Janeiro. [1]

• The chart portended major transformations in the nation (Sun in compromising Libra, located on the 8H of major changes), and a growth in economic prosperity (Sun trine Jupiter; Mars ruler 2H of the economy sextile Jupiter). But this growth has been harmful and brutal for indigenous Indians who live in the Amazon (Mars 1H square 10H planets). They are being driven out of their habitat and killed for the region's wealth.

7. Mudslides, Rio State, 18 January 2011.

Blood Moon eclipse for Mudslide: 21 Dec 2010, 06:13, Rio; around Brazil 1988 natal.

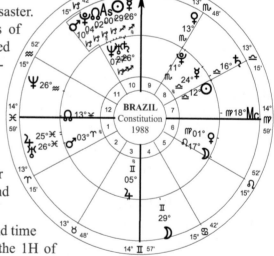

This is the same eclipse that triggered the 2011 Japan tsunami that killed around 20,000 people.

The event was Brazil's worst natural disaster. Unrelenting rain in mountainous regions of Rio de Janeiro triggered floods that caused the mudslide that destroyed villages. Locals think that more than 1,000 people died. About 400 bodies were never found.

• The eclipse stellium is mostly in earthy Capricorn, that rules mountainous terrains. Mars and Pluto in Capricorn are semi-square Neptune, the ruler of major water events, portending the mudslide and mass deaths.

• The sudden catastrophe is shown a second time with Jupiter-Uranus in watery Pisces, in the 1H of the nation, square the Sun, and Mercury that rules the 4H of the land and people.

• The evolutionary pattern shaping events is a Saturn-Pluto square that was just separating when the rains came. This combination causes better structures to be built - in this case, safety precautions - better drainage and containment caps for hills so that heavy rains could be channelled safely away (eclipse Mercury, ruler 4H, conjunct Saturn for infrastructure).

1   Campion, Nicholas. The Book of World Horoscopes, 63.

8. Brazil and Covid-19.

Lunar eclipse for Covid-19: 16 Jul 2019, 18:38,
Rio de Janeiro; around Brazil 1988 natal.

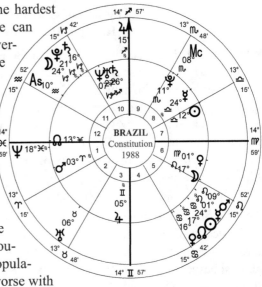

• By the end of 2020, Brazil was one of the hardest Covid-hit nations in the world. The blame can be placed on President Jair Bolsonaro's over-confident approach to handling the virus. He played it down (like Trump in the United States), calling it a "little flu" and accused the media of hysteria (eclipse Jupiter on the MC square Neptune on the Asc).

• Consequently, any protective measures came too little and too late. The virus swept over the nation like a tidal wave (Neptune on Asc, square Jupiter on the MC).

• By 2021, Brazil was ranked 21st in the world for deaths per capita - almost 200 thousand dead and 8 million people infected (population 209 million). And things were getting worse with new, more contagious strains ramping up their assault.

9. The Spiritual Destiny of Brazil.

The personality of Brazil is ruled by Virgo and Ray 2 of Love & Wisdom.

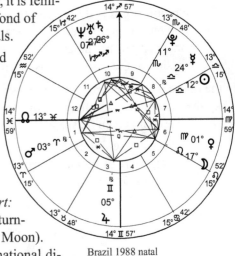

Brazil 1988 natal

• Brazil has a Virgo personality. In its psychology, it is femi-nine, nurturing, intuitive, mystical, alluring and fond of display and colour - as is seen in its many festivals.

• *Problem*: the essential problem that impairs and blocks Brazil's positive growth is greed (a nega-tive trait of R2 and also of Virgo). Avaricious, arrogant leaders (Moon in Leo), who have been selling out the people's rights and well-being to big business interests for profit and gain (Sun semi-square Venus in Virgo, 6H; Leo Moon square Pluto 8H).

• *Changes indicated by the Covid eclipse chart:* these attitudes are targeted for change (eclipse Saturn-Pluto square natal Mercury 8H; inconjunct the Moon). The higher goal of the eclipse is to change the national di-rection so that greater emphasis is placed on the social and cultural needs of the people (Neptune on the Asc, esoteric ruler of Cancer, which the eclipse Sun is in; and Sun, north-node and other stellium planets in the 5H).

• Radical change is coming to Brazil in the unfolding 33-year cycle. If these changes are not done willingly by the leaders, there could be a revolution - one instigated by the soul of the nation. Eclipse Mars and Mercury are in Leo, the sign that rules Brazil's soul, square revolutionary Uranus.

The soul of Brazil is ruled by Leo and the Ray 4 of Harmony through Conflict.

• The soul of Brazil is alive and well in the people, who are warm, inclusive and loving. At the heart of this vast land are a large number of advanced souls who are working for the greater good of the nation and for the world. Because of their work, Brazil has become spiritually advanced and "is on the Path of Probation." [1] This means there are enough people in the nation to start affecting the physical direction in which the nation is being guided. This is important, because Brazil has a very important future ahead. It is one of three major nations tasked with the responsibility of manifesting Christ's work on earth, to demonstrate "the wisdom aspect of love in all its beauty". [2]

• Brazil is a baton-carrier. the United Kingdom has the duty of sowing in the minds of men, the ideal of a world governed by love and wisdom. The United States has to plant this seed in the hearts of men and women. Then, Brazil's task is to manifest this plan physically across its entire people and land. It has to demonstrate through its government a "wisdom [that is] based on true idealism and love." [3] Such a government will be the perfect blend of all that is best in Leo and Aquarius. But all this lies a very long way into the future. Hypothetically, thousands of years.

Brazil's spiritual motto is, "I hide the seed."

The seed that Brazil is tasked with hiding, carries the blue-print of this future glory. All the best that the United Kingdom, the United States and all the other unnamed nations that contribute to world good have created; Brazil will absorb and carry in its heart.

> Symbolising this destiny is *Ankaa* (15 Pisces), located on the nation's ascendant and north-node. The star is in the neck of the mythical Phoenix constellation. In ancient Egypt, this fabulous bird was associated with the worship of the sun, which is a symbol for God.

In the future when the time is right, the seed will flourish and Brazil will reveal to the world - like the phoenix rising; the glory it has been carrying. An expression of love and beauty previously not known en masse in the world.

> The loving, self-conscious Leo soul, identifies both with God and with the beating heart of humanity as a whole. Brazil's spiritual keynote is: "I am That and That am I". [4]

---

1   Bailey, Alice A. The Rays and the Initiations, 625.
2   Bailey, Alice A. The Destiny of the Nations, 55.
3   Bailey, Alice A. The Destiny of the Nations, 54.
4   Bailey, Alice A. Esoteric Astrology, 311.

Canada

Canada's personality is ruled by Libra, its soul is ruled by Taurus. [1]

Canada has the ability to endure through hardships (Taurus) and to build a nation that is fair and just (Libra). With Libra shaping its personality, its leaders have always been aware of the need to be fair and just with all its citizens. But in the past, this impulse was expressed superficially with many injustices - especially those concerning its indigenous people. Now the Taurus soul is becoming more influential, more complete and practical resolutions are being found to settle old injustices and grievances.

Canada is a spiritually advanced nation (all the "children" of Great Britain are), and under the Taurus soul, Canada is becoming a staunch fighter and advocate for human-rights around the world. Because it shares a Taurus connection with the United Kingdom (Taurus personality); Canada will always have a closer psychological connection to "home," Britain, than to the United States.

1. Canada is "claimed" by Jacques Cartier, on 10 May 1534.

Jacques Cartier (1491-1557), was authorized by France's King Francis I, to lead a voyage to the New World to seek gold and other riches and find a new route to Asia. He was the first European to navigate and map the St. Lawrence River. Cartier named Canada, which is derived from the native Iroquoian word "kanata," meaning "village".

Total Solar eclipse for "Claim": 20 Aug 1533, 00:18, St. John's Newfoundland.

• Cartier's arrival and what it represented, was catastrophic for First Nations (FN) people. They lost their lands, their rights and around 60% lost their lives through wars or because they had no immunity to diseases brought in by Europeans.

• This devastation is symbolised by Mercury, which rules the 4H of people and the land, with Virgo on the cusp. Mercury is conjunct *Denebola* - 15 Virgo; that portends despair, dangers, malignant contagious diseases and death. Mercury is also sesquiquadrate Pluto in the 8H of death and transformation.

FN people made treaties with the invaders to protect themselves and their way of life. Even if the Europeans had good intentions there was a gradual loss of hunting grounds and dispossession of lands.

• The star having the greatest effect upon the development of the nation is 1st magnitude *Sirius* (8 Cancer); which is conjunct the ascendant. It is in Canis Major. The Chinese called *Sirius* 'Tseen Lang', the 'Heavenly Wolf'. FN people suffered, probably experienced the newcomers as an invasion of "marauding dogs." Esotericists call *Sirius* the "Star of Initiation." [2] It is the brightest star in the sky and it promised a bright future ahead (eventually), for the nation that was about to form.

---

1 Bailey, Alice A. The Destiny of the Nations, 68.
2 Bailey, Alice A. Esoteric Astrology, 197.

2. Birth of the Dominion of Canada: 1 Jul, 1867, 00:00, Ottawa.

From the 1500s to the 1800s, France, Britain and the United States - with their Native American allies; fought for possession and control of the new colonies.

In 1763, the UK became the preeminent colonial power and on 1 Jul, 1867, 00:00, Ottawa; the Dominion of Canada was proclaimed. The natal chart stemming from that date is the national chart still used today.

• As a child of Great Britain, Canada is a stable democratic nation and will likely have this chart for a long time. Its most powerful and fortunate planet aspect is the Sun in nurturing Cancer conjunct progressive Uranus, trine prosperous Jupiter and in a grand-trine with stable Saturn (if the orbs are extended).

3. Canada in World War I and Spanish Flu.

Blood Moon eclipse for WWI: 15 Sep 1913, Ottawa; around Canada natal.

• In 1913, with the Sun in Cancer and 4H, Canadians still identified strongly with "mother" England and sensed the danger posed by her opponents (eclipse Mars-Pluto conjunct Canada's IC).

Canada entered WWI on 4 August 1914, when Britain declared. Some 619,000 Canadians enlisted for overseas service, an enormous contribution from a population of just under 8 million. Hundreds of thousands of additional Canadians worked on the home front in support of the war (eclipse Jupiter conjunct Canada MC, opposite Sun-Uranus).

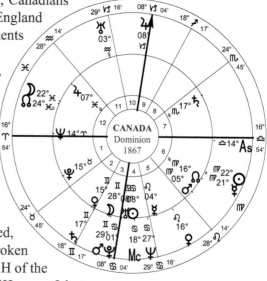

• Close to 61,000 Canadians were killed, 172,000 were wounded including many broken in mind and body (Mars Pluto, ruler of the 1H of the nation and of the 8H of death, conjunct the 4H cusp of the people.

• The Great War changed Canada forever. There was a surge in immigration after it ended. Industries that had been ramped up to service the armies now adapted to normal economic trade. Returning soldiers brought home with them memories of horror but also of a victory and comradeship. But unknowingly, they also brought home an unwelcome hitch-hiker - the Spanish Flu.

Lunar eclipse for Spanish Flu: 14 Jul 1916, 23:40, Ottawa; around Canada natal.

• Two factors make Canada susceptible to viral pandemics. Firstly, natal Neptune that represents viruses; is on the Asc, the "body" part of the chart. Secondly, natal Mercury, which represents the spread of the virus through the air by breathing, and the breathing passages and lungs that the virus attacks; it is conjunct the Sabian Symbol epidemic degree of 2 Leo.

Eclipse Neptune that represents the virus, hit natal Mercury; and the eclipse Sun and Moon formed a t-square with natal Neptune.

• The virus was brought home by returning troops with devastating consequences. It travelled into remote communities (Cancer stellium straddling 3-4 houses). Some entire FN villages were wiped out, children were left parentless and wage-earners died leaving their families destitute. Medical facilities and personnel were overtaxed. Municipal governments closed all non-necessary services and enforced wearing masks in public. The virus remained active in Canada until the mid-1920s. It is estimated about 50,000 people died (Pluto, ruler of the 8H of death, conjunct natal Moon).

4. Canada in World War II.

Blood Moon eclipse for WWII: 3 May 1939, 11:15, Ottawa; around Canada natal.

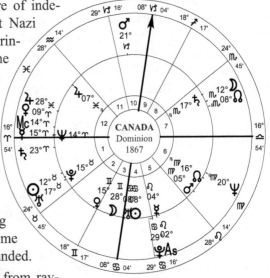

• By 1939, Canada had derived a measure of independence from the United Kingdom. But Nazi Germany's actions violated its ideals and principles and realizing the regime threatened the very existence of Western civilization, on 9 Sep 1939 it declared war on Germany. (Eclipse Asc/ Pluto conjunct natal Mercury; eclipse Mars 10H, conjunct *Sulaphat* - 22 Capricorn, a star associated with Nazism).

• More than 1,000,000 Canadians served, its factories produced planes and arms and it supplied funds, food, clothing and training of airmen, etc. Its efforts were heroic. Some 42,000 died in service and 54,400 were wounded.

• After the war, refugees and immigrants from ravaged parts of the world streamed into Canada, changing its appearance and subsequently weakening its ties to the UK. Canada was growing up.

5. Canada and Covid-19.

<u>Lunar eclipse for Covid-19: 16 Jul 2019, 17:39; around Canada natal.</u>

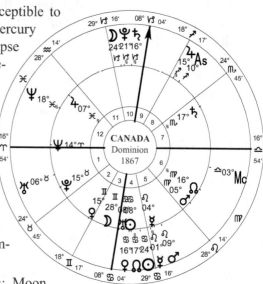

• As previously mentioned, Canada is susceptible to epidemics with Neptune on the Asc and Mercury on the epidemic degree of 2 Leo. This eclipse triggered these points. But authorities, remembering the horror of the Spanish Flu, took protective precautions. Despite substantial outbreaks in Quebec and Ontario, the virus was reasonably well contained.

• It helped that there was respect in the community for social-distancing and for closure of the United States border to all non-essential travel. By January 2021, there were over 16,000 deaths and 659 thousand infected. [1] Still high, but modest in comparison with some other nations.

• *Changes indicated by the Covid eclipse:* Moon, Saturn and Pluto fell in Canada's 10H, indicating that post-virus, there would be a major change in government or in leadership style.

6. Gunman massacres 22 people: 18-19 April 2020.

<u>Lunar eclipse for Massacre: 10 Jan 2020, 16:21, Portapique; around Canada natal.</u>

The deadliest rampage in Canadian history occurred April 18-19 2020, when 51-year-old Gabriel Wortman shot 22 people. He was killed by police.

• The Capricorn eclipse planets are aligned with *Sulaphat* (22 Capricorn), a star that was prominent in WWII and that is associated with Nazism ("Swooping Vulture carrying a lyre"). Based on this, it is likely that Wortman's rampage was inspired by Nazi-inspired, White Supremacist campaigns of terrorism.

The eclipse planets hit this seething vortex of energies and Mars fell in Canada's 8H of death, square natal Mars. The forces struck Wortman's unstable energies, and this triggered his attack.

• The event evoked a powerful response from the government and the world (eclipse stellium in Canada's 10H). On May 1, Prime Minister Justin Trudeau announced an immediate ban on 1,500 makes and models of military-grade "assault-style" weapons, including the types used in these attacks.

---

1   13 Jan 2021: the 35th ranked nation in the world for deaths per capita.

7. The Spiritual Destiny of Canada.

The personality of Canada is ruled by Libra.

• Canada is a progressive nation, very clear about its own identity (Sun-Uranus trine Jupiter). Its ideals are based on fairness and justice (Libra).

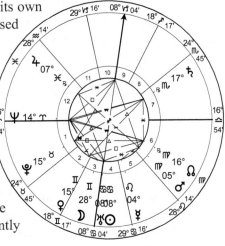

Canada 1867 natal

• Neptune on the Aries Asc emphasises the idealism and devotion of the nation and it shapes the direction in which Canada travels. Neptune in Aries suggests that some of the ideals the nation demonstrates will be pioneering.

• *Problems*: not wanting to deal with deeper, darker issues in life is a trait of air signs (Libra personality, Gemini Moon). The Moon deals with the past and Canada's unresolved issues concern the grievances of its FN people. These issues are currently being dealt with.

The soul of Canada is ruled by Taurus.

• The main configuration in Canada's chart is a Mystic Rectangle (Jupiter to MC, to Mars, to Sun-Uranus). A rectangle is a symbol of strength and stability and its connection to the 4H cusp, indicates that Canada will come into its full strength and stability as a world nation (one point of the rectangle on the MC), when its internal issues with its indigenous people are satisfactorily resolved and healed (other rectangle points in the 6th - 12th health houses.

The work Canada does to legally redress human-rights issues within its own nation and to strengthen the multicultural nature of its society; could prove to be a successful model to be similarly used with all developing nations in the world.

• The goal of fighting for human rights is foundational in Canada's Taurus soul. As it becomes more influential, the power streaming from it through Vulcan [1] (the esoteric ruler of Taurus), will encourage its leaders and people to be more assertive on the world stage for their various causes. Vulcan mythically, was the blacksmith of the Gods. He was tremendously strong with superhuman powers of endurance. These are gifts endowed upon Canadians. Taurus is the fighting Bull, and this rulership ensures that Canada will increase its role in the world as a formidable leader and fighter for human rights and other important causes.

• This task is accentuated by *Nodus II* (15 Aries), which is conjunct Canada's ascendant (the soul-purpose point of the chart). This star lies in the constellation Draco, the Dragon. In one myth, Draco guarded golden apples of the Hesperides, which symbolised fairness and justice. Likewise, this is Canada's task. To become a champion, guarding human-rights in the world.

> When the mind has become a vessel for the light of wisdom, then right-action in the world will follow. Canada's spiritual keynote is: "I see and when the Eye is opened, all is light." [2]

---

1   Vulcan is thought to be conjunct the Sun, and between the Sun and Mercury. Its glyph is the down-turned arrow.
2   Bailey, Alice A. Esoteric Astrology, 403.

China

China's personality is ruled by Libra, its soul by Taurus. [1]

Libra and Taurus combine intelligence with physical practicality. China has long produced brilliant scholars and teachers such as Confucius, Lao Tzu, Shang Yang and Han Fei. With written records dating back 4,000 years, China is recognized as one of the four great ancient civilizations of the world. With Taurus ruling the soul, this intelligence will eventually be used in practical ways to benefit not only China, but the world as a whole.

1. The Bubonic Plague (Black Death): 1345-1351.

Blood Moon eclipse for the Plague: 19 Mar 1345, 04:27, Kunming, Yunnan.

• In the 1st Millennium, plagues wrought havoc across the world. Of them all, the Bubonic Plague was the worst and the 14th Century wave was particularly virulent. Western experts believe that wave originated in Yunnan Province in China.[2]

Scholars at the University of Paris said the Black Death was created on 20 March 1345, from "a major conjunction of three planets in Aquarius." [3] A Blood Moon eclipse on that day (19th in China) had Mars, Jupiter and Saturn conjunct.

• The evolutionary pattern shaping events is a Uranus-Pluto conjunction that had been influencing since 1341. Together, they change the direction of nations by destroying the old so new life can grow.

• Mars - part of the Aquarius stellium, is the most powerful planet in the chart. It is conjunct the Asc, is a lord of the eclipse (Sun in Aries), and disposits Uranus and Pluto. It is also close to the star *Fomalhaut* (25 Aquarius), which brings malevolence of a sublime scope and most interestingly "bites from venomous creatures." As we know, the plague was spread by the bite (Mars) of infected fleas living on rats (Mars also rules small animals).

• With Mars in the 12H of major illnesses and the eclipse Sun ruling the 6H of acute diseases; all omens pointed to an epidemic. Pluto was conjunct the Sun, multiplying exponentially the virulence of this bacterial infection (Uranus), turning it into a pandemic (Pluto).

• With the star *Capella* (13 Gemini) on the IC, the legacy of the disease was domestic disharmony and violent death. Seventeen years after the plague, in 1368, the reigning Yuan dynasty collapsed.

This chart symbolises the effect that all major plagues and famines have upon nations. The death and chaos they bring often causes revolutions that change the destiny of nations.

---

1 Bailey, Alice A. The Destiny of the Nations, 67.
2 Reuters, November 18, 2019.
3 https://sites.uwm.edu/carlin/the-report-of-the-paris-medical-faculty-october-1348/.

2. China 1911-1912 Revolution and the End of the Imperial Dynasties.

The Chinese Imperial Dynasties era began in 221 BC, with the Qin Dynasty (221 BC to 206 BC), though royal houses ruled before that. Subsequent Emperors fought for control of the empire and with the rise and fall of imperial families, innovations and cultural advancements were made.

The Qing Dynasty (1636 - 1912), was the last imperial house. Though powerful and prosperous in its early years, it weakened while making the transition from a closed and medieval society to the modern industrial world. But the main problem came from within - peasant poverty, heavy taxes, greedy local officials and the great famines of 1876 and 1907 that killed millions. When people suffer severely - as they do in such catastrophes, there is often an uprising and so it was in China. The ailing Dynasty fell in the revolution that started in October of 1911.

<u>Total Solar eclipse for the Revolution and end of the</u>
<u>Imperial Dynasties: 29 Apr 1911, 06:19, Nanking.</u>

• The eclipse was a total solar eclipse, where the Moon covers the face of the Sun. It was an important symbol for what was to happen. The darkened Sun represented the dying Imperial Dynasty and as the face of the Sun is uncovered, the rising or birth of the new era.

• The eclipse Sun and Moon are in Taurus, a sign suggestive of longevity and endurance. They are located in the 12H, which indicates old age and the ending of a cycle - a 4000-year dynastic cycle in this case. Further, the Sun and Moon are conjunct Saturn, that rules old-age.

• Uranus dominates the event at the top of the chart in a wide conjunct to the MC. It is the revolutionary planet and is conjunct *Sham* (0 Aquarius), a star in the shaft of the Arrow, of Sagitta. Uranus represents new forces in the nation and progressives with new, modern beliefs and revolutionary ideas picked up from foreign philosophies. It also represents the revolution and its forces that pierced the heart of the Dynasty and killed it.

• The revolution was led by Sun Yat-sen (1866-1925), born into a poor family in Southern China. He became the head of the Nationalist Party that wanted to unify China with a democratic, representative government. He is known as the father of modern China.

• Two "death" stars signify the death of the Dynasty.

(1) *Algol* (25 Taurus), is on the Ascendant, trine Uranus. Its Chinese name is 'Tseih She' (piled up corpses). It is representative of extreme sickness, suggestive of the senility and approaching death of extreme old age.

(2) *Praesepe* (6 Leo), is on China's IC, the legacy part of the chart. Its Chinese name is 'Tseih She Ke' (exhalation of Piled-up Corpses). Praesepe is in the royal constellation, Leo, signifying the dynasty's demise.

3. Birth of the Republic of China: 1 Jan 1912, 12:00, Nanking.

On 1 Jan 1912, the Kuomintang led (KMT) government proclaimed the Republic of China and revolutionary leader Sun Yat-Sen was elected provisional president. This ended thousands of years of monarchy rule in China. A 12-noon time is used.

• The Sun was strong in Capricorn, trine Saturn. Unfortunately, Saturn was located on *Menkar* (13 Taurus), a bright orange star in the jaws of the monster *Cetus*.

• In just over a decade, in 1927, the monster that was eventually to consume the KMT government began its onslaught. This was the Civil War - at first fought intermittently, between the KMT and Communist forces. In 1945, it became a life-or-death struggle for control of China: between KMT nationalists under Chiang Kai-shek, and the Communists under Mao Zedong. Mao's side won and the KMT government relocated to Taiwan.

4. Birth of the People's Republic of China: 1 October 1949, 15:15, Peking.

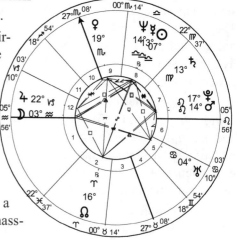

The civil war with the Nationalists ended in 1949.

Then, on 1 October 1949, 15:15, in Peking; Chairman Mao officially proclaimed the founding of the People's Republic of China.

The natal chart for that birth is the national chart used today.

• This incarnation - with the Sun, Mercury and Neptune in Libra; strengthens China's personality and the rise to power of clever, ambitious people who know how to present themselves in a glamorous light to the uneducated and average masses. This was in 1949.

• Moon in Aquarius indicates the priority the new nation placed on raising its masses out of poverty and integrating them into the body of the new state so they could contribute to the nation's greater good and prosperity (Moon conjunct the ascendant trine the Sun; planets in the 8H of international business).

• Taurus which rules China's soul, rules the 3H of education and the 4H of the people. China/ Mao, sensed the needed next step. He and his government initiated the massive effort to educate the masses. Mao knew an industrious workforce was necessary if China was to take its place in the modern world, compete with the west, and become a super-power (which it has).

Mao Zedong: 26 Dec 1893, 07:30, Shaoshanchong (Hunan), China.

The time and chart are from Astro Databank. It has been rectified from an approximate time. [1]

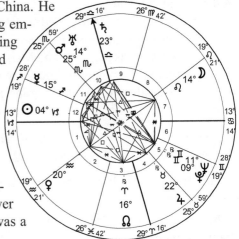

Mao was born into a peasant family in central China. He trained as a teacher, and went to Beijing, gaining employment in the University Library. It was during this period he began to read Marxist literature and became a convert. In 1921, he became a founder member of the Chinese Communist Party (CCP) and its leader from 1935 until his death in 1976.

• Mao was a double Capricorn (Sun and Asc), which gave him leadership ability and great ambition. Additionally, Saturn was the most powerful planet in his chart - exalted in Libra and conjunct the MC. This points to the enduring power of the man. Capricorn rules mountains and he was a formidable mountain of a man.

• Mao was also idealistic (Mercury in Sagittarius opposite Neptune), and fanatically ruthless in the way he drove through his vision (Neptune conjunct Pluto), with violence, difficulties and casualties (*Aldebaran*, 8 Gemini, on Pluto). Western scholars say, no other leader in modern history held so much power over so many people, and inflicted such a catastrophe on them.

• Uranus, the revolutionary planet is exalted in the 10H and conjunct the star *South Scale* at 14 Scorpio. This combination of forces shaped the way Mao pursued his ambitions and led the revolution - intelligently, craftily, revengefully, treacherously and dangerously. He put these skills to use on the "Long March," where he guided his forces that were on the verge of defeat by the Nationalists, to safety in the north of the country. This feat began Mao's ascent to power because it gained him the support of the members of the party. Here is the matter-of-fact way he described a revolution:

> A revolution is not a dinner party, or writing an essay, or painting a picture, or doing embroidery; it cannot be so refined, so leisurely and gentle, so temperate, kind, courteous, restrained and magnanimous. A revolution is an insurrection, an act of violence by which one class overthrows another. [2]

• With Jupiter conjunct the cusp of the 4H of the people, it is likely that ultimately Mao wanted peace and prosperity for the land - with him in control. But he lacked the ability or patience to implement his vision wisely (inconjunct Saturn), and was prepared to sacrifice the people for his ambitions (grand-cross with Mars, Moon and Venus - ruler of the 4th house). This is a hallmark trait of dictators generally.

• All judgments aside, Mao unified his country and dragged it into the modern era. The result is that, barely 50 years later, China is now vying for global - economic, military and political dominance. The means were ugly, and it still has a long way to go in terms of human-rights. But China is now a modern super-power.

---

1   https://www.astro.com/astro-databank/Mao_Zedong
2   "Report on an Investigation of the Peasant Movement in Hunan" (March 1927), Selected Works, Vol. I, p28.

5. The Great Chinese Famine: 1958/9-1962.

Mao's 'Great Leap Forward' policy to rapidly modernise the economy - pulling peasants off food production to work in factories; is the root cause of the famine. It is estimated that he was generally responsible for the death of more than 70 million Chinese. Included in these figures are those who died in the Great Famine, an estimated 36-45 million.

Either his plan was too hasty and Mao did not take into consideration the lives and needs of the people; or he simply did not care (Uranus in a t-square with the Sun and Moon). When personal glory or greater empire goals become more important than people, lives become expendable, are simply collateral damage in the greater scheme of things.

Blood Moon eclipse for the Famine:
7 Nov 1957, 22:32, Peking; around China natal.

• The nation was barely 10 years old when this catastrophe happened.

• The evolutionary pattern shaping events is Uranus square Neptune - they were interacting from 1952 to 1958. Together, they awaken (Uranus) people's minds to new ideals (Neptune). Mao's ideal, governing plan was to make his country competitive on the world stage (eclipse Neptune in China's 9H).

• The famine is shown by the eclipse Moon, which represents food and nourishment. Although it is exalted in Taurus, it is severely afflicted by aspect (conjunct the star *Menkar* {14 Taurus} "crop failures", inconjunct eclipse Saturn {agriculture} and square Jupiter afflicted in Capricorn). Altogether, the pattern portended the gross failure of crops leading to mass starvation. (The Moon also forms a t-square with the natal Asc/ DC axis).

• Mass-deaths were portended. On the eclipse Asc was the Beehive Cluster - *Praesepe* (7 Leo). The Chinese name for this coarse cluster is 'Tseih She Ke', the 'Exhalation of Piled-up Corpses'. An eerie forecast of what was to follow. They (eclipse Asc and *Praesepe*) are conjunct the DC. Planets and points on angles have a powerful effect.

• The legacy of the famine is represented by the IC of the eclipse chart at 22 Libra. The star S*pica i*s located there (23 Libra). It normally represents crop abundance because it is in the sheath of wheat held by the Virgin. But when afflicted, the reverse comes true (the eclipse MC/ IC axis is in a t-square with natal Jupiter, afflicted in miserly Capricorn). People starved because of the famine.

• As a consequence, the ideologies of the Communist Party were modified. In any event, Mao's goal of becoming competitive on the world stage and a world-superpower was a reality by 2020. Mao's dream had manifested. It "only" required the sacrifice of millions of lives (eclipse Neptune, the sacrifice planet; square natal Asc).

6. Hong Kong hand-over on 1 Jul 1997, midnight. [1]

On 1 July 1898, Hong Kong was leased by China to the United Kingdom for 99 years. As agreed under the terms of the lease, it was handed back in 1997.

Total Solar eclipse for Hong Kong Handover: 9 Mar 1997, 09:14, Hong Kong; around British Hong Kong natal: 1 Jul 1898, 00:00, Hong Kong.

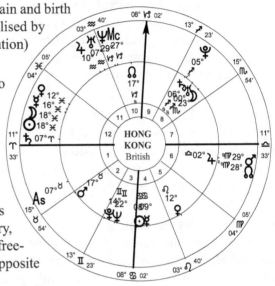

• The dissolution of the marriage with Britain and birth of a new relationship with China is symbolised by the eclipse MC conjunct Neptune (dissolution) and Uranus (going into the new).

• The "one country, two systems" agreed to at hand-over, gave the people some rights. But with the 10H government arm in traditional Capricorn (natal and eclipse), and eclipse Saturn (China) conjunct the Asc in militant and aggressive Aries, people-autonomy was never going to happen.

• The 7H cusp represents Hong Kong's marriage with China. In the 21st Century, China has gradually cracked down on freedoms with an iron fist (Saturn on Asc opposite Mars wide conjunct to the DC).

7. China and Covid-19.

Eclipse for Covid-19: July 17, 2019, 05:39, Wuhan; around China natal.

• With most eclipse planets impacting China's 6th - 12th health houses; Covid would have a massive effect. Not only in China, but on the world (Capricorn planets conjunct Jupiter, the traditional ruler of "the world").

• However, China's Covid statistics were staggeringly successful. With the largest population in the world - 1.4 billion, by 2021 it reported almost 5 thousand dead and 96 thousand infected. Critics accuse it of lying about its figures - quite possible with its personality ruled by the manipulative 3rd ray. In China's defence, because so many diseases have originated from its part of the world over the centuries, China has become adept at suppressing them using any means. For example, a video circulated in 2020, showing Chinese officials welding shut the front door of an apartment complex so the residents could not leave. Such (inhumane) actions certainly would help prevent the spread of the infection.

1 Handover occurred at midnight at the start of 1 July 1997.

8. Spiritual Destiny of China.

The personality of China is ruled by Libra and Ray 3 of Intelligent-Activity.

China is a masculine, mental (Libra and Ray 3), political and governing in its psychology. Djwhal Khul listed four of the major nations in this group:

> China, Germany, Great Britain and Italy are masculine and positive; they are mental, political, governing, standardising, group-conscious, occult by inclination, aggressive, full of grandeur, interest in law and in laying the emphasis upon race and empire. They are more inclusive and think in wider terms [1] [than feminine nations - France, the US, India, Russia and Brazil].

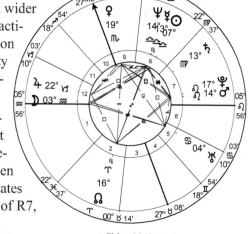

China 1949 natal

The current chart has the Sun, Mercury, Neptune and south-node in Libra, 8H. The ability to think in wider terms and then to apply a plan with clever practicality, has helped to rapidly transform the nation - especially by lifting its people out of poverty and putting them to work to help bring prosperity to China.

• *Problems*: This has come at the cost of individual freedoms and suffering. Under President Xi (and Mao in the past), standardization is being forced upon the people, who are only given freedom if they follow the strict, narrow dictates of the government. "Standardization" is a trait of R7, which Uranus, ruler of chart, carries.

For instance, in 2021, a Social Credit System that tracks citizens via computers was introduced. It rewards or punishes people based on their economic and personal behaviour. But China's most serious breach of human-rights is its "re-education" of the Uyghur people. They have been imprisoned in camps, are being indoctrinated with Chinese propaganda and are forced to work as slaves in Chinese factories. These actions violate Aquarian Age principles and the system and rulership style of Xi is destined to fall in the future.

Changes indicated by the Covid eclipse:

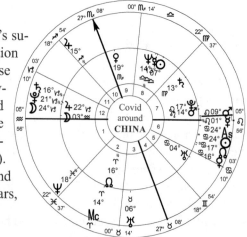

Covid around CHINA

The eclipse does not indicate that President Xi's supremacy is threatened (eclipse in easy opposition with MC, eclipse Jupiter 10H). However, because of the human-rights violations, he and his government are coming under attack from the world community (eclipse Mars on 7H cusp). Pressure is being applied to try to force it to act differently (eclipse Mars opposite natal Asc/ Moon). In the future, there will be further hostilities and possible war (eclipse Mars conjunct natal Mars, 7H).

1 Bailey, Alice A. The Destiny of the Nations, 56.

The soul of China is ruled by Taurus
and Ray 1 of Will and Power.

China's soul is ruled by Taurus and energised by Ray 1 of Will-Power. So, its empire building efforts are in line with what it was born to do in this world period - excepting, its materialistic personality is in control and its current leaders are doing this brutally, through suppression and bullying.

China's spiritual motto is, "I indicate the Way." [1]

China's task is to indicate to the world, how to reach the Aquarian Age. This may seem very odd given its current record of human-rights abuses. But, hypothetically, if a new President comes to power who does a 180-turn on how China engages with the world and how it treats people such as the Uyghurs; then such an example could be set. Specifically, for other developing nations that also struggle with human-rights. The world waits for a wiser China to appear.

China's spiritual keynote is: "I see and when the Eye is opened, all is light." [2]

If it lives up to its promise, China is destined to become a superpower educational and training nation with a curriculum based on Aquarian Age principles. To this end, there are spiritual and esoteric training centres hidden away in the nation, waiting for an enlightened leader so they can make an appearance.

The dragon is a symbol of Chinese culture and China's higher task is to fight for the values and principles of human-rights (north-node in 2H), with the fighting fierceness of a dragon. This destiny is symbolised by *Nodus* II (16 Aries, conjunct China's north node), a star in the Draco (Dragon) constellation. Draco guarded the golden apples of the Hesperides that symbolise fairness and justice and so eventually will China fight for principles such as these.

---

1   Bailey, Alice A. The Destiny of the Nations, 50.
2   Bailey, Alice A. The Destiny of the Nations, 403.

Denmark

Denmark's personality is ruled by Cancer, its soul by Libra. [1]

Scandinavian countries share the same soul and personality rulers. The Cancer aspect was demonstrated powerfully by the Vikings with their very close tribal ties and strong sense of community and self-protection. Libra is an air sign and fosters mental acuity. Ruling the soul of the nation, development along this line is developing in the people a keen sense of what is right and wrong and willingness to ensure that all members in the family of man will be treated fairly and equally.

1. "Great Drowning of Men" Flood, 26 January 1362.

In olden days, Cancer tribalism was essential for survival in the northern winters and to deal with the onslaught of the surrounding oceans. Natural catastrophes such as the one covered here helped to shape these nations. In a region known for flooding, the 1362 Saint Marcellus' flood - it happened around the Saint Marcellus festival date; was a major catastrophe. Reports say it was caused by a cyclone at a new-moon, which places the date on the 26th of January. The flood swept across the British Isles, the Netherlands, northern Germany and Denmark. At least 25,000 people died in the region.

<u>Lunar eclipse for the Great Drowning: 13 Nov 1361, 05:44, Copenhagen.</u>

• Two and a half months after the eclipse, on 26 January 1362, the storm struck on the night of a full-moon. Tide-surges are at their highest at new and full moons. The eclipse omens were exceedingly bad and portended a major water event.

• Firstly, the Sun was conjunct Mars and they are on *Antares* (1 Sagittarius), a 1st magnitude star), that warns of destruction, ruin, and danger of drowning. Mars is a lord of the eclipse, with the Sun's location in its sign Scorpio.

• Opposite the Sun and Mars is the Moon, conjunct 1st magnitude star *Aldebaran* (1 Gemini). This star portends violence and war. The aftermath of the cyclone was like a war-zone.

• Thirdly, these three planets and two stars form a wide t-square to Neptune - in Pisces that rules the oceans. The God of the Oceans was angry. It was a 1st magnitude storm.

• Additionally, rising on the Asc was the malevolent and destructive star *Zuben Elgenubi* (6 Scorpio). So was Mercury - who, because of his speed and rulership of air sign Gemini, is sometimes considered a God of Winds. Therefore, of cyclones - a very destructive one when *Zuben* is factored in. By transit, on the day the cyclone struck, Mercury was midpoint the eclipse Sun and Moon.

• Thousands died. Mercury also rules the 8H of death. Floods like these was the cause of dykes being built in Scandinavia.

---

1   Bailey, Alice A. The Destiny of the Nations, 68.

2. The Birth of Constitutional Denmark: 5 June 1849, 12:15, Copenhagen.

During the Middle Ages, the Danish crown dominated north western Europe and established trading alliances throughout northern and western Europe and beyond. But over time, it lost territories. Notably, in 1814, when a 400-year union with Norway ended. Then, in mid-19th Century wars it lost Schleswig-Holstein to Prussia.

The birth of modern, democratic Denmark took place during its wars with Prussia. It occurred on 5 June 1849, when the first Danish constitution was signed by King Frederik VII - "just after noon." This established Denmark as a constitutional monarchy and the chart is still currently used today. The 5th of June is celebrated as "Constitutional Day."

• Denmark was in a war-like mode when the constitution was signed (Sun sextile Mars in Aries, 8H). Its powerful opponent was Prussia (Saturn in Aries, in the 7H of open enemies, square Mercury 10H).

3. Denmark in World War I and the Spanish Flu.

Blood Moon eclipse for WWI: 15 Sep 1913, 13:46, Copenhagen; around Denmark.

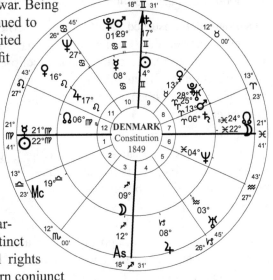

• Denmark escaped the worst effects of the war. Being pragmatic, it declared neutrality and continued to do business with both Germany and the United Kingdom throughout, making a huge profit (eclipse MC in the 2H of the economy).

• The war changed the face of Denmark and all its structures. The eclipse grand-cross (Sun-Mercury, Saturn, Moon and Asc), hit the angles of Denmark's chart. After the war, it regained regions in the Danish Schleswig that pre-war Germany had taken.

• The war also helped the Danes gain a clearer sense of themselves as an identity - distinct from the Germans, and of their national rights (eclipse Sun and Mercury on the Asc, Saturn conjunct natal Sun).

• The key legacy of the war was the alliance that was formed between social liberals and democrats which dominated Danish politics from the late 1920s to the early 1960s and led to the creation of the modern Danish welfare state (eclipse Saturn on the MC, conjunct natal Sun, Jupiter 4H).

Lunar eclipse for the Spanish Flu: 15 Jul 1916, 06:40, Copenhagen; around Denmark.

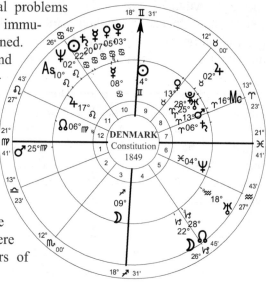

• Although Danes are susceptible to viral problems (Neptune in 6H), during the pandemic the immunity and health of the nation was strengthened. Firstly, by the trine to natal Sun (vitality and immunity) from eclipse Uranus. Natal Uranus rules the 6H of health. Secondly, the Cancer eclipse planets were trine natal Neptune, in the 6H.

• The eclipse Sun fell on Denmark's 11H cusp. The political decision made to shelter Denmark from the effects of the war, also helped protect it from the virus, which was being spread by soldiers returning home after being contaminated in war-zones. There were no outstanding rises in the numbers of deaths in Denmark during the pandemic.

4. Denmark in World War II.

Denmark tried to stay neutral, but Germany invaded on 9 April 1940, on its way to taking Norway. The government cooperated with the occupiers. But when in 1943, Hitler ordered Danish Jews to be arrested and deported, Danish resistance grew and most of Denmark's 7,800 Jews were secretly evacuated to neutral Sweden.

Blood Moon eclipse for WWII: 3 May 1939, 16:16, Copenhagen; around Denmark.

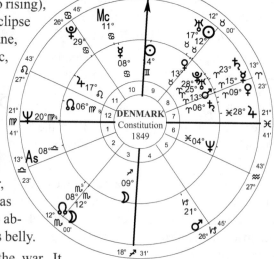

• Denmark demonstrated its intelligent, discriminating and self-interested side (Gemini Sun, Virgo rising), when the King surrendered to Germany (eclipse Sun-Uranus on the 9H cusp; eclipse Neptune, ruler of the 7H - open enemies, on Asc, square natal Sun).

• Denmark was wise to do this. Eclipse Neptune and the nautical star *Avior* (21 Virgo) on the Asc, warned that the nation was in danger of being shipwrecked and drowned. It was in fact by the Nazi occupation. If Germany had won the war, Denmark would not have appeared again as an individual entity. Germany would have absorbed the life essence of the nation into its belly.

• Denmark gave up its neutrality after the war. It wisely made the defence of the nation an important priority - in all probability, to protect itself should aggressive Germany rise again. Denmark joined the United Nations in 1945 and the North Atlantic Treaty Organization (NATO) in 1949. (Eclipse Pluto trine Jupiter in Denmark's 7H of important international relations).

5. Denmark and Covid-19.

Lunar eclipse for Covid-19: 16 Jul 2019, 23:39, Copenhagen; around Denmark.

• Denmark has almost 6 million people and was one of the first nations to apply containment measures. "We have built a bubble around Denmark," said a scientist. Consequently, with over 14 hundred dead and 177 thousand infected,[1] its actions were a model for other hard-hit European nations (eclipse Sun in 10H, conjunct eclipse Venus that rules the 9H of foreign nations).

• *Changes indicated by the Covid eclipse:* Since 2001, far-right politics promoting anti-immigration has heavily influenced Denmark's policies and local attitudes. This has increased race-intolerance in a normally tolerant people. With the eclipse Sun and Moon falling on the 11th and 5th house cusps, these contaminating policies will be challenged. There will be an internal purging and cleansing during the coming 33-year cycle (Saturn-Pluto in 4H); a softening of attitudes towards refugees (eclipse Sun trine Neptune on 7H cusp).

6. The Spiritual Destiny of Denmark.

The personality of Denmark is ruled by Cancer.

• Denmark's Cancer personality is working through a Gemini Sun placed at the apex of a Kite planetary-pattern. This pattern promises success through effort and striving. Gemini cleverness has enabled Denmark to become a prosperous nation and because they look after each other, a generally happy people (Sun sextile Jupiter, ruler Moon and 4H).

• *Problem*: But there is a dark side to this nation. In 2019, Amnesty International reported that Denmark has "widespread sexual violence" [2] and systemic problems in how it deals with rape. Several studies say that Denmark has the highest prevalence of sexual violence in Europe.

Denmark 1849 natal

The violent planets Mars, Uranus and Pluto are in alpha-male Aries in the 8H of sex. Insidiously, they are conjunct two stars in the "chained woman" constellation, Andromeda: *Vertex* (26 Aries) and *Mirach* (28 Aries). This intense, sexual combination portends an entitled, predatory and violent attitude towards women. Some men are feeding off this force, probably via violent internet porn.

1   13 Jan 2021: the 60th ranked nation in the world for deaths per capita.
2   https://www.bbc.com/news/world-europe-47470353

The soul of Denmark is ruled by Libra.

• Since its 1849 birth, Denmark's Libra soul has been working through a Virgo ascendant, which has added a highly discriminating perspective to the way its people view life. With Mercury's location in Cancer in the 10H, this accentuates the Cancer protectiveness in the nation's government and in some nationalistic political groups.

• But following the Nazi invasion despite its neutral status, Denmark made a major shift. Its leaders, influenced by the intelligence and wide-vision of their Libra soul - and Uranus (the esoteric ruler of Libra); ended Denmark's 200 year-long neutrality status. Uranus guides the higher destiny of Denmark through all its various incarnations. Which is why it is such a progressive nation.

Denmark's leaders realised the safety of the nation would be better served by strengthening its alliances with nations that have similar values. Today it pursues an active foreign policy, where human rights, democracy and other crucial values are defended. It has contributed monetarily and has sent peace-keeping forces to troubled areas in the world. This is very much in line with Uranus' placement in military Aries in the 8H of international business and major catastrophes. It also draws upon Denmark's remarkable Viking warriorship past.

• A star that is very influential in this incarnation for Denmark is *Rigel* (15 Gemini), a powerful 1st magnitude star in the constellation Orion, which is conjunct its Sun. Orion constellation is one of the brightest and best-known constellations in the night sky that has been known since ancient times. *Rigel* is an assertive and action-filled star, which compliments the more adaptable and superficial traits of Denmark's Gemini Sun. It will help the nation assert itself positively on the world stage.

• Acting as an arbiter of peace in the world is the higher task all Scandinavian countries are called on to play because of their shared Libra-soul rulership. Denmark will always have very close links with other Scandinavian countries because of this. Their collective higher goal is to become a reconciliating force in world affairs.

> Denmark's spiritual keynote is: "I choose the way which leads between the two great lines of force." [1]

---

1   Bailey, Alice A. Esoteric Astrology, 251.

Finland

Finland's personality is ruled by Aries, its soul by Capricorn. [1]

With powerful rulings signs - Aries and Capricorn governing its nation, Finland is destined to take the lead in some area of human living. It has been unable to do this in the past because it is one of the world's most northern and remote countries and has been dominated by Russia to the east and Sweden to the west. However, it is closer to Scandinavia than to Russia, because for centuries it was part of Sweden and its roots lie there.

Finland is the only country in 'Destiny of the Nations' that was given a Capricorn soul. This means that when it matures spiritually and starts to express its higher force, its government style - how it supports the wishes and rights of the people will likely be pioneering, a model for other nations to follow. The clue to the form this might take began in 1996, with the introduction of flexible work hours. Employees can start or finish work 3 hours outside the normal schedule and this apparently has produced a happier workforce and increased productivity. It is a model that workers around the world would welcome.

1. Finnish Famine, "the Great Hunger Years," 1866-1868

European nations were constantly wrought with famines during the Middle Ages. But the famine in Finland from 1866 to 1868 was the last major naturally caused famine in Europe.

<u>Blood Moon eclipse for the Famine: 31 Mar 1866, 06:11, Helsinki.</u>

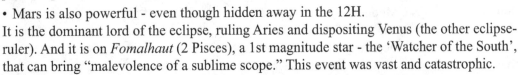

• Extreme rains caused staple crops to fail in 1866, and the following winter in 1867 was freezing. Subsequently, the crops failed two years in a row. About 10% of the entire Finnish population died of hunger. Consequently, the chart is dramatic with the Lord of Death, Pluto, on the Asc, and on the star *Menkar* (12 Taurus), that brings great trouble and crop failures.

• Lord of Winter, Saturn, is opposite, on the DC (and star *Zuben Elgenubi*, 13 Scorpio). He was hard, cold, pitiless and freezing in 1867. Crops failed for the second straight season and people starved and began to die in their droves (Saturn, disposits Jupiter, ruler 8H; opposite Pluto).

• Mars is also powerful - even though hidden away in the 12H.
It is the dominant lord of the eclipse, ruling Aries and dispositing Venus (the other eclipse-ruler). And it is on *Fomalhaut* (2 Pisces), a 1st magnitude star - the 'Watcher of the South', that can bring "malevolence of a sublime scope." This event was vast and catastrophic.

• The eclipse fell across the 6-12 houses. With the Moon on the star *Algorab* (11 Libra), in the Corvus constellation, people were scavenging, and crime rose in the major towns.

• Saturn and Pluto were shaping events. But it took 50 more years and another famine - in Russia this time, before Finland gained its independence.

---

1 Bailey, Alice A. The Destiny of the Nations, 68.

2. The Birth of Independent Finland: 6 December 1917, 15:00 at Helsinki.

After the devastating famine, came the huge upheaval of WWI. To add to the turmoil, the Russian Revolution erupted and the Spanish Flu was circulating. Finland had not been born when the war broke out. It was occupied with its own struggle to survive in the hostile environment in which this was taking place. Russia had annexed it in 1809. Taking advantage of its distraction with the revolution, Finland broke free.

On 6 December 1917, 15:00 at Helsinki, a new government formed in Finland and it formally declared its independence. This national chart is still used today.

• Efforts to defend itself is shown in this 1917 chart with the Sun on the 7H cusp of international relations, square Mars.

3. Finland Civil War, January to May 1918.

Blood Moon eclipse for Finland Civil War: 28 Dec 1917,
11:33, Helsinki:around Finland natal.

• The early years were tough. Secession from Russia left a power vacuum. Shortly after independence was declared on 6 December, civil war broke out - on 27 January 1918 (when the eclipse Moon was conjunct Pluto).

• The battle was a fight for control between the "White," upper, conservative, rural classes - strongly influenced by Germany (eclipse Sun in Capricorn); and the "Red," city, socialist city workers (opposite Moon). The White army won.

• It was a brief but vicious struggle for dominance (eclipse Moon conjunct Pluto, opposing the Sun in the 8H of death). However, it seemed that the struggle was important, that differences needed to be sorted out, before the nation could move forward (Sun conjunct the north-node).

• More than 38,000 people died - many from malnutrition and Spanish Flu in prison camps. Eclipse Neptune that rules the 12H of internment and major health problems - with Pisces on the cusp; is conjunct the malevolent star group of *Praesepe* and the *Aselli* (7 and 8 degrees Leo).

• Although its birth was hard, Finland did come safely through this period. The eclipse chart held a promise for better things to come. Pluto that is conjunct the eclipse IC, the legacy part of the chart, is also conjunct *Dirah* at 4 Cancer. It is a little star in the right heel of Castor in the constellation Gemini. It promises power and protection after brutal oppression.

• Though the conflict left deep scars, a culture of working together helped former enemies co-operate in the nation-building process. Finland's postwar reconstruction benefitted greatly because of the demand for its timber pulp, which smoothed its way through the Great Depression. (The 7H of open enemies is ruled by Jupiter, the planet of abundance and prosperity, trine natal Venus in 10H).

4. Finland in World War II.

Finland's participation in WWII was complicated and a sad story of a fight for survival to keep its independence. The choices it made were designed to protect it from its superior and bullying neighbour Russia, which wanted to annex its territory again. On 30 November 1939 - after WWII had started, Russia crossed the border and attacked. In the face of defeat, Finland signed a peace treaty with Russia. But fearful of its continued bullying, Finland sought aid from the UK and Sweden. When this was not forthcoming (the UK was embroiled in the war and Sweden had declared its neutrality), it turned to Germany and fought with it against Russia. When the war turned, in September 1944, Finland switched sides to the Allies. Still, it lost land and had to make war reparations when the war ended.

Blood Moon eclipse for WWII: 3 May 1939, 17:16, Helsinki; around Finland natal.

• The WWII eclipse chart warned of an invading beast of war - *Menkar* (13 Taurus), a star in *Cetus*, the Sea Monster. *Menkar* is conjunct the eclipse Sun. *Cetus* was sent to devour the chained woman. For Finland, the invading beast was Russia, wanting to put it back into chains again. Russia is represented in the chart by eclipse Mars in the 9H, a foreign power violating Finland's borders.

• Mars is on *Sulaphat* (21 Capricorn), a star in the Lyra constellation, also known by the name the "Swooping Vulture or Eagle," an apt description for the avaricious seizing of prey (other states and territories), by Germany and Russia in and after the war.

• The eclipse Sun and Moon fell in the 6-12 health houses. The stresses of the war and the invasion by a hostile power, these took a deep toll on the spirits, physical and psychological health and the welfare of the people.

• In post-war years, Finland has struggled to find its identity and remains afraid of the threat of the dangerous Bear on its border (Sun on the 7H cusp of open enemies). It should, with *Grafias* (16 Sagittarius) a star in the stinger of the *Scorpion* located there as well.

5. Finland and Covid-19.

Lunar eclipse for Covid-19: 16 Jul 2019, 23:39, Helsinki; around Finland natal.

• Finland is a smaller European nation of 5.5 million people. Officials locked-down quickly to contain Covid and this vigilance paid off. By 2021 the virus was under control with 580 dead and over 37 thousand infected.[1] Finland was helped by eclipse Jupiter falling on its Sun, boosting the nation's vitality and resistance to the disease.

• *Changes indicated by the Covid eclipse:* With the eclipse Moon, Saturn and Pluto in the 9H of foreign nations, the crystallised pattern that most needed addressing concerned its foreign relations - most likely that with Russia. Finland has made major concessions to keep its freedom. To the extent that the derisive term "Finlandisation" was coined to describe the situation when a small country allows its policies to be significantly influenced by a powerful neighbour.

6. The Spiritual Destiny of Finland.

The personality of Finland is ruled by Aries.

• *Problem*: The major problem for Finland - in terms of the natural and spontaneous expression of its personality, is its fear of Russia. This was covered in the Covid section. This fear is shown in the 1917 chart with the Moon conjunct Mars in finicky, ultra-cautious, modest Virgo; in a t-square with the Sun and Asc. There are deep wounds to heal.

• Finland will be a vastly different nation when it overcomes this fear. It has an Aries personality, a Sagittarius Sun and *Hoedus I* (17 Gemini) on the ascendant. This star is in Auriga, the Charioteer constellation, which is of the same nature as Mars and therefore complimentary with Aries. These forces gift Finns with courage, forthrightness and a willingness to fight for what is right. It will be wonderful to see these characteristics emerge through the people.

Finland 1917 natal

• Finland considers itself part of the west and since the war, it has shown greater willingness to engage with the world. It is now a member of the EU and is gaining confidence. Over the next 33-year cycle, it will have an opportunity to establish its own independent and unique identity.

---

1   13 Jan 2021: the 76th ranked nation in the world for deaths per capita.

The soul of Finland is ruled by Capricorn.

• Finland's Capricorn soul is working through a Gemini ascendant, which is interesting - the lightness of Gemini balancing the serious and conservative Capricorn.

Venus is a special planet for Finland, because it is helping to shape its spiritual goals and direction (it is the esoteric ruler of Gemini). Like a good-luck talisman, it was shining over the nation when it declared independence in 1917. The beauty of Venus is reflected in the national flower, which is the glorious Lily of the Valley. Finns are asked to be true to their highest spiritual and cultural values, to radiate the exquisite beauty of its soul to the world, to be a messenger (Gemini) for humanitarian values.

• With two planets in Aquarius, Finland is an agent nation that is helping the New Age to come in. Uranus is conjunct the star - *Nashira* (21 Aquarius). It is in the tail of the Sea Goat, Capricornus, the constellation that rules Finland's soul. Two of its names are the 'Fortunate One', and the 'Bringer of Good Tidings.' It gifts the nation with "integrity and justice" and portends that it will come to "hold a position of trust" in the world community (Uranus and *Nashira* in 11H trine Asc).

• Saturn, the esoteric ruler of Capricorn that guides the nation's higher destiny through all its various incarnations, is in Leo in the 4H of the people. This emphasises the need to shore up the confidence of the people and to build a solid and integrated community. This is essential if the nation is to move towards its higher destiny, which is to demonstrate to the world, wise governance that embraces the talents, leadership qualities and individual rights of all its citizens. These are qualities associated with Aquarius, the age of brotherhood.

> When a true sense of reality supersedes both earthly and spiritual ambition. The man (nation) can then say with truth "Lost am I in light supernal, yet on that light I turn my back." There remains now no goal but service. He (the nation) has become a world server in Aquarius. [1] Finland's spiritual task is to be a world server.

---

1   Bailey, Alice A. Esoteric Astrology, 173-174.

France

France's personality is ruled by Leo, the soul by Pisces. [1]

France's history has been coloured by its Leo personality and by magnificent royal houses and leaders. For instance, Charlemagne who reigned from 774-814. He united major duchies and principalities in Europe to form France, making it one of the oldest nations on earth. In later centuries were the glamorous Valois and Bourbon dynasties. This Leo past collided with the growing influence of its Pisces soul at the French Revolution and the progressive forces won. Pisces is a sign associated with the inclusive love and compassion of Jesus Christ and France's future lies in establishing a future "kingdom" based on higher Pisces values. Overlaid with the glamour of Leo.

1. Great French Famines, 1693-1694, 1709-1710.

Along with other European nations in the Middle Ages, France suffered its share of plagues and catastrophes caused by natural disasters. The famine of 1693 to 1694 was one of these.

Blood Moon eclipse for the 1693-1694 Famine: 22 Jan 1693, 04:09, Paris.

• Decades of war brought foraging armies who seized all meagre food supplies. The summer of 1692 brought heavy rains and hailstones that destroyed crops. Saturn rules agriculture. It is in a t-square with Neptune and Jupiter-Uranus, indicating stormy and unpredictable weather patterns that caused the damage.

Bread-prices were exorbitant, rulers did not help and the masses began to die - estimated at 1.3 million people (Moon - the masses, conjunct Pluto, in the 8H of death).

• The dire omens were multiplied exponentially by the Moon's conjunction with the Beehive cluster *Praesepe* and the *Aselli* (3-4 Leo), in the constellation Cancer. They are often involved when mass deaths occur. The Moon was at 2 Leo, which is the Sabian Symbol epidemic degree. This added to the toxicity.

• In the period preceding this famine and a later one in 1709, France was in religious turmoil. Protestants were persecuted and forced to convert to Catholicism. Those who did not wish to do so were forced to flee France to save their lives. Saturn square Neptune was shaping events - crystallising religious beliefs prior to their shattering later in the French Revolution (Uranus).

The famine of 1709 to 1710.

Fifteen years later, the winter of 1709 struck. It was called the Great Frost - 3 months of deadly cold that ushered in a year of famine and food riots. Everything turned to ice. The sea froze, so did lakes, rivers and the soil froze a metre deep. Livestock died from cold in their barns and trees exploded. France was hard-hit. Approximately 600,000 people died.

---

1   Bailey, Alice A. The Destiny of the Nations, 67.

Lunar eclipse for the 1709-1710 Famine: 29 Sep 1708, 21:19, Paris.

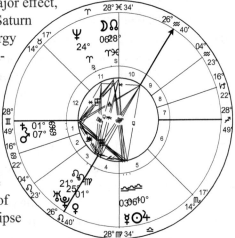

• The planet again having the most immediate major effect, is Lord of Winter, Saturn that rules agriculture. Saturn is malevolent in Cancer (summer). Its frigid energy dominated the chart from the ascendant and temperatures plummeted (Saturn conjunct Mars and square the Sun - two planets that represent heat and warmth). The country-side froze. Crops could not be grown.

• Weather patterns were further disrupted by the star *Porrima* at 6 Libra, conjunct the Sun; portending an evil environment. People took to the streets, begging for food. The social structures of society were totally disrupted (Sun and Moon eclipse across the 5th - 11th houses).

• There were mass deaths (Pluto-Uranus on *Adhafera*, 24 Leo, "The Funeral Pyre"), and the misery continued into the future. On Pluto and the IC, the legacy part of the chart was *Regulus* (26 Leo), that heralds plague, acute sickness and fever.

A dangerous follow-on effect of famines, is that the people are left vulnerable to epidemics. After the second great famine came the last major outbreak of bubonic plague in western Europe. It arrived in Marseille in 1720 (the 'Great Plague of Marseille'), killing 100,000 people: 50,000 in the city during the next two years and another 50,000 to the north in surrounding provinces and towns.

• The evolutionary pattern shaping events is Uranus conjunct Pluto on the IC. Not only were they influential in the famine, they sowed the seeds for what was to come - the infamous or famous French Revolution (depending upon one's point of view).

2. The French Revolution, 1789-1794.

The preceding famines had fomented a rage in the people who blamed the ruling classes for being selfish and indifferent to their suffering. This was honed by activists such as Maximilien Robespierre and Jacques Pierre Brissot. Napoleon Bonaparte was also involved, helping France win the Revolutionary Wars.

This rage exploded with the storming of the Bastille prison on 14 July 1789. Then on 5 October 1789, women from the marketplaces of Paris who were enraged because of the high price bread and its scarcity; marched towards Versailles. This forced the royals to return to Paris. This is considered a key moment in the revolution.

In 1791, because of increasing trouble, the royal family tried to leave Paris. But they were stopped. On 21 January 1793, after being put on trial for various offences, King Louis XVI was found guilty and executed. The Reign of Terror had begun, lasting until July 1794. About 40,000 people died. Although bloody, it was a momentous day for human rights. Ordinary people rising up to overthrow cruel and indifferent leaders.

> The importance of the rights of humanity, as a whole, came to the world via France at the French Revolution. [1]

1   Bailey, Alice A. The Destiny of the Nations, 75-76.

Partial lunar eclipse for the French Revolution: 9 May 1789, 09:28, Paris.

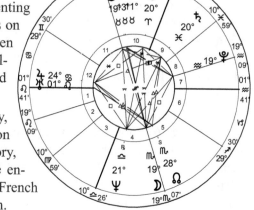

• The forces were potent due to Pluto joining the Sun and Moon to form a t-square in fixed signs.

• The Moon is in the 4H of the people, representing civil unrest. Severely afflicted in Scorpio, it is on *Unukalhai* (18 Scorpio) a dangerous star when afflicted. It is in the neck of the Serpent constellation and portends an evil environment and bad domestic relations.

• The cry of the revolution - "Liberty, Equality, Fraternity," rose up from the heart of the nation and its people. At this moment in human history, the force of the Aquarian Age dominated the environment (Uranus on the Asc). Through the French people, the world soul cried out for its freedom.

• Pluto, acting under Aquarius, fomented rage in the people (square Moon). They rose up to destroy the structures of society that kept them shackled in poverty (square Sun). The revolution that began as a flood of human anger and despair ended with blood running in the streets (Pluto aligned with the star *Sadalsuud* - 20 Aquarius, that is associated with continuous rain, hence "blood running in the streets").

• The revolution brought to the people of Europe, the notion that they could be free of autocrats who screw them down to keep themselves in comfort. It ended the French monarchy, feudalism and curbed the repressive powers of the Catholic church. It led eventually to the abolishment of slavery and more liberal rights for women. These new ideas flooded across the world, radically changing the direction of humanity.

2a. Maximilien Robespierre: 6 May 1758, 02:00, Arras.

• Robespierre was a revolutionary activist who became the symbol of the French Revolution. He is described as a fanatical idealist (Neptune conjunct Mars in Leo), who was incorruptible (Taurus Sun in the 2H of values, square Mars-Neptune).

• He directed the masses towards revolution through his writings and speeches. Here is a quote: "Kings, aristocrats, tyrants are slaves rebelling against the sovereign of the earth, which is the human race, and against the legislator of the universe, which is nature." [1] (Pluto-Jupiter in Sagittarius, conjunct MC).

• But in 1794, parliament turned on him and he was executed on the 28th of July, guillotined in Paris. His Sun had progressed to 20 Gemini, conjunct a star *Alnilam* that portends violent death.

---

1 Robespierre on Property (24 April 1793).

2b. Napoleon Bonaparte: 15 Aug 1769, 11:00, 1 Ajaccio, Fr.

• Bonaparte's name is synonymous with military genius and political power. This genius can be found in his Jupiter, Uranus, Mercury pattern.

• Jupiter rising endows wisdom. Conjunct *North Scale* (16 Scorpio), in the constellation Libra; this star's symbolic name is, "The Full Price." It gives the gift of honour, good fortune and an acute intellect which has a great sense of proportion and balance.

• Uranus gifted Bonaparte with intellectual brilliance and genius, which he turned to practical and tactical use (Uranus in Taurus, square Mercury). Uranus is conjunct *Menkar* (11 Taurus), a star in the Sea Monster, *Cetus*. In his heyday, Bonaparte must have appeared an unstoppable and devouring monster to his enemies.

• But Uranus is in his 7H of open enemies and his nemesis - the Duke of Wellington was also gifted militarily. The latter was born just 3 months before Napoleon on a full moon. His Sun was conjunct Uranus in Taurus, falling in Napoleon's 7H of enemies.

<u>Blood Moon eclipse for Napoleon's retreat from Russia: 22 Aug 1812, 17:32, Moscow; around Bonaparte's natal chart.</u>

• Bonaparte dominated European affairs for almost two decades, winning most of his battles in the Napoleonic Wars. His blunder - as it was with Hitler just over a 100 years later, was to invade Russia. He took Moscow, but intransigent locals set fire to the city, denying Bonaparte a base to work from. Then "General Winter" (the Russian winter) interceded in 1812, and lacking supplies Napoleon abandoned his army and retreated back to Paris.

• The end for Bonaparte's supremacy and dominance was in sight. The eclipse Uranus-Mars square attacks Bonaparte's Sun, symbolising this defeat. Uranus is conjunct *Unukalhai* (19 Scorpio), a star in the neck of the Serpent. It creates an evil environment and has a dangerous bite. Perhaps this star represents Russia's winter.

• Bonaparte's ultimate defeat was at the Battle of Waterloo on 18 June 1815. He was exiled to St. Helena where he died on 5 March 1821, aged 52.

1 Bonaparte's birthtime is estimated. "The mother having gone into labor while in church."

3. Birth of the 3rd Republic of France: 4 Sep 1870, 16:00, Paris

When the government of Napoleon III collapsed, the 3rd Republic of France was proclaimed, on 4 September 1870, at the speculative time of 16:00 hours in Paris.

• This chart had a volatile mix that hinted of the future World Wars that were just a few decades away. War comes up several times.

• Firstly, aggressive Mars is conjunct Uranus, square Neptune in military Aries in the 3H. People were thinking about war.

• Secondly, Mars and Uranus were conjunct *Procyon* (24 Cancer) and *Aludra* (28 Cancer), two stars in the Dog constellation Canis Major, which warns of being bitten by a dog. "Dog" is a metaphor for the coming Nazi danger, with these planets located in the 7H of open enemies.

• Thirdly, Pluto is conjunct the IC, the legacy point of the chart. Its alignment with *Botein* (19 Taurus), a star in war constellation Aries is the main omen that relates to the coming World Wars and the blood-baths they would turn out to be.

4. France in World War I and the Spanish Flu.

Blood Moon eclipse for WWI: 15 Sep 1913, 12:45; around France natal.

• France had a huge toll in WWI. Its forces were the most numerous of all allied troops, and of the 8 million who went to war, 1.3 million were killed and over 4 million wounded (eclipse Sun and Mercury were in the 8H - Mercury rules the 8th; in a t-square with the Moon and Mars-Pluto).

New lethal weapons were being developed by all combatants (eclipse Uranus 1H, opposite natal Mars-Uranus 7H), and they took their toll on French troops - the 1H is "the body", the 7H is "the enemy." France's bloodiest battle was that of Verdun, fought over a gruelling 10 months. France eventually won, but in that battle alone there were half a million casualties and more than 100,000 died.

• The war eclipse chart with Mars and Pluto in the 6H of health, warned that the war would bring disease to France. Oxford researchers believe that the Spanish Flu was born in France (eclipse Moon trine Mars-Pluto 6H).

Spanish Flu lunar eclipse, 15 Jul 1916, 05:40 BST, Etaples; around France natal.

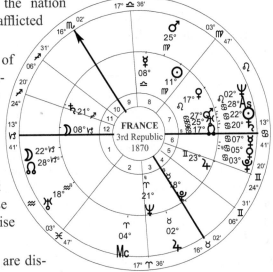

• The virus would be catastrophic on the nation (eclipse Moon 1H, co-ruling 6H of health, afflicted in Capricorn, opposite Saturn).

• Eclipse Mercury (ruler of France's 6H of health), and Pluto (representing the unstoppable toxicity of the virus and its lethal effect) are in the 6H. Deaths were estimated to be in the hundreds of thousands, including 30,000 soldiers.

• Though severe in France, some believe the virus was worse in Germany - that it knocked that nation out of the war because it decimated its troops. A blessing in disguise (Neptune square Jupiter).

• It is estimated 17 to 50 million (figures are disputed) died globally (Pluto sesquiquadrate Uranus in the 8H), around 400,000 died in France alone.

5. France in World War II.

Blood Moon eclipse for WWII: 3 May 1939, 16:16 BST, Paris; around France natal.

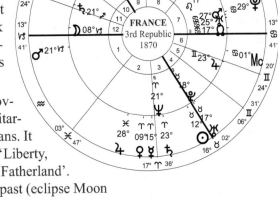

• Germany attacked in May 1940 and France was outgunned and out-thought by its superior military opponent (Mars 1H, opposite Pluto 7H conjunct natal Mars). France had built the expensive Maginot Line - concrete fortifications, obstacles and weapon installations to rebuff Germany. The Germans simply went around it. The defeat led to the Dunkirk evacuations. Since then, the line has become a metaphor for expensive efforts that offer a false sense of security.

• After the invasion, the French Vichy government came to power. It was an authoritarian body that collaborated with the Germans. It went as far as replacing France's motto - 'Liberty, Equality, Freedom' with 'Work, Family, Fatherland'. It was an ugly retrogressive step into the past (eclipse Moon in Scorpio on MC).

• The eclipse Sun and Uranus hit the bottom of France's chart (and Pluto), representing the shattered foundations of French society as a consequence of the war - and then later, its transformation and rebuilding of its identity, its sense of self, as it rose out of the ashes.

• In London, Charles de Gaulle, a French army officer and statesman, organised French Resistance against Nazi Germany.

6. Birth of the 4th Republic of France: 28 Oct 1946, 00:00, Paris.

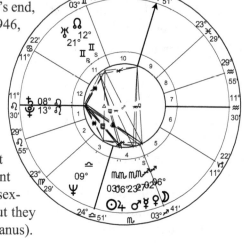

After the Vichy Government went out at the war's end, the 4th Republic was born, on 28 October 1946, 00:00 in Paris.

• The new government was born with a Saturn-Pluto conjunct the Leo Asc. This indicated the great pressure on the government to lift France out of the ashes of the war.

• In a sense, it was ahead of its time. It brought into government men and women with different ideas, ideals and goals (Uranus in Gemini, 11H, sextile the MC), and huge egos (Leo influence). But they could not work together (Sun sesquiquadrate Uranus).

• After an unpopular war in Vietnam and turmoil in Algeria, the government cracked under the strain and it collapsed. At the time, Uranus was transiting over Saturn, Pluto and the ascendant; square the natal Sun.

7. Birth of the 5th Republic of France: 6 Oct 1958, 18:30, Paris.

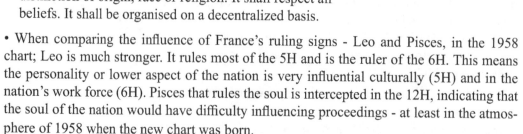

Wartime leader Charles de Gaulle came out of retirement to help design a new French constitution and the 5th Republic was born on 6 October 1958, at 18:30 in Paris. This chart is still current today.

• The new chart reflected the spirit of compromise that existed at the time with the emphasis in Libra. This was also reflected in the new constitution, which was very Aquarian (Sun in Libra sextile Uranus). Here is an important excerpt:

> France shall be an indivisible, secular, democratic and social Republic. It shall ensure the equality of all citizens before the law, without distinction of origin, race or religion. It shall respect all beliefs. It shall be organised on a decentralized basis.

• When comparing the influence of France's ruling signs - Leo and Pisces, in the 1958 chart; Leo is much stronger. It rules most of the 5H and is the ruler of the 6H. This means the personality or lower aspect of the nation is very influential culturally (5H) and in the nation's work force (6H). Pisces that rules the soul is intercepted in the 12H, indicating that the soul of the nation would have difficulty influencing proceedings - at least in the atmosphere of 1958 when the new chart was born.

8. France and Covid-19.

Lunar eclipse for Covid-19: 16 Jul 2019, 23:39, Paris; around France natal.

• France with a population of 67 million people, had the first recorded case of Covid in Europe, brought in by a person who had been to China. The virus made a major impact.

• Firstly, the eclipse and Saturn-Pluto planets fell across the 4th and 10th houses - square natal Sun and Mercury in the 6H of health. These two latter planets rule France's 6H. The huge toll on the nation's health will eventually have a major impact on government (10H emphasis).

• Secondly, Neptune that rules the virus is located in the 12H of major illnesses, square Jupiter that multiplies, in the 8H of death.

• By 2021 Covid was still virulent with a new wave driving figures up - over 66 thousand dead and 2.7 million infected. Lock-downs were applied to try to contain the virus. [1]

9. The Spiritual Destiny of France.

The personality of France's is ruled by Leo and the 3rd Ray of Intelligence (R3).

• Psychologically, France is a nation of contrasts. It is feminine in its psyche, alluring, beautiful, intuitive and mystical (Libra emphasis, Cancer Moon). It is also dominant and assertive, can be arrogant and bullying (Leo influence). Its people are highly individualistic (Sun sextile Uranus in Leo, 5H).

> Historian Jules Michelet remarked: "England is an empire, Germany is a race, France is a person." [2]

The nation's most outstanding quality is the scintillating and rationalising intellect of its intelligentsia (Sun, Mercury, Venus in Libra, sextile Uranus; 3rd and 5th rays). For example, Voltaire, Denis Diderot, Rene Descartes, Jean-Jacques Rousseau, Simone de Beauvoir and Christine Lagarde. France's spir-

France 1958 natal

itual task is to "release the Light" (wisdom is synonymous with "Light"), and its intellects do just that - bring the light of reason and clear thought to the world.

---

1 13 Jan 2021: the 17th ranked nation in the world for deaths per capita.

2 https://www.britannica.com/place/France

• *Problems:* the impediment to France's spiritual progression is the attempt by some to take France back to its past glory-days, to try to recreate these in the present. Nationalist politics tries to do this (Moon in Cancer 4H, inconjunct Saturn in Sagittarius).

• *Changes indicated by the Covid eclipse:* the Covid-19 eclipse pattern (see chart on the previous page), formed a grand-cross with the angles of France's chart, indicating major changes ahead. The people are unhappy. The economy is struggling, there is high unemployment, civil unrest and an increase in far-right populism. This great nation that has led the way in fighting for human freedoms is going through a major upheaval. Eventually, new progressive leaders with the outstanding French wit, will rise to help put the nation back on track (eclipse Uranus 1H, trine MC).

The soul of France is ruled by Pisces and the 5th Ray of Scientific-Mind.

• The soul is currently working through an Aries ascendant and Mercury (the esoteric ruler of Aries). This compels progressive French people and its leaders to use reason and argument to promote harmonious relations between the conflicted nations in the world.

• Another area of importance for soul growth is represented by Pluto, the esoteric ruler of Pisces that rules the nation's soul. The reason France goes through such powerful and at times brutal upheavals, is due to this powerful 1st ray planet guiding its spiritual destiny through all its various incarnations. In this chart, Pluto is located in Virgo in the 6H that represents the workers of the nation. The soul is currently directing much of its force through this section of the community. They have been taking to the streets in recent times in unruly mob-like demonstrations (typically Plutonic - as was the French Revolution); to criticise government policies and demand changes. It will be perilous for the government to ignore them.

France's spiritual motto is, "I release the Light." [1]

• As previously mentioned, the French nation has produced some of the most brilliant intellects in the world. People who have brought enlightening reason to the world with their progressive thoughts and ideas. In the future, its thinkers will introduce new bodies of thought that bring amazing revelations about the existence of the soul and its effect on human consciousness.

> From France will come a great psychological or soul revelation which will bring illumination to world thought. [2]

• France's soul is ruled by Pisces - the only major nation that is. This means it is on the Path of the World Saviour and its high goal is to walk the same path as the Christ, with the goal of nurturing human souls and lifting them up into the light. (Neptune the Christ, conjunct expansive Jupiter in the 7H of its relationships with the world; sextile the MC). This higher manifestation lies far into the future (Pisces intercepted in the 12H).

> France's spiritual keynote is: "I leave the Father's Home and turning back, I save." [3] In the future, if France lives up to the opportunity, it will lead the world spiritually as it did in the past politically and culturally.

---

1   Bailey, Alice A. The Destiny of the Nations, 50.
2   Bailey, Alice A. The Destiny of the Nations, 73.
3   Bailey, Alice A. Esoteric Astrology, 654.

Germany

Germany's personality is ruled by Pisces, its soul by Aries. [1]

Germany is a masculine nation and Germanic tribes in the past demonstrated the aggressive and warlike side of Aries. They were a diverse migratory group of peoples with common linguistic and cultural roots. Warriors who were fiercely devoted to their military leaders and chiefs, they migrated across Europe competing for territories. This fluid movement of people across natural and human borders is a manifestation of the Pisces force that knows no boundaries. In the past, aggressive leaders such as Bismarck and Hitler channelled this force to promote their ideals and ambitions for the nation. But, in recent decades more progressive German leaders have taken Germany in a new and higher direction. This is evidence that the Aries soul of the nation is becoming influential.

1. "Great Drowning of Men" Flood, 11-12 October 1634.

Pisces rules the oceans of the world and all water-ways. Germany has had its share of disasters related to the water element and all coastal areas in the region of this flood were susceptible. The Burchardi storm-tide struck coastal Frisia and Dithmarschen in Germany on the night of 11 October. It breached existing dykes and 8,000 to 15,000 people died. Here is an eyewitness account.

> At six o'clock at night the Lord God began to fulminate with wind and rain from the east; at seven He turned the wind to the southwest and let it blow so strong that hardly any man could walk or stand; at eight and nine all dikes were already smitten. The Lord God [sent] thunder, rain, hail lightning. [2]

<u>Lunar eclipse for the Flood: 7 Sep 1634, 10:51, Busum.</u>

• The malevolence of the storm is shown by Neptune (God of the Oceans) and Mars (God of War) on the ascendant, conjunct malevolent and treacherous *Zuben Elgenubi* (10 Scorpio). This star was also rising when the Saint Marcellus storm struck Denmark in 1362.

• Also, very powerful and influential is Saturn, in a t-square with the eclipse. It is opposite *Bellatrix* (16 Gemini), that "Swiftly Destroys" and brings violent death. The storm killed, swiftly.

• When *Capella* at 17 Gemini is added, a grand-cross is formed with the eclipse and Saturn. This star is in the Charioteer constellation and negatively, brings cyclones and tsunamis that kill many. *Capella* is in the 8H of death.

• On the day, the storm built as the Moon transited *Capella* and Mercury (God of the Winds), connected with tempestuous Uranus. The storm surge and winds devastated the region. People called it "The great drowning of men flood."

---

1 Bailey, Alice A. The Destiny of the Nations, 67.
2 Peter Sax from Koldenbüttel (Riecken, p. 35).

2. Birth of the German Empire: 18 Jan 1871, 13:00, Berlin.

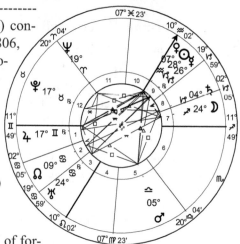

For 800 years, the Holy Roman Empire (HRE) controlled most of Europe. With its dissolution in 1806, there was a scramble to control its former territories. From 1815 to 1898, Prussia's Otto von Bismarck - responding to the nation-building forces flowing via Aries and the 1st ray, freed German states from the control of Denmark, Austria and France. Then he unified them into the German Empire - the 2nd Reich. The empire was officially proclaimed on 18 January 1871, at 13:00 hours in Berlin.

• The Sun was in ambitious Capricorn in the 9H of foreign nations. It represented Germany's formation at the death of the HRE, which was ruled from Rome.

• On the ascendant was Jupiter, the personality ruler of Pisces, that represents the materialistic side of this sign. Germany was going through a fortunate period as Bismarck fulfilled his political ideals and ambitions (Jupiter sextile Neptune 11H), and fused the nation together. Now the Germanic state was a force to be reckoned with and in the coming decades its leaders turned their eyes to other states in Europe that were ripe for the taking.

3. Germany in World War I and the Spanish Flu.

Germany had an alliance with Austria-Hungary in 1882 and when the latter declared war on Serbia on 28 July (for the killing of Austria's Archduke Ferdinand), Germany stepped in as well. Within a week, Russia, Belgium, France, the UK and Serbia had lined up against Austria-Hungary and Germany. WWI had begun. Some commentators speculate that this was the intention of the Serbian activists who carried out the assassination all along. Pulling in other nations to fight Austria provided them with an opportunity to take back "Serb lands" held by Austria-Hungary. In this, they were successful

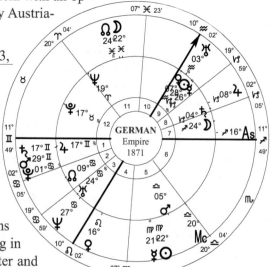

Blood Moon eclipse for WWI: 15 Sep 1913, 13:35, Berlin; around the German Empire.

• Rising on the Empire's ascendant is militant *Aldebaran* (9 Gemini). But this was also a warning for Germany. If it instigated war, it would face an enemy of the nature of Aldebaran's sister star - *Antares* (9 Sagittarius), a force more lethal and cunning than the Bull. This proved to be true.

• In 1939, Germany's war-like inclinations were triggered by eclipse Mars-Pluto falling in the Empire's 1H, and Saturn on natal Jupiter and the ascendant. When war is unleashed, its violence becomes an unstoppable force. Saturn is on two stars from Auriga the Charioteer - *Hoedus I* and *II* (7-18 Gemini). Auriga's four steeds are related to war and to the Four Horsemen of the Apocalypse:

> The Charioteer (Auriga) lifts his team from the ocean (where icy Boreas lashes with his bitter blasts), holding in check the 4 mouths curbed with foam-flecked bits the spirited steeds outstrip the winds. [1]

• Saturn is Lord of Karma and Germany paid a heavy karmic price for the carnage it unleashed. 1.7 million service-people died and 430,000 civilians. The global death number is around 20 million with many more casualties.

<u>Lunar eclipse for Spanish Flu: 15 Jul 1916, 06:40, Berlin;
around the German Empire natal.</u>

Some military experts are of the opinion that the Spanish Flu altered the course of the war and of world history. As 1918 opened, the fate of WWI hung in the balance. Germany, with many more troops than the Allies was preparing its biggest offensive against France. Then the flu struck. Within months, troop mortalities were so high Germany was forced to negotiate an armistice and the war ended. These experts are of the opinion, that without the virus, things could have ended differently.

• By the time the virus hit, troops on both sides were exhausted by the ghastliness of the war. In German troops, this was represented by the eclipse Moon and stellium that crowded over and opposite Germany's natal Sun - a debilitating and weakening effect on the vitality of the nation and its people.

• The virus is spread by people, through breathing, coughing and touch (stellium in the 3-9 houses of travel). The 3H is related to Gemini and breathing and consequently, the masses were infected. (The stellium and Venus and Pluto - rulers of the 6H of health; are in Cancer. This sign rules the masses).

• The Empire chart had an unfortunate group of stars stationed near its IC - *Praesepe* and the *Aselli* (6-7 Leo) in the constellation Cancer. The eclipse stellium impacted and channelled these forces, in particular Neptune that rules viruses and is conjunct the Sabian Symbol epidemic degree of 2 Leo. Afflicted, these stars bring major catastrophes such as a pandemic and mass deaths. So it was for Germany.

• Nature's goal when a pandemic strikes is to rid the planet of toxins that poison the planet - physically and atmospherically. Unfortunately for the world, after the war, the atmosphere remained toxic. This was fuelled by German anger for being beaten and humiliated - first in the war, then at post-war talks at Versailles. This poisonous and festering mix is symbolised by the toxic star groups the *Aselli* and *Praesepe* on the IC. From that poison, German Nationalism, Adolf Hitler and the Nazi Party rose.

1 Manilius, Marcus; Astronomica, 305-309.

4. Birth of the Weimar Republic: 9 Nov 1918, 13:30, Berlin.

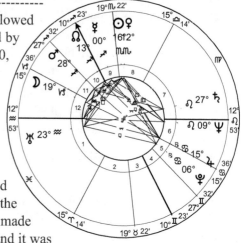

The German civil Revolution (1918–19) followed WWI. The monarchy was deposed and replaced by the Weimar Republic, born on 9 Nov 1918, 13:30, at Berlin.

• Deep hatred was festering away in the "guts" of a section of the German community; those who felt humiliated by the defeat in WWI (Mars opposite Pluto in Cancer).

• With the great military/ war stars *Antares* and *Aldebaran* (9 Sagittarius-Gemini), located on the Empire's MC/ IC axis, their intentions were made clear. The Republic was born on a war-footing and it was just a matter of time before the drums of war would beat again.

5. Birth of Nazism and the 3rd Reich: 30 January 1933, 11:15, Berlin.

After WWI, Hitler joined the German Worker's Party. In 1921 "strong arm" squads were recruited to protect Hitler and to bully opponents. In that same year Hitler became the leader of the party and from then on, his magnetic mystique fostered a fervent and adoring response in everyone who was susceptible to his message - a message based on the notion that there are superior and inferior races and that is just a natural part of nature. Hitler convinced his followers that the Germanic or Aryan Race was the master race and all other races were inferior. The Nazis gained power during the depression and by the 30s was a force to be reckoned with.

Hitler became German Chancellor of the Weimar Republic on 30 January 1933. This is the date that is given for the birth of the 3rd Reich, the Nazi regime and government. According to reports, Hitler became chancellor at 11:15.

• The most dominant planets are Venus in ambitious Capricorn, opposed by powerful Pluto in tribal Cancer. They dominate the MC/ IC axis, and represent the avaricious (the Taurus ascendant) goals of the Nazis and their desire to control the world through mayhem and murder (Pluto).

• The chart predicted Hitler. Pluto is conjunct *Castor* (21 Cancer), a 1st magnitude star that is called, "A Ruler Yet to Come." A blood-thirsty and unprincipled leader, Hitler established an absolute dictatorship and turned his avaricious eyes upon greater Europe.

Adolf Hitler: 20 April 1889, 18:30, Braunau am Inn, Austria.

Blood Moon eclipse for WWII: 3 May 1939, 16:16, Berlin; around Adolf Hitler natal.

• Hitler's determined Taurus Sun was strengthened by *Tyl* (1 Taurus), a star in Draco. Just as the Dragon guarded the golden apples of the Hesperides, so was Hitler determined to guard and bring to the fore the might and grandeur of his German Master-race heritage. This ambition was seeded in his early school years and his preoccupation with the myths and legends of German warriorship and racial superiority.

• Hitler has the peace-making sign Libra rising. But it can represent war when peace-making efforts fail. This happened with Hitler. His Venus (ruler of Libra), was conjunct military Mars. Compromise was not part of his makeup. These forces were subverted to Hitler's aspirations for military power and dominance.

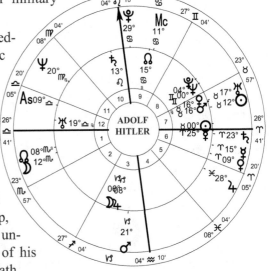

• However, Libra gifted Hitler with incredible charm. People found him charismatic and this benefitted his ambitions. He also wielded a powerful mystique and ability to mesmerise people through the power of his words and thoughts (Neptune-Pluto in Gemini). Some believe he was a practitioner of the dark arts.

• But the war eclipse held a fateful omen for Hitler. Eclipse Pluto was on his MC and Saturn was on his open enemies 7H cusp, conjunct his Sun. The war would have an unfortunate karmic ending for him - defeat of his ambitions by his mortal enemies and his death.

6. Germany in World War II.

Some historians are of the opinion that WWII was a continuation of WWI. [1] Eastern Teacher, Djwhal Khul, agrees with this but said the wars were more than that. They were the final battles in a war that started aeons ago. [2] Here is the quote:

> That great struggle [in] the Atlantean civilization [where] the forces of light, and the forces of darkness, were arrayed against each other. The struggle still persists, and the World War through which we have just passed was a recrudescence of it. [3]

The very life and existence of humanity's soul was at stake and WWI - "the war to end all wars," was only the first battle. The second battle just 21 years later (WWII) was even more catastrophic.

> Germany's attack on Poland on 1 September 1939, started WWII. The eclipse selected to represent the gathering of malevolent forces that foreshadowed the bloodiest war in recorded history, was aptly - a Blood Moon eclipse.

1 Encyclopaedia Britannica.
2 The writings of Djwhal Khul are reported to have originated from ancient Buddhist sacred books.
3 Bailey, Alice A. Initiation, Human and Solar, 35.

Blood Moon eclipse for WWII: 3 May 1939, 16:16, Berlin; around the German 3rd Reich natal.

• Hitler drew on occult knowledge to formulate his plans for world dominance and it is likely the 3rd Reich chart date and time was planned by astrologers. This is because, on the ascendant is *Algol* (25 Taurus), "the most evil star in the heavens." Its Chinese name is 'Tseih She', Piled up Corpses.

• *Algol* represents the Medusa's head - all who looked upon it were turned to stone. An analogy it seems to the might of the Nazi war-machine. All who stood in its way would be destroyed. This bloodthirsty star typifies Nazi intent and its evil.

• The belief that Germany was a master race was embedded in the German psyche (natal Pluto in Cancer on the 4H cusp). That belief had been dealt a severe blow in WW1. Now a new attempt was being made by the universe to destroy that toxic belief again (eclipse Pluto conjunct natal Pluto). It was only partially successful.

• The eclipse was devastating for the 3rd Reich and Hitler did not factor this into his formulations or he may have delayed the start of the war (Mars opposite Pluto, hit the Reich's MC/ IC axis). The war destroyed German leadership, the people and its lands.

• Natal Sun is in the 10H of power, conjunct conservative power-planet Saturn. They are conjunct *Albali* (11 Aquarius) in the Aquarius constellation known for great deluges. Hitler hoped his reign would prove to be a great deluge, that Nazi power would flood the earth. Instead, the 3rd Reich was washed away in a sea of blood.

• Eclipse Uranus, that rules the natal Aquarius Sun in the 10H - and therefore Hitler and the Nazi leadership; was on *Rucha* (17 Taurus), a star on the knee of the constellation Cassiopeia, the Ethiopian queen. In mythology, because of her pride, Cassiopeia was bound to her chair by the Gods and condemned to circle the pole head downwards as a lesson in humility.

There is a very clear moral and karmic message here for the Nazis (Uranus square Saturn). "Those who live by the sword (Mars on the MC), die by the sword." As a consequence of the evil actions by Hitler and the Nazis, they and Germany as a whole were destroyed and humbled.

• Finally, the legacy of WWII is symbolised by the eclipse IC at 12 Capricorn. The star *Pelagus* (also known as *Nunki*), was stationed there. According to Ptolemy, *Pelagus* is of the nature of Jupiter and Mercury and it gives "truthfulness and a religious mind." This IC is located in the 3rd Reich's 9H of morals and beliefs. So, the promise was that the nation would go through a spiritual and moral epiphany (IC 9H, trine eclipse Sun-Uranus), because of the ugly revelations about the Reich's actions, the devastation to the land, and suffering of the people. The hope was that in time, this would lead to the moral rehabilitation of the nation and put it on the right track. This has happened.

7. Birth of Independent West Germany: 5 May 1955, 12:00, Bonn.

The Russians remained in East Germany and Berlin at war's end and from the annexed state proclaimed the birth of "The German Democratic Republic" on 7 October 1949.

The Americans remained in West Germany, and the Federal Republic of Germany was born on the 23rd of May in 1949, operating legally on the 24th.

Then, Germany went through another rebirth in 1955 when the allied powers handed power to the West German Government.

Consequently, independent West Germany was born on 5 May 1955 at 12-noon, in Bonn. The chart for this rebirth is shown here.

• The chart is powerful with Leo rising and Pluto in Leo conjunct the Ascendant. Germany was to rise in glory from the flames of defeat (Pluto, ruler of Scorpio with its phoenix symbol).

• Then followed a period of tremendous reconstruction for the people and its land, and economic growth (Taurus Sun in a t-square with Saturn 4H and Pluto).

8. Birth of the unified Republic of Germany: 3 October 1990, 00:00, Berlin.

Unification of Germany required the East German government's demise and the fall of the Berlin Wall that divided East and West Germany. The Berlin Wall came down on 9 Nov 1989.

On 3 October 1990, the East German government and its states joined the Federal Republic of (west) Germany. This happened at 00:00 hours in Berlin. This date and time marks the rebirth of the Germany we know today.

• The new chart retained the Leo Asc, which was greatly beneficial for Germany's autonomy and sense of independence and identity. This is the nature of Leo, but importantly, Leo rules Berlin, [1] which greatly helped the nation's recovery from its difficult past.

• Most importantly, the chart promised prosperity, growth and a growing sense of confidence and well-being for its people (Jupiter in Leo rising, sextile the Sun and Mars).

• Saturn and Pluto are at work. Saturn rules dividing walls and Pluto their destruction. In this case, the destruction was constructive and had an immediate positive outcome (Saturn in Capricorn, sextile Pluto in the 4H).

1   Bailey, Alice A. The Destiny of the Nations, 69.

9. Germany and Covid-19.

Lunar eclipse for Covid-19: 16 Jul 2019, 23:39, Berlin;
around German Unity natal.

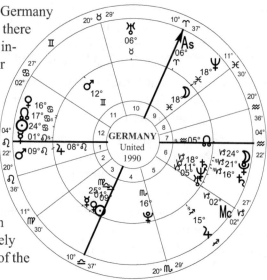

• With a population of 83 million people, Germany did well in containing the virus. By 2021 there were over 38 thousand dead and 1.8 million infected. Compare this to France with a smaller population and its 66 thousand dead and 2.7 million infected. [1] Things could have been worse with the toxic point of the eclipse - the Moon, Saturn and Pluto located in the nation's 6H of health. These forces portended that the virus would take a high toll on the nation. But, because Germany had a robust health system, it did a lot of testing and officials move quickly to contain outbreaks, Germany managed Covid relatively well. However, in 2021, new mutant strains of the disease threatened.

10. The Spiritual Destiny of Germany.

The personality of Germany is ruled by Pisces and Ray 1 of Will & Power.

• Germany is a mental, alpha-male nation, that is political and aggressive (power ray). It is also empire-building and under the Pisces influence, many of its leaders have had a vision of a Germany that rules the seas and entire world.

• *Problems:* Hitler subjugated this power to build a world conforming to his warped vision. He wanted to remake Germany and the world into a white-supremacist Germanic model. But this brought a karmic backlash and physical Germany was destroyed. Though hard, it has helped to break down and destroy its ancient tribal beliefs and traditions, which Hitler represented.

Since 1990, the nation's limiting pattern remains its aggressive tribal past and dreams of racial superiority that are still held by some (Moon in Pisces, 9H, square

Germany 1990 natal

Mars 11H). This pattern has continued to infect people around the world with its poison.

• *Progressive growth:* since reunification, German aggression has been modified by a mediating Libra Sun. It changed the whole tone of the nation and enabled the political rise of Angela Merkel (she has Neptune in Libra conjunct her MC). Under her wise helm, Ger-

---

1   13 Jan 2021: the 40th ranked nation in the world for deaths per capita.

many's power has been directed into building political alliances that benefit the well-being of the nation and the world community.

Germany's power has also been directed into economic prosperity - the Sun that rules the Asc and the 2H of the economy, is conjunct *Vindemiatrix* (10 Libra). This bright yellow star (the colour of gold), is in the right arm of the Virgin (Merkel at the helm). Known as "The Gatherer of the Grapes, from its rising in the morning just before the time of the vintage," [1] it is a symbol of prosperity when well aspected. Today, Germany is one of the most prosperous and spiritually progressive nations in the world (Leo rising and Jupiter in Leo conjunct the Asc. Jupiter sextile the Sun).

• *Changes indicated by the Covid eclipse:* (see chart on the previous page). There is trouble ahead (eclipse Uranus 10H square Mars, conjunct natal Asc and Jupiter). Far-right politics in Germany has been growing and there are some who want to take the nation back to its Nazi past. Chancellor Merkel's tenure ends later in 2021 and the new leader will be crucial for Germany's future direction.

The soul of Germany is ruled by Aries and Ray 4 of Harmony & Conflict.

• Aries, which rules the nation's soul is on the MC of the 1990 chart. Germany is one of the leading nations in the world in terms of its progressive government style. One of its duties is to model to developing nations, wise democratic government (Jupiter on Asc, trine MC).

• Germany's Aries soul is coloured by the harmony-conflict ray. This explains why so much good has come from the various conflicts that its people have initiated and which have torn the country apart. This nation grows spiritually through its conflicts. But it also means that the nation has a duty to help settle world disputes and bring peace and harmony. Germany took an important step towards this goal when it got its own house in order by unifying west and east Germany. This act gave the nation a peace-making Libra Sun in the new chart.

> Experience leads to rulership and in Aries, the man (nation) of power who has controlled his mind and has learned to act with love; has earned the right to guide the affairs of the world. Germany's spiritual keynote is: "I come forth and from the plane of mind, I rule." [2]

Germany's spiritual motto is, "I preserve." [3]

Germany's spiritual task is to preserve "the pattern of the superman". [4] This is its ultimate destiny. The "superman" referred to is the wise and loving soul. It is man's spiritual prototype. Hitler who sensed this goal, thought it referred to a physical super-race. He butchered the vision and subsequently all those who stood in his way.

The "pattern of the superman," the archetypal pattern of man's spiritual glory, may come through Germany's music. The 4th ray is the pre-eminent ruler of artists and artistic creations and in the past, Germany expressed its soul-genius through amazing artists such as Wagner and Beethoven and many others. It could do so again.

---

1 Hinckley Allen, Richard; Star Names, 471.
2 Bailey, Alice A. Esoteric Astrology, 108.
3 Bailey, Alice A. The Destiny of the Nations, 50.
4 Bailey, Alice A. Esoteric Psychology I, 392. Written in 1942.

Greece

Greece's personality is ruled by Capricorn, its soul by Virgo. [1]

With two earth signs ruling its destiny, Greece will always take a pragmatic and practical approach to life. A reaction to the centuries its lands and people were controlled by other nations. As time goes by and the lasting effects of the repressions that subjugated its people fade from the public consciousness (Capricorn); a new wave of intellectual brilliance (Virgo), which distinguished its glorious past will arise.

Greece's governing signs are the same as Australia's. This has created a magnetic resonance between the two nations. As a consequence, in the mid-19th Century, over 200,000 Greek migrants went to Australia. The two countries have a close bilateral relationship that will likely become closer in the future.

1. Earthquake of Crete, 21 July 365 AD.

The entire north side of the Mediterranean Basin is earthquake prone. When this one struck, Crete was a backwater state in the Roman Empire. It happened around sunrise, a magnitude eight earthquake with its epicentre under Crete.

<u>Solar eclipse for Crete Earthquake: 6 Jun 365, 03:10, Heraklion.</u>

• Under immense stress (transit Mars moving over Pluto in fiery and violent Aries); the tectonic plates in the earth's crust (Saturn) released suddenly with shattering force (square Uranus on the IC).

• A devastating tsunami followed (Neptune dominant in the 10H, in a t-square with Uranus and Saturn).

• Additionally, the Venus, IC, Uranus conjunction straddle *Pherkad* (28 Cancer), a star linked to massive sea events by Shakespeare. The "guards" in the quote refers to the stars *Pherkad* and *Kochab*.

> It is a high-wrought flood. The wind-shak'd surge, with high and monstrous mane seems to quench the *guards* of the ever-fixed pole. [2]

• Nearly all of the towns on Crete and other areas of Greece were destroyed. The tsunami killed thousands. [3] The physical event mirrored what was to happen in the region and to any hope of Greek independence after Roman rule ended (around 180 AD). The region was overrun by warring factions that included Arabs and Crusading Normans. In the 14th Century it was brought under Ottoman Empire rule. But by the 17th and 18th Centuries, the Empire was crumbling and the flickering flame in Greek hearts for independence (Uranus on the IC), became a flame.

---

1   Bailey, Alice A. The Destiny of the Nations, 68.
2   Quote from Shakespeare, Othello, Act II. Scene I. (* the guards are Pherkad and Kochab)
3   https://en.wikipedia.org/wiki/365_Crete_earthquake

2. Battle for Independence from the Ottoman Empire.

Lunar eclipse for Greece Independence: 17 Feb 1821, 02:19, Athens.

This eclipse represents the beginning of the end for Ottoman Empire control in Europe. This is emphasised by Pluto, in the final degrees of Pisces, on the IC of the chart. It is on *Scheat* (27 Pisces), that warns of danger from tidal waves and violent storms. The eclipse portended what came to pass - a tidal wave of change was about to engulf and destroy the empire (Pluto inconjunct the Moon, ruler of the 8H of death).

• As the empire crumbled, Greek hearts cried out for freedom and independence (Sagittarius Asc and Uranus-Neptune rising).

• They drew on their valour from the past (Moon on *Regulus,* 27 Leo, the Lion's Heart). On 21 Feb 1821 - 3 days after the eclipse, Alexandros Ypsilantis (1792-1828) gave this wonderful address:

> Cast your eyes toward the seas, which are covered by our seafaring cousins, ready to follow the example of Salamis (an ancient naval battle that Greeks won). Look to the land, and everywhere you will see Leonidas (Spartan King) at the head of the patriotic Spartans (courageous Greek warriors).

• The evolutionary pattern is Uranus (representing the Greek cry for independence), conjunct Neptune (freedom from the decaying Islamic caliphate).

3. Birth of the Kingdom of Greece: 3 February 1830, 12:00, Athens.

The Kingdom was created on 3 February 1830 and given a 12-noon time.

When the UK, France and Russia declared it to be an independent, sovereign state, they also in their "wisdom", put in a foreigner to rule - Otto of German-Bavaria. It was an ill-conceived move that caused lasting trouble.

• Through the centuries, the Greeks had managed to maintain a sense of nationality, their Greek Orthodox religion and language. They resented having autocratic and conservative European customs being foisted upon them, which Otto proceeded to do (Sun-Uranus opposing Saturn in the 4H of the people).

People rebelled and Otto was driven into exile in 1862. From then on, Greece-national politicians began to rule the nation, alternating with periods of further monarchies.

• A 1920 referendum brought back the Monarchy (Constantine I), but was abolished again in 1924. Greeks wanted to rule themselves and bring back their Hellenic customs and religion (Sun-Uranus; Mars in Sagittarius, opposite Moon. Mars is on *Grafias*, 15 Sagittarius, a star in the warlike, Scorpius constellation).

• Finally, in 1974, with Constantine II on the throne (the Duke of Edinburgh's cousin), the Monarchy was formally abolished by a military junta.

4. Greece in the two Balkan Wars, 1912 to 1913.

Lunar eclipse for the Balkan Wars: 26 Sep 1912, 13:08, Athens;
around Greece natal.

• Greek independence had been gained under a Uranus-Neptune conjunction. Now, 82 years later, transit Uranus opposed Neptune, bringing about another stage in the development that began in 1830. Greece, Serbia, Bulgaria and Montenegro went to war against the crumbling Ottoman Empire. It was an opportunity for Greece to take back territories it had historical links to.

• Many nations were involved in the Balkan wars (eclipse Uranus in the international 9H), and they gained the support of European super-powers who hoped to benefit commercially and in any other way they could, from the carve-up.

Like hungry wolves they circled the Empire. The Sun is on one of the wolf stars - *Nodus I* (2 Libra); and Mars was on the other - *Nodus II (*16 Aries).

• For such a short war, death-totals were horrendously high, over a quarter of a million troops died and tens of thousands of civilians. Deep-seated hate had condensed over the centuries (eclipse Mars conjunct the eclipse south node), and butchery was committed (Pluto on the eclipse DC, in a t-square with the eclipse Sun and Moon; opposing natal Jupiter, multiplying the malevolence of the forces).

• Land taken in the first war (8 Oct 1912 to 30 May 1913), was shared among the victors. Greece greatly benefitted in the territories it gained. It almost doubled its size. (Eclipse Saturn on the natal Asc, trine the eclipse Sun, that rules the 4H of land territory; sextile eclipse Moon that naturally rules the 4H).

2nd Balkan War. Bulgaria, unhappy with its share, started the second Balkan War on 16 June 1913. It attacked its former allies, Serbia and Greece. But it was an ill-conceived and poorly-planned move and Bulgaria was quickly defeated - within 13 days, on 29 June 1913. There was relative peace for a while.

However, the Balkan troubles led to the greatest carnage the world had known. They triggered WWI.

5. Greece in World War I and the Spanish Flu.

Blood Moon eclipse for WWI: 15 Sep 1913, 14:41,
Athens: around Greece natal.

• Greece declared neutrality. Then in June 1917, King Constantine I was ousted and Eleftherios Venizelos was installed as prime minister.

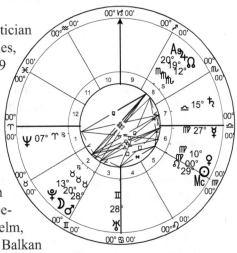

• On 29th June 1917, Greece declared war on the side of Britain. It was a strategic move. Greece's first goal was to keep the land gained in the Balkan Wars and to stop Bulgaria causing trouble.

• The war took its toll - the eclipse Sun-Moon form a grand-cross with Greece's Moon and other planets. Many thousands of Greek soldiers died.

• The Spanish Flu appeared in Greece in 1918, but tuberculosis, typhoid fever and malaria were causing more deaths. In Athens 1,668 people died and 5,284 in Thessaloniki. The only recommendations were social distancing and natural remedies.

> Avoiding gatherings. This is the only remedy. Garlic, ouzo and other nostrums claiming to prevent the influenza are comical. [1]

Eleftherios Venizelos: 23 Aug 1864, 12:00, Mournies.

(Time unknown, 12:00, Aries rising chart).

Venizelos was probably the most significant politician of modern Greece. Born in the village Mournies, he became famous for his leadership in the 1889 and 1896 uprisings against the Ottoman Empire. Venizelos became the island's first independent prime minister in 1905 and served for 15 years.

• Highly intelligent (Mercury in Virgo) he had a mind like a rapier. An idealist, he promoted liberal-democratic policies to help his nation move forwards into the modern age (Neptune in Aries, Sun sextile Uranus). He is credited with being the maker of modern Greece and under his helm, Greece doubled its area and population in the Balkan Wars (Mercury trine Mars).

• Venizelos' Sun was on *Megrez* (29 Leo), a star that in China was called 'Tien Kuen' - 'Heavenly Authority.' Sadly, by the 1930s, Venizelos had become very unpopular. Consequently, he went into exile where he died.

---

1 Embros Newspaper, 17 October 1918.

6. Greece in World War II and the Greek Famine.

Blood Moon eclipse for WWII: 3 May 1939, 17:16, Athens; around Greece natal.

• Greece was violently impacted by the war (the eclipse Sun and Moon formed a grand-cross with Greece's Sun-Uranus and MC/ IC axis).

• The Germans invaded in April 1941. Hitler wanted to stop the Allies using Greece's airports to bomb Romanian oilfields, which fuelled the Nazi war-machine.

• Reaching Athens, the Germans ordered that the Greek flag flying over the Acropolis be removed. A soldier guarding the flag took it down, wrapped himself in it, then leapt from the walls of the ancient fortress to his death. It was the first public act of resistance in Athens and a warning to the Germans they would not have an easy time. Nor did they. Greek resistance was one of the strongest in Nazi-occupied Europe. The Greek love of independence and freedom enshrined in their souls (as well it should be after almost 2,000 years of occupation), is well represented in the chart by the Sun-Uranus conjunction on the MC.

Lunar eclipse for the Greek War Famine: 13 Mar 1941, 13:46, Athens.

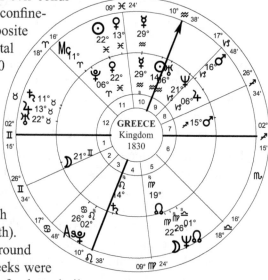

• The Germans imprisoned the Greeks in evil conditions. (a). Eclipse Saturn in the 12H of confinement, in a t-square with natal Sun opposite Saturn. (b). Eclipse Sun-Moon square natal Moon, conjunct the war star *Bellatrix* (20 Gemini), portending war and carnage.

• The Nazi invaders raped the land, plundered produce to feed their troops and left locals without food (eclipse Pluto-Asc, conjunct 4H cusp)

• Food shortages became critical by the middle of 1941 and by the end of the year and in 1942, people were starving to death (Pluto inconjunct Jupiter in 8H of death). More people died from starvation (around 300,000), than from other causes. The Greeks were so traumatised by the famine, after the war, food-stockpiling became common. A fear that locals called "occupation syndrome."

> "Occupation syndrome", the fear of not having enough to eat [is] still affecting how people perceive poverty today. [1]

---

1   History, Time, and Economic Crisis in Central Greece, Knight, Daniel M., p.xi

7. Birth of Democratic Greece: 24 July 1974, 04:00, Athens.

In 1952, Greece became a kingdom ruled by parliamentary democracy. In 1964, King Constantine II succeeded to the throne. Then in 1967, a far-right military junta took over and ruled until 1973-74. In 1974, the democratically elected Prime Minister, Konstantinos Karamanlis, called a referendum which formally abolished the Monarchy.

Greece became a Democratic Republic on 24 July 1974, at 04:00 when Constantine Karamanlis was sworn in as prime minister. This chart is still used today.

• The chart reflects the violence and tumultuous forces that preceded the birth of the democratic nation (Moon conjunct Pluto, 4H; Sun square Uranus).

8. Greece and Covid-19.

Lunar eclipse for Covid-19: 16 Jul 2019, 23:39, Athens; around Greece natal.

• Greece has been bailed out 3 times from threatened bankruptcy, an action designed to maintain the integrity of the eurozone. Bailout lenders were bankers who imposed austerity conditions to force Greece to live within its means. Consequently, the nation's health system was under-funded.

Recognizing this, when the first Covid cases appeared in March 2020 the government imposed a preemptive national lockdown. Restrictions were gradually eased and by 2021 there were almost 5 thousand deaths and 140 thousand infected.[1] Greece's population is 11 million.

Greece's leaders did well. With natal Sun conjunct the 2 Leo epidemic degree, things could have been much worse.

• Greece will walk a more independent road in the future (natal Sun conjunct eclipse Sun and square eclipse Uranus). This will be a good thing for Greeks. Now it is time for its people to remember the words of Alexandros Ypsilantis, when he said:

> Look to the land, and everywhere you will see Leonidas at the head of the patriotic Spartans.

------

1   13 Jan 2021: the 41st ranked nation in the world for deaths per capita.

9. The Spiritual Destiny of Greece.

The personality of Greece is ruled by Capricorn.

• *Problem*: the 1974 rebirth chart with Saturn afflicted in Cancer was not helpful for Greece's progression. It indicated that regressive forces in the nation were bent on blocking forward progression and wanted to return to the old ways (Saturn conjunct Asc). Greece is an ancient nation whose roots are still embedded in its past. Influenced by Saturn and Capricorn, Greece remains very patriarchal, traditional and conservative, especially in rural areas where women largely adhere to their traditional, domestic roles. The repression of women is likely an inheritance from the Ottoman days (Moon conjunct Pluto Saturn). By the 21st Century, women still only made up around 30% of the work force.

Greece 1974 natal

Another manifestation of this problem is poverty, exacerbated by austerity measures applied by EU monetarists in 2010. Recent reports say almost a 1/4 of the nation was unemployed and about 1/3 live below the poverty line. This includes a high proportion of the elderly because 1 in 5 Greeks are over 65. Greece's elderly have the worst quality of life in Europe. [1]

• *Changes indicated by the Covid eclipse:*
The shape of the nation, its economy and its relations with its neighbours are destined to drastically change in the coming 33-year cycle with the main eclipse planets falling in the 1st and 7th houses and the Sun ruling the 2H of the economy.

The death of an important relationship will occur (Pluto 7H). Possibly, Greece will sever its ties with the EU or with eurozone and revert back to its own currency. As painful as this will be it is a real possibility with eclipse Mars in the 2H of the nation's wealth and currency, square the planet of extreme measures - Uranus in the 11H of friends and politics.

The hardship that Saturn on the Asc represents is a current problem. A major constitutional change, rebirth of the nation and therefore a new national chart, would remove Saturn from this prominent position. Positively however, Saturn's trine to Neptune in the 9H, promises that Greece will eventually move through this period. What it learns about itself as it does so, will contribute to its higher spiritual and philosophical destiny, which is covered in the next section.

1   https://www.huffpost.com/entry/greece-elderly-poor-study_n_560e96c1e4b076812701a102

The soul of Greece is ruled by Virgo.

• Greece has a Virgo soul, the sign that traditionally rules teaching and healing. In the future, as the nation comes into its spiritual maturity, Greece could go through a revival of its past greatness. Advanced Greek scholars, bringing to the world new and higher forms of the great sciences that it had previously shared with the ancient world.

• This is particularly so in medicine and healing, because of the association of the asteroid Chiron with Virgo. In mythology, Chiron was a very wise teacher and healer, who dedicated himself to healing because of his great compassion for the suffering of others. In the chart, this destiny - Greece pioneering new and higher schools of education, medicine and healing is shown. Chiron is in Aries, in the 10H; trine the north-node in the 6H of health.

• Another reason that strengthens this line of thought, is because of the Sun's conjunction with *Talitha* (2 Leo), a star associated with the power to heal and to raise the dead to life. "Talitha" means "Daughter of the assembly," and it was mentioned in the Bible. A young girl was dying, when Jesus took her hand and said, "Talitha Cumi" - "daughter arise". [1] She was healed and she did arise.

• At the higher level, Virgo is the sign that represents the purification of consciousness as well as of the body. Certain groups in the nation are spiritually developed and in the future a mystery school that teaches higher wisdom will open. All those who pass through this higher level of training will help Greece achieve its ultimate destiny, which is to contribute to the healing of humanity and its enlightenment.

> When that spiritual reality, spoken of by St. Paul as "Christ in you, the hope of glory," is released in man and can manifest in full expression. When a sufficient number of people have grasped this ideal, the entire human family can stand for the first time before the portal which leads to the Path of Light, and the life of Christ will flower forth in the human kingdom. [2] Greece's spiritual keynote is: "Christ in you, the hope of glory."

---

1   Bible, Mark 5:41.

2   Bailey, Alice A. From Bethlehem to Calvary, 18.

Iceland

Scandinavia-Iceland's personality is ruled by Cancer, its soul by Libra. [1]

The Icelandic Vikings were protective and tribal (Cancer) in their formative years, which was essential for their survival in the long, dark and glacial conditions of northern winters. They were also an emotional and mystical people who were influenced greatly by their pagan myths and beliefs (Cancer is a water sign that is related to the emotions).

Their higher development is along the Libra-line with this sign ruling the nation's soul. Libra is an air sign that fosters mental acuity - the very opposite of feeling-driven Cancer. Development along this line has fostered in the people a keen sense of what is right and wrong. Values that will help the world at large develop similar qualities.

1. The World's Oldest Democracy

Iceland is distinguished by the fact that it has the longest running parliament in the world. The Icelandic Althing (Alþingi), the national parliament of Iceland, is the oldest legislature. It was founded in 930 A.D. at Thingvellir (45 km from Reykjavík), a date considered to be the beginning of Iceland as a country.

Total Solar eclipse for Icelandic Althing: 29 Jun 0930, 00:12, Thingvellir.

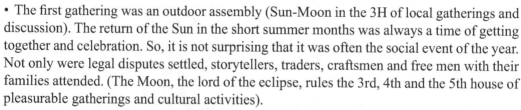

• The evolutionary pattern behind the event is Saturn trine Uranus. They portend the establishment of a form of government (Saturn in Capricorn on MC), which came naturally to the people and was democratic (trine Uranus). Democracy is government (Saturn) by the people, for the people (the eclipse Sun and Moon are in family-oriented Cancer, opposite Saturn).

• The country's most influential leaders met to discuss the community's affairs (Pluto in communicative Gemini rising in the 1H of "the nation"). They formed laws and dispensed justice (Saturn-Uranus for legislation. Saturn semi-square Jupiter, the natural ruler of the 9H of the high court; Jupiter trine Mercury).

• The first gathering was an outdoor assembly (Sun-Moon in the 3H of local gatherings and discussion). The return of the Sun in the short summer months was always a time of getting together and celebration. So, it is not surprising that it was often the social event of the year. Not only were legal disputes settled, storytellers, traders, craftsmen and free men with their families attended. (The Moon, the lord of the eclipse, rules the 3rd, 4th and the 5th house of pleasurable gatherings and cultural activities).

• The Althing was so useful for governing the community's affairs, it became a custom. It ran until 1800 when it was discontinued, but was restored in 1844 and still runs today. This power to endure can be attributed to powerful Pluto conjunct *Alhena* (24 Gemini), a brilliant white star (1.9 magnitude), on the left foot of Pollux - the immortal Twin.

---

1 Bailey, Alice A. The Destiny of the Nations, 68.

2. Eruption of Grímsvotn Volcano and Laki fissure, 8 June 1783.

Iceland is a volcanic island sited between the North American and Eurasian tectonic plates, so volcanic eruptions are common - once in every 4 years on average. One of the worst on record is the Grímsvotn eruption that started on 8 June 1783. With the adjoining Laki fissure, the eruptions continued for 8 months, spewing out lava and volcanic ash that poisoned the land and sea.

Total Solar eclipse for Eruption: 6 Oct 1782, 23:21, Vatnajokull National Park.

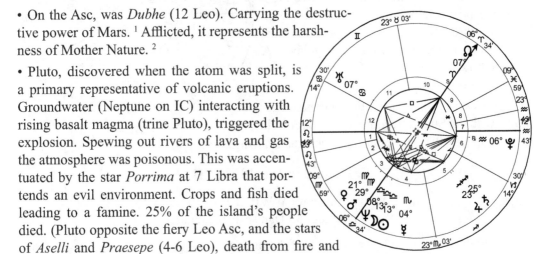

• On the Asc, was *Dubhe* (12 Leo). Carrying the destructive power of Mars. [1] Afflicted, it represents the harshness of Mother Nature. [2]

• Pluto, discovered when the atom was split, is a primary representative of volcanic eruptions. Groundwater (Neptune on IC) interacting with rising basalt magma (trine Pluto), triggered the explosion. Spewing out rivers of lava and gas the atmosphere was poisonous. This was accentuated by the star *Porrima* at 7 Libra that portends an evil environment. Crops and fish died leading to a famine. 25% of the island's people died. (Pluto opposite the fiery Leo Asc, and the stars of *Aselli* and *Praesepe* (4-6 Leo), death from fire and stones and piled-up corpses. Here is an eyewitness description:

> The flood of fire flowed with the speed of a great swollen river. Great cliffs and slabs of rock were swept along, tumbling about like large whales swimming, red-hot and glowing. [3]

• As for the legacy, Neptune is on the IC. So is the star *Vindemiatrix* (7 Libra), called 'The Grape Gatherer' by the ancients. Afflicted, it is a symbol of famine. The poisonous effects affected the world's weather. From 1783 to 1785, it led to droughts, exceptionally cold winters and disastrous floods around the world that resulted crop in failures and starvation.

3. Iceland in World War I, the Spanish Flu and Independence.

Iceland was ruled by Denmark when the war broke out, which remained neutral. But it is estimated that 1,200 Icelanders fought in the war - mostly Canadian immigrants. The Great War coincided with a rise of nationalism in Europe and Iceland gained sovereignty, in personal union with Denmark through a common monarch, on 1 December 1918.

The World War may have left Iceland relatively untouched, but the unseen enemy - the influenza virus, did not. The infection arrived in Iceland on two ships from Copenhagen on 19 October 1918. It spread rapidly. Two thirds of Reykjavík caught the virus. Overall, 540 people died. Attempts to halt the spread of the epidemic to the northern and eastern parts of the island were successful.

---

1 Ebertin-Hoffman, Fixed Stars, 43
2 Brady, Bernadette. Solar Fire software interpretations
3 Pastor Jón Steingrímsson who was a witness,

4. Birth of Danish-Iceland: 1 December 1918, 12:00, Reykjavik.

Iceland was an Independent Republic from 930 to 1264, then it was briefly ruled by Norway before coming under Danish rule in 1381. In 1874, it was granted home rule

After WWI, through an Act of Union, Denmark recognized Iceland as a fully sovereign and independent country in personal union with Denmark through a common monarch. This happened on 1 December 1918, at Reykjavik. A 12-noon time is used.

• Iceland's new, though partial independence, is shown with the Sun in freedom loving Sagittarius, trine Neptune in Leo, 7H. The latter represents the Danish Crown.

5. Iceland in World War II.

Blood Moon eclipse for WWII: 3 May 1939, 14:16, Reykjavik; around Danish-Iceland natal.

• Mythologically, this eclipse warned of being devoured by the monster *Cetus,* a symbol for the bestiality of Nazi Germany. Iceland declared its neutrality. But it was invaded anyway (Mars 1H), by the British on 10 May 1940, who feared it would be taken by the Germans who were invading Denmark at the time.

• Just 230 Icelander lives were lost in the war, most killed on cargo and fishing vessels sunk by the Germans. It could have been worse with the eclipse Mars in the 1H of the nation and the eclipse hitting the natal Moon in Scorpio in the 8H of death.

• The eclipse IC, the legacy of the war, fell on 9 Sagittarius, conjunct Iceland's Sun. It promised major changes to the nation's identity as a result of the war. One way this happened was by Icelandic women fraternising with British and American soldiers - they had mixed-blood babies. Another way the occupation transformed the country was due to the engineering projects (Mars 1H) and other modern developments brought in by the British and Americans.

• With 5 eclipse planets in Iceland's 2H of values, and two of them - Venus and Mercury forming a grand-trine with the Sun and Neptune, occupation was beneficial in the long term. It led to full independence from Denmark (eclipse Sun-Uranus square natal Neptune 7H).

6. Birth of the Iceland Republic: 17 June 1944, 14:00, at Reykjavik.

A referendum held after the war - at the end of May 1944, resulted in voters overwhelmingly voting to abolish the union with Denmark and adopt a new republican constitution.

The natal chart still current today is set for that rebirth, on 17 June 1944, at 14:00 when the republic was formally inaugurated.

• The urge for independence is represented by Uranus. It drives the stellium of planets through Gemini - that represent the intense negotiations that preceded the act. The last planet in the group is Saturn, representing the new government taking power (conjunct the MC).

7. Banking Crisis: 8 October 2008.

Total Solar eclipse for 2008 Stock Market Crash: 1 Aug 2008, 10:12, Reykjavik: around Iceland natal.

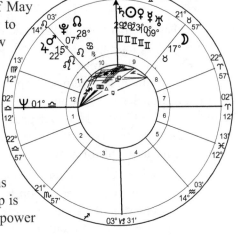

• The 2008 global financial crisis hit Iceland hard. The eclipse impacted natal Pluto, and was semi-square natal Venus, which rules the 2H of the economy.

• Uranus rules the 5H of share-market speculation; and Mars rules the 8H of international finance, major financial losses and bankruptcies.

In the eclipse chart, they both square mega-powerful Pluto on *Acumen* (29 Sagittarius). It is a star north of the stinger of the Scorpion that portends "bloodshed and carnage," [1] which is what occurred financially.

• The currency crashed, businesses went bankrupt, unemployment soared and the stock market was more or less wiped out. Iceland's three major banks were too big to bail out. So they failed and 36 bankers were convicted and jailed for negligence (eclipse Mars, ruler 8H, in the 12H of incarceration).

• Banks were forced to decrease household debt so people would not be driven into bankruptcy and could apply for debt forgiveness. Supportive Jupiter is in the 4H of the people, trine Saturn (the courts and government). Iceland set the example for how world governments should deal with corrupt bankers and banking institutions.

1 Manilius, Marcus; Astronomica, 239-240.

8. Iceland and Covid-19.

Lunar eclipse for Covid-19: 16 Jul 2019, 21:39, Reykjavik; around Iceland natal.

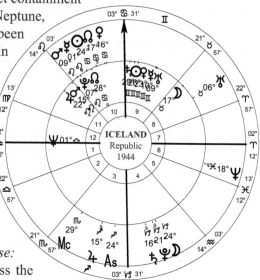

• Informed and vigilant, Iceland applied strict containment measures (natal Sun-Saturn square eclipse Neptune, which represents the virus). It could have been much worse with firstly, eclipse Neptune in the 6H of health. Secondly, eclipse Mars and Mercury (on the 2 Leo epidemic degree of the zodiac), conjunct natal Pluto, square eclipse Uranus in the 8H of death.

• These precautions allowed tourism, a main source of income for the nation to continue. It worked well. By 2021 there were 29 dead from 5.7 thousand infected (the island's population is 357 thousand people).

• *Changes indicated of by the Covid eclipse:* with the eclipse axis of planets falling across the 10th - 4th houses, some adjustments will be made in the government and across the people of the land generally.

9. The Spiritual Destiny of Iceland.

The personality of Iceland is ruled by Cancer.

• Iceland's Cancer personality, is currently working through a Gemini Sun. The Gemini stellium in the 9H indicates a nation of world travellers and seekers who want to understand themselves and the world they live in.

• Iceland places great importance upon education (Gemini, 9H). Its website states that, "everyone should have equal opportunities to acquire an education, irrespective of sex, economic status, residential location, religion, possible handicap and cultural or social background." A 2016 study ranked, Iceland the third most literate nation in the world.

Iceland 1944 natal

• *Problem*: Iceland has a Taurus Moon. Negatives that are often associated with Taurus are greed and over-eating and Icelanders are getting fat. Records from 2008 show that 58.4% of the adult population were overweight and almost a quarter were obese. [1] Another reported problem is a growing incident of rape (Taurus Moon in the 8H of sex, square Mars).

---

1 https://www.euro.who.int/__data/assets/pdf_file/0015/243303/Iceland-WHO-Country-Profile.pdf

The soul of Iceland is ruled by Libra.

• Iceland is a very progressive nation and as previously mentioned before, it is the world's oldest democracy. Due to the Libra influence and its advanced spirituality, it has maintained the title of the most peaceful country in the world since the first the Global Peace Index launched in 2009. It helps that it is so isolated and is not a crossroads of many diverse cultures, races and ideologies.

• God of the Oceans, Neptune, is rising on the ascendant, which is perfect for this oceanic island. It squares the Gemini planets in the 9H, perhaps reflecting the challenges to survival caused by being so far from other world nations. But Neptune is also an energy that represents the mystical and spiritual side of life and it draws people into alternate or higher worlds of discovery. There are many Icelanders who still believe in elves, trolls, and other figures from Norse myths.

Neptune is trine Uranus, the esoteric ruler of the nation (with Libra ruling the soul). Uranus rules "the new" and science, and the aspect to Neptune indicates islanders building upon their myths and legends of the past to develop their own unique form of spirituality and worship.

• Uranus guides the higher destiny of the Scandinavian nations through all their various incarnations. Uranus is conjunct the powerful military star *Aldebaran* (9 Gemini). It is a pale rose star that marks the right eye of the Bull, and is one of the Four Royal Stars in ancient Persia. Its name is 'The Watcher of the East'. When its forces are harnessed and are being used positively as they are by Iceland (Uranus/ *Aldebaran*, sextile Mars in Leo; Mars conjunct Jupiter); there is tremendous energy available for outer and inner growth.

• With a Libra-ruled soul, when the Scandinavian countries come of age spiritually, they will play an important harmonising role in the world and be powerful advocates for human-rights. Iceland will always have very close links with other Scandinavian countries because of this. Their collective higher goal is to become a reconciliating force in world affairs.

> Iceland's spiritual keynote is: "I choose the way which leads between the two great lines of force." [1]

---

1 Bailey, Alice A. *Esoteric Astrology*, 251.

India

India's personality is ruled by Capricorn, its soul by Aries. [1]

India has two very strong signs ruling its psychology - Capricorn and Aries. They both carry the power ray which indicates that in the future, as the nation matures, integrates and learns to handle its power wisely; it is destined to be a world super-power.

India's Capricorn personality indicates that generally, its leaders will take a conservative approach to guide the nation and repress dissent through strict laws and controls. The Mughal Empire that governed most of the subcontinent (1526–1761), is an example. It was influenced by the conservative grandeur, pomp and tradition of Capricorn. Fabulously wealthy, it produced glorious architecture - the Taj Mahal being the most famous.

Advanced members of the nation who tap into its soul-force, use Aries leadership power to bring about the greater good. Mahatma Gandhi was such a man.

1. The Sepoy Uprising - the First War of Independence, 1857-1858.

India and its style of government was changed profoundly by the British influence. The first major British presence in India was the East India Company (1608-1858), London merchants who started trading in Western India. From there the company's influence grew. Using its army (260,000 men at its greatest), it forcibly subjugated provinces, rulers and any dissent until it controlled most of India. This Sepoy outbreak was the first major challenge to British rule and it started over religion. To load the new Enfield rifles, sepoys (Indian soldiers), had to bite the ends off cartridges first. But they were lubricated with a mixture of pig and cows' grease and making oral contact with this grease violated Hindu religious principles. Many refused to do so and were jailed - for years. This triggered the insurrection.

Lunar eclipse for Uprising: 9 Apr 1857, 14:39, Meerat.

• The eclipse Sun was in Aries, fuelling the Indian urge to be free of repression. It was also conjunct *Baten Kaitos* (20 Aries), a star in the belly of *Cetus*, the Sea Monster. The aggrieved soldiers saw the British as foreign monsters (Mars in 9H), who were forcing them to violate their religious principles and values (9H emphasis, Moon 2H).

On 10 May 1857, the British were attacked. The conflict spread to Delhi and other areas in northern India.

• The conflict was brutal (Mars and Pluto conjunct violent *Hamal* - 5 Taurus 39; Sun in 8H). The sepoys and townspeople slaughtered British officers and families. The British retaliated with similar cruelty and terrible atrocities were committed by both sides. It is estimated almost 6000 British were killed and many more thousands of Indians. The fiasco caused the British government to act and it brought India under the direct rule of the British crown in 1858.

1 Bailey, Alice A. The Destiny of the Nations, 67.

2. Birth of the Indian Empire: 1 January 1877, 00:00, Delhi.

The British raj period of direct British rule began in 1858 and lasted until the independence of India and Pakistan in 1947.

On 1 January 1877, at 00:00 hours in Delhi, India went through a rebirth when Queen Victoria was proclaimed "the Empress of India." On that day it became the "Indian Empire" under the British Crown. This title and act were gestures to bind India more closely to Britain. The empire at that time consisted of the whole of India that included the modern states of Pakistan, Bangladesh and Myanmar.

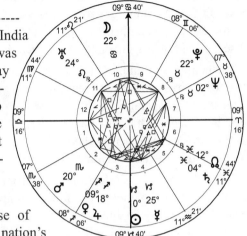

• The chart was beneficial for India because of the Sun's location in Capricorn that rules the nation's personality. It helped the integration of the nation. But the "mother-country" was firmly in control (Moon in 10H). Under the guiding presence of the raj, British political, social and economic influence began to change the nation.

3. India in World War I and the Spanish Flu.

Although Indians wanted independence, there was deep admiration for the British. Consequently, there was enthusiastic support for the war when it broke out. Almost 1.5 million troops enlisted and the nation provided monetary and practical support. Field-Marshal Sir Claude Auchinleck, Commander-in-Chief of the Indian Army from 1942 asserted that the British "couldn't have come through both wars [WWI and II] if they hadn't had the Indian Army." [1]

Blood Moon eclipse for WWI: 15 Sep 1913, 18:15, Delhi; around the India Empire.

• The war eclipse made a powerful impact on India's chart (Mars-Pluto on the MC, opposite Jupiter on the IC; forming a t-square with all angles). The war extracted a heavy toll on the nation.

• Fighting in the trenches in a foreign and cold land and amongst people who did not speak their language was miserable. Many expressed their thoughts in letters sent home. For example:

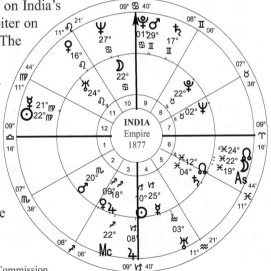

The shells are pouring like rain in the monsoon," and

"The corpses cover the country, like sheaves of harvested corn. [2]

---

1   "Indian Army in WWII". Commonwealth War Graves Commission.
2   https://www.bbc.com/news/magazine-33317368

Lunar eclipse for the Spanish Flu: 15 Jul 1916, 10:10, Delhi; around India Empire.

• About 50,000 Indian troops died in the war. But many more Indians were to die as a consequence of the Spanish Flu. Neptune governs viruses and the nation easily succumbed to the disease with Pisces - Neptune's sign, on the 6H of health.

• The eclipse stellium, contained by Neptune (the virus) and Pluto (mass deaths), opposite to the natal Sun; dominated the Empire's chart. This can be interpreted as the virus over-powering the health and well-being of the nation (Sun)

• Soldiers brought the infection home from foreign lands (9H planets). The first cases appeared in Bombay in June 1918, then spread. It killed about 12 to 13 million people in India alone.

During the war, there was a big demand for Indian cotton jute and rubber. This initiated an industrial boom which continued once the war and epidemic years subsided. But all too soon, WWII broke out.

4. India in World War II and Indian Independence.

Blood Moon eclipse for WWII: 3 May 1939, 20:35, Delhi; around India Empire.

• India again made a huge contribution to Britain's war effort. It sent over two and a half million soldiers and lent billions of pounds (eclipse Sun-Moon in the Empires 2-8 money/ resource houses).

• The war reached India's north-east territory (Mars in 4H), when the Japanese attacked Kohima in the Himalayan foothills. It took 3 months, but eventually the British-Indian army drove them out.

• Over 87,000 Indian soldiers (including those from modern day Pakistan, Nepal, and Bangladesh) and 3 million civilians died (8H emphasis).

• WWII - and the growing independence movement led by Mohandas Gandhi; forced Britain to give India its independence. The war destroyed Britain's economy so that it was no longer able to financially maintain its military force in India. In 1946, the British Viceroy, Archibald Wavell, announced to London that India was no longer governable.

Total Solar eclipse for Independence: 20 May 1947, 19:13, Delhi; around India Empire.

• India gained independence on 15 August 1947. The Sun and Moon were conjunct the Pleiades (29 Taurus), stars long associated with loss and bereavement. So is Neptune, which was conjunct the Asc. Although a later eclipse is used for Gandhi's assassination; this one also reflects the great sorrow that many in the world felt when he died.

• Independence was a hard birth (eclipse Sun-Moon conjunct natal Pluto 8H, and Pluto-Saturn conjunct). Violence flared when the nation was partitioned into India and Pakistan. Between 200,000 thousand to 2 million people were killed in the conflict.

• But there was a promise that the nation would survive. On the eclipse IC (8 Pisces), the legacy of the trouble, are *Skat* and *Situla*. These two small stars are in the constellation Aquarius (at 9 Pisces). This constellation, though it is associated with the deluge in Noah's time, it promises survival.

Mohandas Gandhi, 2 October 1869, 07:08, Porbander, India.

• Gandhi, born a Hindu, was peaceful and bridge-building by nature (Sun and Asc in harmonising Libra). By 1919 and 1920, he was prominent, loved and respected as a Mahatma, a saintly and humble soul.

• He felt a deep personal responsibility for his country-men, as advanced souls always do (Capricorn on 4H, Saturn sextile Sun). He wanted to guide his people onto the higher way (Saturn in Sagittarius), instil right and spiritual values and principles to live by (2H).

• Gandhi supported the United Kingdom in WWI, hoping that unconditional support in that nation's hour of need would result in support for home rule. Instead, the British extended martial law when the conflict was over. So, Gandhi became political to lead the fight for independence (Mars trine Uranus on the MC). He launched an anti-British civil disobedience but non-violent campaign called 'Satyagraha', non-cooperation. He was jailed for 6 years. Then on 12 March 1930, Gandhi began a "salt march" in defiance of British monopoly on salt. This act is seen as the beginning of the civil disobedience revolution. Gandhi was jailed for a year (Sun 12H). But such was his success in galvanising support for his cause, on his release in 1944, the UK at last began to make plans to withdraw from the Indian subcontinent. Independence was finally granted in August 1947.

Lunar eclipse for Assassination: 28 Nov 1947, 14:16, Delhi.

Gandhi was assassinated by a Hindu extremist on 30 January 1948, who belonged to a group that objected to Gandhi's insistence of non-violence. The people he represented wanted to fight and kill.

• Violence was a theme of the eclipse chart. The eclipse Sun was in the 8H of death, and with the Moon, was in a conflicted t-square with violent Mars. Militant Aries was rising, on *Algenib* (8 Aries) that warns of sudden and violent death.

• The assassin was a religious (Neptune) fanatic (semi-square Mars). He shot Gandhi in the heart (square Sun). It was a form of regicide, the slaying of a "king". Mars was on the royal star *Regulus* (29 Leo).

• Gandhi's legacy inspired non-violent civil-rights actions around the world. In particular, Martin Luther King Jr. in the United States. With Neptune located in the 7H of open enemies and with the volatile forces around at the time, Gandhi knew he was at great risk of being killed. But - as is the manner of all advanced souls, he was prepared to sacrifice himself for the greater cause.

5. Birth of the Republic of India: 26 January 1950, 10:15, Delhi.

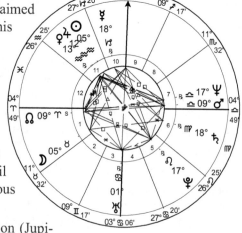

India gained its independence in 1947 and proclaimed itself a republic on 26 January 1950 at 10:15. This is the national chart used today.

• The new chart featured Aries on the ascendant, the sign that rules India's soul. But in the formative years of a nation, when there are major upheavals and turmoil; the lower nature of the people - and of the signs, usually dominate what is happening. So it was in India. The civil war that accompanied independence was vicious (Uranus square Mars on the angles).

• Religious and political divisions split the nation (Jupiter, ruler 9H of religion, in the political 11H - square the Moon. Uranus on the MC/ IC axis).

• Despite the catastrophes of the earlier 20th Century, India's Sun was starting to rise. Inspired by its soul, India was beginning to find its forwards direction (north-node conjunct Aries Asc, sextile the Sun, rising in the 11H).

• Gaining momentum during the war and demand for its products, industrial growth boomed and the economy grew (Venus, ruler of the 2H of the economy, conjunct generous Jupiter and the Sun).

6. India and Covid-19.

Lunar eclipse for Covid-19: 17 Jul 2019, 03:09, Delhi; around India natal.

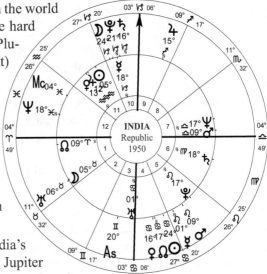

• India, the second most populous nation in the world with 1.4 billion people, was destined to be hard hit by the effects of the virus with eclipse Pluto-Saturn falling in the 10th (government) and 4th (people) houses.

• India has a developing health system, so was not able to respond as well to pandemics as western nations. It went into lock-down 2 months after its first case was reported. But by then, the virus had spread across the nation. By 2021, over 150 thousand were dead with 10 million infected and the virus was accelerating. [1]

• After the Covid-driven recession, India's economy will forge ahead again (eclipse Jupiter in the 9H of international affairs, sextile Venus, ruler of the 2H of the economy).

7. The Spiritual Destiny of India.

The personality of India is ruled by Capricorn and Ray 4 of Harmony through Conflict.

• India's Capricorn personality is still developing and integrating. Coloured by the conflict ray, its history has seen many violent civil conflicts within its borders. But the 4th ray artistic personality has also created a nation of artists and musicians, people who are intuitive and mystical, alluring and beautiful, that are fond of display and colour.

• *Problems*: Taurus Moon square Jupiter indicates an over-emphasis of the material side of things, a trait that is shaping modern politics (Moon square Sun conjunct Jupiter in Aquarius 11H). This is emphasised by two stars in the materialistic constellation Capricorn, which are conjunct the Sun - *Bos* and *Oculus* (4 Aquarius).

India 1950 natal

Although the Sun in Aquarius promises liberal freedoms, the nation has yet to move past its materialistic side. This is inevitable at this stage of its development as the nation's leaders try to lift the masses out of poverty. The gifts that *Bos*, *Oculus* and Capricorn give to the nation are skills to cleverly manage the resources of the material world so that prosperity can be achieved.

---

[1]   13 Jan 2021: the 75th ranked nation in the world for deaths per capita.

The current chart also warns against partisan fanatics who would violate human and other civil rights in order to get power (Mars conjunct Neptune, square Uranus, opposite Asc). It also warns against ambitious and avaricious Capricorn-type leaders who gain popularity by telling lies about their opponents (Saturn, ruler of the Capricorn personality, in Virgo trine Mercury square Neptune).

• *Changes indicated by the Covid eclipse:* (see the chart on the previous page). There will be repercussions in the future as the people vent their anger on leaders for the way they perceive the crisis was handled - or mishandled (Moon, Saturn, Pluto in 10).

New political leaders will rise (Uranus rising trine MC), introducing changes to improve the health system generally and to formulate a more progressive response to future pandemics (square natal Sun, ruler of the 6H of health).

India's soul is ruled by Aries
and the 1st Ray of Will and Power.

• Governed as it is by powerful political and militant signs (Capricorn and Aries), and the 1st Ray of Will and Power, India is destined to play a prominent political and governing role in the world. This destiny is assisted in the current chart with Aries rising. But first, the government has to demonstrate wise action in handling the affairs of the country.

> Experience leads to rulership and in Aries, the man (nation) of power who has controlled his mind and has learned to act with love; has earned the right to guide the affairs of the world. India's spiritual keynote is: "I come forth and from the plane of mind, I rule." [1]

• Harmony in the nation will follow when spiritually advanced leaders appear who can wield the higher Aries and 1st ray forces benevolently for the good of all its people (Mercury in Capricorn 10H, trine Saturn functioning at its higher level). Such leaders will be recognised by the lighted wisdom of their words.

> Harmonising light is sorely needed in India and when it has been manifested it will bring about the right functioning of the 1st Ray of Power or Government. The will of the people will then be seen in the light. [2]

India's spiritual motto is, "I hide the Light." [3]

India's mission in the world is to be the custodian for the light of the Ageless Wisdom. The teachings of Raja Yoga, the Vedas and esoteric Buddhism represent aspects of this wisdom. Drawn to this Light, for decades westerners have made pilgrimages to India seeking understanding and wisdom. The Light of the Ageless Wisdom has been India's major contribution to the spiritual development of humanity. Here is how the Master Djwhal Khul describes this destiny.

> India hides the light and that light, when released upon the world and revealed to humanity, will bring about harmony. Things will then be clearly seen [and people] will be freed from glamour and illusion. [4]

---

1 Bailey, Alice A. Esoteric Astrology, 108.
2 Bailey, Alice A. The Destiny of the Nations, 52-53.
3 Bailey, Alice A. The Destiny of the Nations, 98.
4 Bailey, Alice A. The Destiny of the Nations, 52-53.

Ireland

Ireland's personality is ruled by Pisces, its soul by Virgo. [1]

The Irish are a mystical and magical people of great beauty - a gift from its ruling sign Pisces. Introverted, they love the freedom and privacy that the greens of the forests, the mists of the seas and grandeur of the mountains, gives them.

Engagement with the world, with the English, has been a painful experience and as Ireland has progressed into the modern era; it has become more worldly and discriminating. This is a necessary development for a nation whose soul is ruled by Virgo - the sign directly opposite to Pisces.

1. The Irish Potato Famine, "the Great Hunger": 1845 - 1848.

In 1845, most Irish Catholics were poor, landless and worked as tenant farmers for their English and Anglo-Irish overlords. That year, Ireland had unusually cool moist weather, in which a fungus-like organism, a water mould or blight thrived. Much of that year's (and subsequent years) potato crop rotted in the fields. Because it was the main staple food it had a catastrophic impact, resulting in the death of roughly one million Irish from starvation. Another million were forced to leave their homeland as refugees.

Blood Moon eclipse for the Famine: 21 May 1845, 15:34, Dublin.

• The eclipse Moon is on *Dschubba* (0 Sagittarius), which is on the forehead of the Scorpion. In an eclipse, this star portends an evil environment and that bad things are coming for the people.

• Constant rain promoted the spread of the water mould, which turned the potato crop to mush (Saturn that rules agriculture was conjunct Neptune that rules water).

Saturn squares Mercury in the 8H of death. The latter is conjunct *Menkar* (12 Taurus), a star that has an evil effect when afflicted. It is often active when crops fail.

• Then people began to starve (Saturn-Neptune) and die. The eclipse Sun was in the 8H of death, forming a t-square with Neptune conjunct Saturn. Millions of Irish were driven away from their homes and forced to relocate - many as migrants to the United States (Mercury that rules the 9H of international travel, squares Saturn).

• On the IC was *Sulaphat* (20 Capricorn), a star in the Lyra or musical constellation. As a consequence of the catastrophe, the Irish took their songs and music to other parts of the world.

• The evolutionary pattern was the Saturn-Neptune conjunction, that causes the slow dissolving of crystallised structures. The famine and its effects lasted for another 7 years - until the Saturn-Neptune square. The Irish now form a vital part of the United States nation. Perhaps the famine was nature's way of leading these people to a better way of life.

---

1   Bailey, Alice A. *The Destiny of the Nations*, 68.

2. The Irish War of Independence, 1919-1921.

By the 20th Century, the desire by Irish Nationalists for home rule was growing. The Irish Republican Army (IRA) was formed with the specific purpose of driving the British out of Ireland. On 24 April 1916, at noon in Dublin, Nationalists proclaimed Ireland Independence. This initiated the Easter Rising (24 to 30 April 1916), which the British put down. But this was just the beginning of decades of war.

Lunar eclipse for Irish War of Independence:
17 Dec 1918, 19:16, Tipperary: around UK natal.

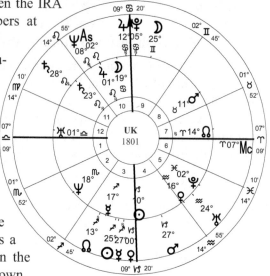

• The war started on 19 January 1919, when the IRA shot two Royal Irish Constabulary members at Tipperary.

• The conflict was ugly (eclipse Pluto and Jupiter in Cancer, in a wide conjunct to the Moon; on the UK MC). There were riots, burning of homes and property and vicious, retaliatory killing raids by both sides. Around 1,500 people were killed in the fighting.

• A truce was called in July 1921 and at the end of 1922 an Irish delegation signed a treaty with the United Kingdom that gave Ireland British Dominion status. There was a clause in the treaty that infuriated some in the IRA - an oath of allegiance to the British Crown.

3. Birth of the Irish Dominion of the UK: 6 Dec 1921, 17:00, Dublin.

The Anglo-Irish Treaty was signed on 6 December 1921 at 17:00 hours in Dublin, by Michael Collins and an Irish delegation.

Michael Collins was a leading figure in the struggle. He was an Irish revolutionary and soldier and was instrumental in the formation of the IRA. Also a politician, he was Chairman of the Provisional Government of the Irish Free State. The clause in the treaty that required an oath of allegiance to the British Crown brought about his death. Collins was assassinated by anti-Treaty IRA soldiers on 22 August 1922.

• The Uranus-Moon conjunction in the 10H shows the volatile nature of the community with the British government around the time the treaty was signed.

• Death is in the chart (Pluto rising square Mars in Libra), and killing continued.

4. Irish Civil War, 1922-1923

Lunar eclipse for Civil War: 13 March 1922, 11:15, Dublin.

• As previously mentioned, the Anglo-Irish Treaty fuelled further violence. The previous solid IRA movement split and the Irish Civil war broke out (revolutionary planet Uranus in 10H square Mars). On 22 June 1922, republicans killed the Ulster Member of Parliament, Sir Henry Wilson. Michael Collins responded by attacking the republican-occupied courts in Dublin and the war erupted.

• Vicious killings and retaliations broke out (Pluto on Asc, inconjunct Mars). Friends turned on friends (Mars, ruler 11H square Uranus). Then, in August 1922, the anti-Treaty IRA killed Michael Collins.

• By 1923, the conflict was spent and fighting finished. Around 2,000 were killed in the war and many thousands were left injured and imprisoned. The war left feelings of sadness and shame in many Irish, because they had turned on their own. However, though the fighting was over, efforts to gain full separation from Britain never wavered.

• Eamon De Valera (1882-1975), an active revolutionary turned politician, was trusted by the people to guide them towards becoming a republic in a united Ireland. When it became clear the Ulster unionists (states in Northern Ireland) would never join a united Ireland, Valera presided over the Republic of Ireland Act on 21 December 1948.

5. Birth of the Republic of Ireland: 18 April 1949, 00:00, Dublin.

On 18 April 1949, at 00:00 hours in Dublin, the Republic of Ireland Act became law. Full separation from Britain was gained and the Irish Republic was born. This is the national chart for Ireland still used today.

• The stellium in military Aries carries the tone of the nation and the struggle that led up to the creation of a free Ireland (Sun, Mars, north-node in Aries; opposite visionary Neptune).

• The people were united in their dream of being free of an oppressive regime. This compelled them to take up arms and die for the cause if necessary - and many did (Mars opposite Neptune, and Neptune sextile Pluto in the 8H of death). There was an element of fanaticism to the republican cause, which is reflected in the chart (Neptune - Mars, Sagittarius rising).

6. The Troubles of the 1960s - the Northern Ireland Conflict.

But trouble rumbled on in the north of the country. Catholic Nationalists who lived there never gave up the hope that their states would rejoin the Irish Republic. They also accused the dominant Protestant Government and the Constabulary of discriminating against them. When a Catholic campaign was met with police force, trouble erupted again.

Blood Moon eclipse for the "Troubles":
6 Oct 1968, 12:45, Belfast: around the UK natal.

• A vicious 3 decades long guerrilla war was triggered (1968-1998) - portended by this Blood Moon eclipse. The eclipse chart shows a battle between the mainly Protestant ruling faction (Sun in the 10H, in the eclipse chart), and the militarised Republicans (Moon in Aries, eclipse chart 4H).

When the eclipse chart is placed around UKs, the same story is shown again. By the eclipse Sun on the UK Asc (representing the English side), opposing the eclipse Moon in Aries in the 7H (the republican "open enemies").

• Terrorism was used during the trouble by both sides. One infamous IRA attack was the bombing of Lord Mountbatten.

> Earl Mountbatten was killed today when his fishing boat was blown up in the sea, apparently by terrorists of the Irish Republican Army. A 14-year-old grandson and a 15-year-old passenger were also killed [1]

• The IRA also took their fight onto the British mainland in retaliation for the British sending their army to Ireland. The most infamous attack was the Brighton hotel bombing.

> It was one of the most audacious plots against the British Government, coming ''within an inch,'' of assassinating Prime Minister Margaret Thatcher and much of her Cabinet. Although Mrs. Thatcher was uninjured, the bomb that shattered a Brighton hotel during a Conservative Party conference in 1984 killed five people and seriously injured 30. [2]

• The impact on ordinary people on both sides has been compared to that of the Blitz on the people of London. Around 3,600 people were killed in the troubles. (*Jabbah* - 4 Sagittarius, was on the eclipse Asc, a star in Scorpius "that creates natures ardent for war and a spirit which rejoices in plenteous bloodshed and in carnage"). [3]

• But eventually, dialogue and shared rulership brought peace. Since the Good Friday Agreement of 1998, Unionists and Sinn Fein (IRA political arm) have been co-operating to govern Northern Ireland.

1 NY Times: August 28, 1979
2 NY Times: June 15, 1986. Patrick J. Magee, the accused leader of an IRA Army cell was convicted.
3 Manilius, Marcus; Astronomica, 239-240.

7. Ireland and Covid-19.

Lunar eclipse for Covid-19: 16 Jul 2019, 22:39, Dublin; around Ireland natal.

• Ireland was at the forefront of European nations to apply containment measures so that by the end of 2020, its statistics were modest compared to other European states - with over 3 thousand dead and almost 150 thousand infected. But, after relaxing restrictions over Christmas, by mid-Jan 2021 infections rose making Ireland the 42nd most affected nation in the world for deaths per capita.

A high Covid toll was always a potential with the eclipse stellium falling in the 8H of death, square the natal Aries stellium in the 4H. This placement also means that Ireland will go through major transformations over the next 3 decades as a consequence.

• With the Moon, Saturn and Pluto in the 2H of the economy, there will likely be financial disruptions because of Covid and Brexit. But the important change concerns its values. As Ireland becomes more integrated into the EU, the nation is changing, its people are becoming more cosmopolitan.

8. The Spiritual Destiny of Ireland.

The personality of Ireland is ruled by Pisces.

• The 1949 birth gave the Irish a military chart, with Aries emphasised, Sagittarius on the ascendant (the Archer) and Libra on the MC - a sign of peace that is often involved in wars. The chart represents pictorially the intense armed struggle for home rule.

Personality integration always precedes spiritual development and positively, the war years and struggle for independence bonded the people together.

• *Problem*: Ireland's limiting pattern is that some people still live in the past (Moon in Capricorn in the 1H), they cannot release themselves from their hatred for the British. This is holding the nation back. With the planet emphasis in military Aries, there is always the danger that hot-heads will start a new war rather

Ireland 1949 natal

find other avenues to address their grievances. This happened with the Troubles of the 60s.

Changes indicated by the Covid eclipse: another serious problem that needed to be addressed in 1949 was the unhealthy control exerted by the Catholic Church over the nation. Natal Neptune exalted in the 10H represents Ireland's mystical roots and its religious orientation. During the Church's years of control, many institutions had become abusive and even murderous. The separation of church and state took a big step forward in 1973, when the Catholic Church's control over education and health was removed from the Irish Constitution. The exposure of sex scandals in the 90s hastened this process. The Covid eclipse carried another message - the final death pangs of the church's absolute control (the Sun that rules the 9H of religion/ the Catholic Church, in the 8H of death). The arrangement also promises the rebirth and transformation of the church as a purified and healthier entity (8H Cancer planets square Neptune).

The soul of Ireland is ruled by Virgo.

• The Aries stellium promised that new ways of settling conflicts would be developed. The first planet in a stellium (going anti-clockwise through the chart), is the "driver" of the stellium - this is Mars. The Irish are motivated by Mars' fire and passion.

The end planet is Mercury, which rules Virgo. Its intelligent forces have been revealing themselves through the nation since the 90s. The race is maturing, is less emotional and more thoughtful about its internal problems. The people now are debating and discussing and have stopped killing each other. They are becoming more discriminating. This is evidence of the increasing influence of Ireland's Virgo soul.

• Virgo is a great healing and teaching sign, and Ireland's contribution to world good in the future will be along these lines. Apart from the traditional sciences, a medical college that specialises in spiritual healing techniques will become renowned.

> This destiny is highlighted by *Marfik*, a star in Ophiuchus, the Serpent Charmer constellation that represents the God of Medicine and Healing. *Marfik* is conjunct the ascendant (at 5 Sagittarius), the spiritual destiny part of the chart.

• The Irish are a naturally mystical people and Neptune on the MC represents its past religious and spiritual emphasis. But a new chapter will be written in the future along these lines. Ireland's spiritual sign Virgo is intercepted in the 9H of higher teaching, religion and philosophy, indicating new spiritual developments in the future. One of these concerns a new mystery school that trains its students in spiritual development. Such a school is destined to rise in Ireland at one of the magnetised spots where the ancient mysteries previously were founded. All those who pass through this higher level of training will help Ireland achieve its ultimate destiny, which is to contribute to the enlightenment of humanity.

> When that spiritual reality, spoken of by St. Paul as "Christ in you, the hope of glory," is released in man and can manifest in full expression. When a sufficient number of people have grasped this ideal, the entire human family can stand for the first time before the portal which leads to the Path of Light, and the life of Christ will flower forth in the human kingdom. [1] Ireland's spiritual keynote is: "Christ in you, the hope of glory."

---

1   Bailey, Alice A. *From Bethlehem to Calvary*, 18.

Italy

Italy's personality is ruled by Sagittarius, its soul by Leo. [1]

Italy is a masculine, empire-building nation and the Romans responded to this force and travelling Sagittarius by expanding the country's borders to encompass much of Europe. Sagittarius also rules formal religion, and the Catholic Church did the same, excepting its borders expanded to include many parts of the world and the empire still exists today.

Italy is a spiritually advanced country and when Leo comes to the fore again on a higher turn of the spiral, powerful and charismatic leaders that work for the higher good will stabilise the nation and help do the same for the world.

1. Mt Vesuvius eruption and destruction of Pompeii, 24 August 79 AD.

By 200 BC, Rome had conquered the Italian Peninsula and over the following centuries much of Europe. The Romans were explorative - great nation-builders and road builders. They had a tremendous cultural impact on many nations. The demise of the Roman Empire began in the AD centuries with the rise of Christianity. The influence of this new religion was as powerful and as devastating for pre-Christian religions as a volcano eruption is on the surrounding countryside. Perhaps the eruption of Vesuvius and the destruction of the Roman city Pompeii, portended what was to come.

Solar eclipse for Vesuvius: 20 Apr 0079, 04:14, Pompeii.

This volcanic eruption is one of the most famous disasters in world history. Here is an eye-witness account:

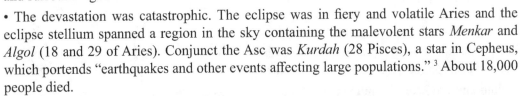

A cloud shot up to a great height like a very tall trunk, which spread out at the top into sort of branches, broad sheets of fire and leaping flames blazed, buildings were shaking. Outside, there was the danger of failing pumice stones, flames and smell of sulphur. [2]

• From the bowels of the earth erupted a deadly cloud of super-heated (Jupiter) gases and ash (Neptune, a gas-giant). It was a 'plinian' eruption that produces plumes of ash that can ascend 45 kilometres into the stratosphere. Poisonous vapours, molten debris, ash, rocks and pumice suffocated Pompeii and surrounding towns.

• The devastation was catastrophic. The eclipse was in fiery and volatile Aries and the eclipse stellium spanned a region in the sky containing the malevolent stars *Menkar* and *Algol* (18 and 29 of Aries). Conjunct the Asc was *Kurdah* (28 Pisces), a star in Cepheus, which portends "earthquakes and other events affecting large populations." [3] About 18,000 people died.

• The evolutionary pattern shaping events was Saturn square Neptune. They dissolve out-

1   Bailey, Alice A. The Destiny of the Nations, 67.
2   Account is from Pliny the Younger, a Roman historian who escaped the disaster with his mother.
3   Noonan, George; Fixed Stars and Judicial Astrology, 12.

dated beliefs and religions so new ones can emerge. Jesus' disciples Peter and Paul spread the Christian message across the Roman Empire - seeding the Christian era. Pisces, a sign associated with Christ is on the ascendant.

2. The Power of the Catholic Church and rise of Protestantism.

Solar eclipse for Luther's challenge to the Church: 19 Jun 1517, 06:28, Wittenberg.

The Catholic Church is arguably the most powerful ruling throne the world has known. The pope (father), the head of the Church, ruled the Medieval kings and emperors of Europe who believed the Pope represented God and he had the power to send them to hell. This kept them obedient and noncritical - at least in public.

• Renaissance man, Martin Luther, is one of the most influential and controversial figures in the history of Christianity. He was a humble German friar who challenged the Church's teachings. Legend has it that on 31 October 1517, he nailed to a church door in Wittenberg, his argument against the Church's right to "sell better treatment after death" - which the church had been doing. From then on, his "95 Theses" rapidly spread, converting many to Protestantism and this led to the split in the Church. Luther died of a stroke in 1546.

• Saturn conjunct Pluto indicated the destruction of the Church's decaying foundations and the birth of a new, more humanistic branch (Pluto opposite Sun-Moon 12H, sextile Neptune in Aquarius 8H, trine Uranus 10H).

Blood Moon eclipse for Act of Supremacy: 25 Jul 1534, 06:08, Westminster, Eng.

• King Henry VIII extinguished Catholic power in England, when the first Act of Supremacy was passed on 3 November 1534. From then on, Papacy power in Europe began to subside. It was telling when Napoleon Bonaparte I refused to kneel to the pope when being crowned. He snatched the crown from the pope and crowned himself.

• The eclipse is a Blood Moon. Millions died in subsequent Catholic-Protestant wars. Saturn and Pluto are now opposing - Saturn with the Leo planets in the 12H, representing the advanced age and decrepitude of the Church at that time.

• Pluto and the Moon in humanistic Aquarius, represent the release of the masses from the shackles of religious superstition (Moon inconjunct Mars, ruler of 9H of the Church).

• The Holy See still wields temporal power in the modern age. For instance, Pope John Paul II helped bring down the Iron Curtain with his support of the Solidarity movement in Poland. Even today, State heads call on the See's assistance in any part of the world, when their political actions have become compromised.

3. Birth of the Kingdom of Italy: 2 July 1871, 12:30, Rome.

The important events prior to and including this event concerned the rise of the Italian "Risorgimento" unification movement. It was the social and political process that eventually succeeded in the unification of many different states into the modern nation of Italy.

The northern and southern Italian states were unified on 17 March 1861. The ceremonial celebration of this occurred when Victor Emmanuel II, King of a united Italy, arrived triumphantly in Rome at 12:30 on 2 July 1871. The Kingdom of Italy chart commemorates that date and time.

• Unification is commemorated in the chart with the Cancer Sun (the motherland) conjunct Jupiter, which is the "fusing" planet. Sun-Jupiter conjunct the north-node indicates that this was the right direction for the nation to proceed towards.

• But Mars conjunct the ascendant portended future conflict, the impending WWI.

4. Italy in World War I and the Spanish Flu.

<u>Blood Moon eclipse for WWI: 15 Sep 1913, 13:46, Rome;
around the Kingdom of Italy natal.</u>

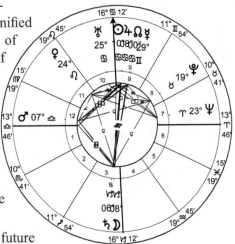

• Italy's prime motive in entering the war was to regain north-east Italian-speaking regions annexed by Austria. Initially allied with Germany and the Austria-Hungary Empire, it secretly switched sides when it saw they were losing (eclipse Sun-Mercury in the 12H of hidden things). It openly entered the war (on May 23 1915) on the side of the United Kingdom, France and Russia. The strategy worked and Italy did regain these disputed regions at war's end. (Jupiter conjunct natal Saturn - widening structural boundaries).

• Italy paid a price. Approximately 460,000 Italians were killed and 955,000 were wounded (eclipse Venus, ruler of the 8H of death, square natal Pluto in that house).

Lunar eclipse for Spanish Flu: 15 Jul 1916, 06:40, Rome; around the Kingdom of Italy

• The eclipse stellium dominates the chart, indicating the virus would have a major impact on the nation - and Italy *was* severely affected.

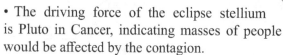

    The main indicator is the eclipse Moon. It is severely afflicted - in Capricorn, opposing the Sun and Saturn, and square natal Neptune. On its own, a highly afflicted Moon can indicate serious illness in the community. With Neptune included in the pattern, a highly contagious infectious virus was portended, which would severely affect Italian health. Neptune rules the 6H of health, with Pisces on the cusp.

• The driving force of the eclipse stellium is Pluto in Cancer, indicating masses of people would be affected by the contagion.

• The end planet - the outcome of the trouble, is Neptune.
Neptune is on the Sabian Symbol epidemic point of 2 Leo "The school, closed by an epidemic." Deaths due to the virus were estimated to be about 466,000 - including 70,000 in the military.

5. Italy in World War II.

Blood Moon eclipse for WWII: 3 May 1939, 16:16, Rome; around the
Kingdom of Italy natal.

• The Kingdom chart was not fortunate for war. Natal Mars - the military, fighting planet, is very weak in Libra in the 12H of hidden things. It is in a grand-cross with the angles, indicating extensive weakness.

• Defeat was imminent. Saturn, in the eclipse t-square (with Mars and Pluto), fell in the 7H of open-enemies on Neptune. Reality ended dreams of grandeur based on old Roman glories.

• The war would change Italy at all levels and in all areas of life. The eclipse angles are very close to the Kingdom's angles. One of the casualties was the end of the royal dynasty (eclipse Pluto in Cancer, in the 10H; disposited by the Moon that rules the 10H).

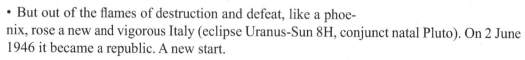

• But out of the flames of destruction and defeat, like a phoenix, rose a new and vigorous Italy (eclipse Uranus-Sun 8H, conjunct natal Pluto). On 2 June 1946 it became a republic. A new start.

Benito Mussolini, 29 Jul 1883, 13:10, Predappio, Italy; his effect on Italy.

Mussolini natal   around the Kingdom of Italy natal.

• Mussolini was a Fascist Dictator who allied with Adolf Hitler. His Leo Sun is on *Praesepe* (6 Leo), a dangerous star if misused. The choices he made led to his death and that of many others.

• However, fortune smiled on him for a while with his stellium in the Kingdom's 10H and Jupiter on the MC. He became popular by improving public services and creating jobs and drew people to him with the power of his oratory (his Jupiter rules the 3H of communication and transport).

• When Hitler offered an alliance, Mussolini accepted, hoping to gain booty from a Nazi victory. But over-confident and seduced by unrealistic dreams of creating a new and powerful Roman-type state (his MC square Neptune), he invaded Greece. It was disastrous. The ferocious Greeks drove his army out in a week.

In 1943, with the tide of war turning, King Victor Emmanuel III had Mussolini arrested. But on 10 July 1943, Germany invaded, rescued Mussolini and set up a puppet fascist Republic. The rest of Italy signed an agreement with the allies, who landed on the peninsula. Germany was defeated in 1945 and Mussolini was executed on 28 April 1945 by Italian partisans.

6. Birth of the Republic of Italy: 10 June 1946, 18:10, Rome.

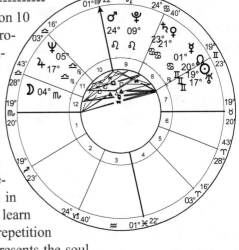

After the war, King Emmanuel III abdicated and on 10 June 1946, the Italian Supreme Court formally pronounced the establishment of a Republic. The announcement was made around 18:10. This date and time are used for the birth of the Republic and the chart is still used today.

• War planet Mars' close proximity to the MC, affecting all the angles, indicates that it would take some time for Italian life on all levels to recover from the effects of the war. But Mars is in Leo, Italy's soul sign. Italians were asked to learn from the lessons of the war and to avoid the repetition of these (Mars square the Scorpio Asc, that represents the soul purpose of the nation).

• The Sun-Uranus conjunction (sextile Mars and trine Neptune), promised that rapid and exciting renewal and regrowth would occur, and it did.

7. Italy and Covid-19.

Lunar eclipse for Covid-19: 16 Jul 2019, 23:39, Rome; around Italy Republic natal.

• Covid reached Italy in late January 2020 and it began containment measures in March. It was too late and its astrology portended a high infection and death toll.

Eclipse Mercury is the transporter of airborne viruses and its location on the 2 Leo epidemic point in the zodiac represents the contagious toxicity of this virus. Mercury is midpoint natal Saturn and Pluto, doubling the malevolence of the transit Saturn-Pluto effect and the virulence of the infection. Mercury also rules Italy's 8H of death (with Gemini on the 8H cusp).

Consequently, by the beginning of 2021, Italy was one of the worst Covid-affected nations in the world - over 77 thousand dead and 2.2 million infected. [1] This in a nation of 60 million people. As if this was not bad enough, by March 2021 a 3rd Covid wave was ramping up.

• Italy's economic crises were exacerbated by Covid-19 (so have all other world states). Its struggle to "balance the books" will be ongoing for generous-spending Italy (eclipse Saturn in the 2H, square natal Jupiter, ruler of the 2H of money).

• *Changes indicated by the Covid eclipse:* (see the chart on the previous page). Italy's values are being questioned at this time in history, with the eclipse Moon, Saturn and Pluto located in the 2H. Far-right parties with anti-immigrant policies have been gaining ground and these issues will likely be fought out in the following 33-year cycle.

• Paying back national karma is also part of Covid's effect with the eclipse Sun conjunct natal Saturn. The devastating effect of the pandemic - death, grief and loss, will help to release toxins buried in the psyche of the nation that may be connected with church abuse (eclipse Mercury in the 9H of religion, on the epidemic degree of 2 Leo; midpoint Pluto and Saturn). With poison released, the vitalising eclipse Sun on the 9H cusp indicates a healed nation moving forwards with increased faith and hope into the future.

8. The Spiritual Destiny of Italy.

The personality of Italy is ruled by Sagittarius and Ray 4 of Harmony through Conflict.

• Italy's Sagittarius personality is currently working through a Gemini Sun. This gives the nation intellectual brilliance and creative flair. But the downside of this mutable and highly adaptable energy, is a lack of integration and stability at the nation's core. There is also a tendency to over-react and create conflict when things are not flowing smoothly (the ray 4 effect).

---

1   13 Jan 2021: the 3rd ranked nation in the world for deaths per capita.

• *Problems*: The Moon's location in the 12H, indicates that the nation's limiting pattern involves Vatican-connected people whose under-handed and hidden machinations behind the scenes have desta-bilised the nation (Moon 12H, square Pluto in Leo 9H). This is the reason why Italy has had 68 differ-ent governments in 73 years. (Mars conjunct MC, square Asc. Jupiter, ruler of Italy's Sagitta-rius personality in the 11H semi-square MC and trine chaotic Uranus).

Italy 1946 natal

• Because Italy is masculine-ruled in its psy-chology, its politics are patriarchal, men fighting for dominance and control (Mars in Leo on MC). Italy has never had a female candidate for the top political job (Moon hidden in the 12H).

However, Italy's leadership style is about to change. In August of 2020, the progressed Sun moved from autocratic Leo, into reliable and discrimi-natory Virgo. Simultaneously, it is moving into the 10H of leadership. Virgo, a feminine sign, is opening the door for more women to make their way to the top and to bring much needed balance to the nation's politics and direction. It will be interesting also, to see if the church liberalises its rules regarding sex and women.

• The conflicted and artistic ray 4 runs through the blood of Italians. Italy grows through pain and conflict, which it expresses through its cul-ture, art, literature and music. Consequently, It-aly has produced some of the world's greatest artists

Italy's transits and Progressions Jan 2021

- Leonardo da Vinci, Michelangelo and Enrico Caruso to name a few. Their creations have lifted the hearts and souls of the world. The 4th Ray is beginning a new round of influence from 2025,[1] and this will bring a resurgence of the nation's creative and artistic brilliance.

The soul of Italy is ruled by Leo and Ray 6 of Idealism and Devotion.

• Italy's Leo soul is coloured by the devotional ray, which explains why so much of Christi-anity's strength and power is rooted in the leadership in Rome. The 6th ray rules Christian-ity. However, the revelations of paedophilia and other abuses in the Church in the latter 20th and early 21st centuries has greatly damaged its reputation.

Mars and Pluto, the two rulers of the Scorpio ascendant (which is the soul-purpose point in the chart for the current incarnation), are both in Leo that rules Italy's soul. Their brutal and uncompromising forces are being wielded by its soul to bring about the needed purifica-tions. In time, when this healing process has been completed, Italy is destined to once again be a dominant force in the world. This time through a spiritually rejuvenated church. On this theme, here is an interesting prediction:

---

1 Bailey, Alice A. Esoteric Psychology I, 26

The whole field of religion will be re-inspired and re-orientated from Rome because the Master Jesus will again take hold of the Christian Church in an effort to re-spiritualise it and to re-organise it. From the chair of the Pope of Rome, the Master Jesus will attempt to swing that great branch of the religious beliefs of the world again into a position of spiritual power and away from its present authoritative and temporary political potency. [1]

Italy's spiritual motto is, "I carve the Paths." [2]

Rome was a great road and bridge builder. The motto "I carve the Paths" can be interpreted as building progressive pathways that help humanity to move forwards into the Aquarian Age. This is Italy's major work and it lies through a rejuvenated and purified church and new higher-type leaders like Pope Francis.

The loving, self-conscious Leo soul, identifies both with God and with the beating heart of humanity as a whole. Italy's spiritual keynote is: "I am That and That am I". [3]

---

1   Bailey, Alice A. The Destiny of the Nations, 59.
2   Bailey, Alice A. Esoteric Astrology, 50.
3   Bailey, Alice A. Esoteric Astrology, 311.

Japan

Japan's personality is ruled by Capricorn, its soul by Scorpio. [1]

Japan has a masculine, mental and political psychology, not surprising since it is ruled by two powerful signs - Capricorn and Scorpio. It is aggressive and nation-building but its ambitions were blocked by its defeat in WWII, which included the humanising of its royal dynasty.

This is interesting, given that Japan has the warrior-sign Scorpio ruling its soul, which mean its ultimate destiny is to fight to the death to protect the freedoms and rights of the world's masses. When the nation takes up this task, it will fight as hard and for as long as it did in WWII, this time to establish and protect individual human rights. In the 21st Century - in light of China's sabre-rattling; Japan was given the legal right to build a defence force. Perhaps this is the germ-beginning of its eventual world role.

1. Great Kan'ei Famine: 1640-1643.

In Japan's early history, political unification occurred under the Yamato court and it developed a great civilization. Between 1603 and 1868 - during which this famine occurred; Japan was under the rule of the Tokugawa (military) shogunate. The ruling shogun during the famine was Tokugawa Iemitsu. The famine itself was named after the Kan'ei sub-era that lasted from 1624 to 1644.

Solar eclipse for Famine: 21 May 1640, 05:53, Komagatake, Hokkaido.

• The famine occurred on the island of Kyushu, which is well known for its natural hot springs and active volcanoes. It was the end result of a series of events that were triggered by the eruption of Hokkaido Koma-ga-take in June 1640.

It was a *plinian* eruption that produces plumes of ash that can ascend 45k into the stratosphere. Similar to the eruption of Pompeii, molten debris, ash, rocks and pumice poured over the countryside. This resulted in plants being poisoning and crops dying. On top of this, in 1641, flooding, drought, frost and insect damage sent food reserves plummeting.

• Tension in the bowels of the earth and the massive explosion is shown by Pluto (bowels) square to Saturn (earth). It was a massive explosion. Pluto was conjunct *Prima Hyadum* (1 Gemini), which warns of an evil disposition, violence, injuries and sudden death.

• Due to the eruption fallout and evil weather conditions (Saturn rules agriculture, square Neptune); crops died (Saturn square Pluto); causing a catastrophic famine.

• This was followed by starvation - Neptune (slow) opposite Pluto (death). An estimated 50,000–100,000 people died from the explosion and famine.

---

1 Bailey, Alice A. The Destiny of the Nations, 68.

Tokugawa Iemitsu, born 12 August 1604, 12:00, Tokyo.
Birthtime unknown, 12 pm time, 0 Aries chart.

• Shogun ruler Iemitsu was a man of principle, a visionary and outstanding leader (Sun in Leo, trine Jupiter-Saturn in Sagittarius)

• He implemented progressive policies (Uranus sextile Moon) such as setting up food kitchens, provided shelters for the starving, ensuring rice distribution was fair, and punishing profiteers.

• Jupiter was conjunct the star *Sabik* (14 Sagittarius), which gifted him with "moral courage, material success and promotion in the church or law." To protect the nation's Buddhism religion, Iemitsu killed or expelled Christians (Saturn conjunct Jupiter in Sagittarius; sesquiquadrate Pluto). It may seem brutal today, but he was a man of his time and that was the way things were done then.

2. The deadliest Volcano Eruption in History - Mt. Tambora: 5 April 1815.

Historians agree, for its after-effects, this eruption of Mount Tambora on the island of Sumbawa, Indonesia; is the deadliest in history. It is included in this Asian section because Indonesia is not covered in this book.

Solar eclipse for Eruption: 10 January 1815, 21:55, Sumbawa Besar, Indonesia.

• The most powerful planet in the eclipse chart is Pluto, because it is located on the chart-angles. Pluto rules volcanic explosions and its mega-explosive force (representing the gathering forces in nature), is multiplied exponentially because of its aspects and involvement of some malefic stars.

• Firstly, Pluto is conjunct *Markab* (21 Pisces), a star in the constellation Pegasus. It portends danger from fire - hence a volcano eruption. Stars in Pegasus can cause changes in the weather. [1] Massively and adversely so with Pluto conjunct *Markab*.

• Secondly, Groundwater (Neptune on IC) interacting with rising basalt magma, triggered the massive explosion. (square Pluto, semi-square Saturn, and Saturn is midpoint Pluto and Uranus).

• Thirdly, Saturn, the lord of the eclipse (because it occurred in Capricorn), is conjunct *Giedi Prima* (2 Aquarius). *Giedi* is in the constellation Capricornus, which can bring "major changes in climate". [2] The eruption did exactly that.

---

1 Noonan, George; Fixed Stars and Judicial Astrology, 29.
2 Noonan, George; Fixed Stars and Judicial Astrology, 51.

[The eruption] unleashed the most destructive wave of extreme weather the world has witnessed in thousands of years. The volcano's massive sulphate dust cloud enveloped the earth, cooling temperatures and disrupting major weather systems for more than three years. Communities worldwide endured famine, disease, and civil unrest on a catastrophic scale.

• Finally, Pluto was also aligned with *Denebola* (20 Virgo), on the chart ascendant. At its worst, *Denebola* portends misfortune from the elements of nature, and violent, malignant and contagious diseases.

> The colder temperatures caused by the eruption led to the development of a new strain of cholera. [1] Few people had immunity and it spread throughout the world, killing thousands. [2] (Uranus, ruler of the 6H of health rules bacterial infections; is conjunct Mars that rules the 8H of death).

Roughly 100,000 people died in the immediate aftermath. But far more died over the next several years, due to secondary effects that spread all over the globe. The eruption happened two months before Napoleon's final defeat in 1815. Sumbawa was the site of the most devastating volcanic eruption on earth in thousands of years.

3. Birth of Meiji Japan: 11 Feb 1889, 12:00, Tokyo.

In the 1850s, western powers used their superior military strength to force Japan into trade and the nation's outdated military was unable to cope. This initiated the fall of the Tokugawa shogunate in 1868, returning nominal control of the country to imperial rule under emperor Meiji (1852-1912). This contact with the West and the major reforms it initiated - politically, economically and socially; these became identified with the Meiji Restoration.

The Meiji Constitution of Japan, formalised on 11 Feb 1889, was created to help Japan modernise and westernise. The constitution was modelled on that of Germany's. (Time unknown, 12-noon).

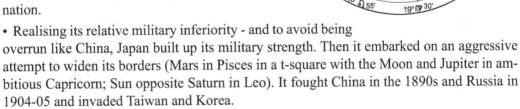

• Significantly, the ascendant of the Meiji chart was conjunct the great military star *Aldebaran* (8 Gemini). Thus the rebirth of the nation emphasised its military and warrior past. The view then was that militarism should dominate the political and social life of the nation, and that the strength of the military is equal to the strength of a nation.

• Realising its relative military inferiority - and to avoid being overrun like China, Japan built up its military strength. Then it embarked on an aggressive attempt to widen its borders (Mars in Pisces in a t-square with the Moon and Jupiter in ambitious Capricorn; Sun opposite Saturn in Leo). It fought China in the 1890s and Russia in 1904-05 and invaded Taiwan and Korea.

---

1   Gillen, D'Arcy Wood, 'Tambora: The Eruption That Changed the World.
2   Ibid

4. Japan in World War I and the Spanish Flu.

Lunar eclipse for Spanish Flu: 15 Jul 1916, 13:40, Tokyo, Japan; around Meiji Japan.

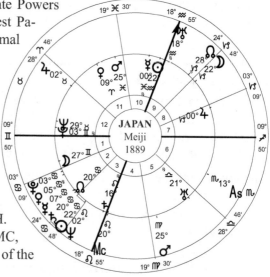

Japan was a partner with the Allied Entente Powers and helped to secure sea routes in the West Pacific and Indian Ocean. Its losses were minimal compared to other nations - 1,000 died.

• This figure pales in comparison to the devastation that Spanish Flu caused. Whole villages were wiped out. Modern scholars estimate that nearly 470,000 people on Japan's four main islands died either due to the flu or because of secondary cases of pneumonia that followed. (Saturn rules the 8H of death and it was conjunct the eclipse Sun, opposite the Moon in the 8H. Additionally, eclipse Uranus hit Japan's MC, and eclipse Pluto squared natal Venus, ruler of the 6H of health).

5. Japan in World War II.

Lunar eclipse for Pearl Harbour: 6 Sep 1941, 02:36, Tokyo; around Meiji Japan natal.

• When WWII started, Japan invaded Indochina. But America and the United Kingdom objected and restricted Japan's oil and rubber imports. This was a major blow for Japan because the oil it needed to drive its war efforts came from the US and rubber from British Malaya. These events preceded and initiated the attack on Pearl Harbour.

• The evolutionary pattern shaping this period was Uranus conjunct Saturn. They travelled together through 1941 and 1942, and hit Japan's natal Neptune-Pluto at the September 1941 eclipse; stimulating its warlike impulses.

• Japan attacked Pearl Harbour on 7 December 1941 and in retaliation, extensive and destructive change came to Japan, to its land, people and to its leaders. (Eclipse t-square: Sun, Moon, Saturn-Uranus, hit the 10H of government, 4H of people, wide conjunct to Asc).

• Two atom bombs later and it was all over. (Eclipse Pluto that rules nuclear power is on malevolent *Praesepe* and *Aselli* (7-8 Leo). About 3 million Japanese died in the war.

6. Birth of post-war Japan: 3 May 1947, 12:00, Tokyo.

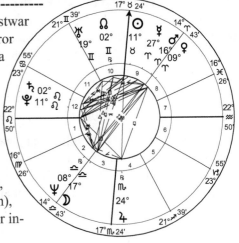

On 3 May 1947 at 12:00 noon, Tokyo Japan's postwar constitution came into effect. It stripped Emperor Hirohito of all but symbolic power, stipulated a bill of rights and outlawed Japan's right to make war.

• Japan was chastised and put on a good behaviour program. Pluto and Saturn in Leo represent the might and omnipotent power of the victorious United States. From behind the scenes (12H), they held the reins of power over Japan (the Sun), and monitored its behaviour. This incarnation - or incarceration, lasted for 5 years.

7. Birth of Sovereign Japan: 28 Apr 1952, 22:30, Tokyo. [1]

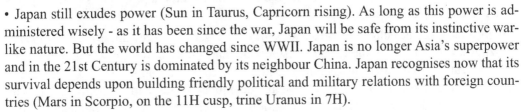

Japan's status was affected again in 1952, with "The Treaty of San Francisco," in which the Allied powers finally declared peace with Japan. Japan's sovereignty was restored and its independence gained. It was signed in San Francisco on 8 September 1951 and legally came into force on 28 April 1952, at the local Tokyo time of 22:30.

Many Japanese, ashamed of losing the war do not like to acknowledge this day. But it happened.

• The Treaty clarified Japan's rights to foreign territories, confiscated all its assets in colonized or occupied countries and restricted its military to a defence force only.

• Japan still exudes power (Sun in Taurus, Capricorn rising). As long as this power is administered wisely - as it has been since the war, Japan will be safe from its instinctive warlike nature. But the world has changed since WWII. Japan is no longer Asia's superpower and in the 21st Century is dominated by its neighbour China. Japan recognises now that its survival depends upon building friendly political and military relations with foreign countries (Mars in Scorpio, on the 11H cusp, trine Uranus in 7H).

• Spiritual and idealistic Neptune placed on the MC changed the whole tone and orientation of the nation, which now has a more sensitive attunement to the world as a whole. Under this influence the goals and values of the people have gradually changed (Neptune trine north-node in Aquarius 2H). The government became more sensitive to what was going on in the world and adapted to fit in with the progressive nations.

---

1 Campion, Nicholas. The Book of World Horoscopes, 174.

8. Tsunami hits Japan: 11 March 2011 at 14:46 JST.

The earthquake is now referred to as the "Great East Japan Earthquake." It was a magnitude 9, with the epicentre 70 kilometres east of the Oshika Peninsula on Japan's main island. The country literally shifted more than 5 meters, and is now slightly closer to North America. It initiated a series of large tsunamis that killed around 18,000 people around the Pacific Ocean rim.

Blood Moon eclipse for Tsunami: 21 December 2010, 17:13, epicentre 38N06, 142E51: around Japan Sovereignty natal.

(1) *The earthquake*. The evolutionary pattern shaping events in the eclipse chart is a Saturn-Pluto square that was exact in late 2009, early 2010. They were just separating when the earthquake struck. Two formidable forces fighting each other, mirrored in the earth's tectonic plates that smashed their way to release. Pluto was conjunct Mars and the eclipse Sun, multiplying exponentially the power of the earthquake and of the eclipse.

(2) *The tsunami*. It is symbolised by Jupiter-Uranus in Pisces, dominating the event from the eclipse MC. Jupiter is a ruler of Pisces and therefore of the ocean. It creates sudden and powerful water catastrophes. They are 3 degrees off the star *Scheat* (29 Pisces), which Uranus reached by transit on the day of the event. *Scheat* is "especially unfortunate regarding the sea, bringing danger from that element and tidal waves." [1]

• On the eclipse Asc was *Sirius* (14 Cancer), a star associated with flooding. In ancient Egypt its helical rising marked the annual flooding of the Nile. The tsunami invaded the coastline, up to 10 km in Sendai, flooding the land and destroying all before it.

• The devastating effect of the tsunami on the people and the land can be gauged by the eclipse stellium falling over Japan's Asc/ DC axis and forming a grand-cross with Japan's natal planets. In particular the natal Moon.

• Interestingly, on the eclipse IC (in Japan's 9H); the legacy of the event, is the star *Labrum* (27 Virgo). It is situated in the Crater constellation that some call the Holy Grail that "purifies to salvation." This ambiguous phrase could be used in relation to the future of nuclear energy in the country, a 2H matter (eclipse IC inconjunct Neptune in the nation's 2H). The tsunami damaged the Fukushima power station and there was release of radioactive contamination. Now, many view nuclear energy as dangerous and unstable. Consequently, the government has pledged to increase renewable energy sources to 25% of its needs by 2030. An important resource change. This is the way for Japan to go - Neptune that also represents the tsunami is conjunct Japan's north-node.

---

1   Noonan, George; Fixed Stars and Judicial Astrology, 30.

9. Japan and Covid-19.

Lunar eclipse for Covid-19: 17 Jul 2019, 06:39, Tokyo;
around Japan Sovereignty natal.

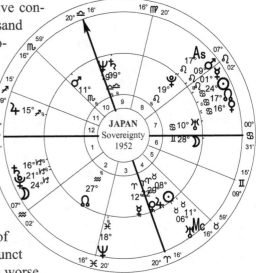

• By 2021, Covid seemed to be under relative control with 3.4 thousand dead and 247 thousand
infected. [1] This in a nation of 126 million people. But by late January and early February
- with new variant strains wreaking havoc
around the world, numbers began climb-
ing. At this stage the government did not
impose strict lock-downs, apparently to
try to balance the health of the people
with support for the business community.

Japan should be careful. Firstly, the
eclipse stellium impacts the 1H of the nation. Secondly, Mercury, the ruler of the 6H
of health is conjunct the cusp of the 8H of
death. Thirdly, the eclipse ascendant is conjunct
natal Pluto in the 8H. Things could get much worse.

• Karma from Japan's warlike past will likely be paid off by
the nation as a consequence of its suffering during the pandemic (Saturn-Pluto-Moon in
1H).

• *Changes indicated by the Covid eclipse:* with the stellium falling in the 1st - 7th house
axis; the nation and how it responds to the world will be reconstructed.

10. The Spiritual Destiny of Japan.

The personality of Japan is ruled by Capricorn:
and Ray 6 of Idealism and Devotion. [2]

• Japan's Capricorn personality is currently working through a
Taurus Sun, which is located in the 4H of the people. This
emphasises the change of tone in the nation when,
post-war, power in the nation was taken away from
the emperor and given to the people (the Sun in
the 4H).

Double earth emphasises the practical side
of the nation and the willingness to accept reality as it is (the loss in the war), and to move on
to build for a prosperous future. This has distinguished Japan's progress since the war.

• A Capricorn ascendant posed both a problem
and an opportunity for the nation. An opportunity if
it focused on building peaceful relations with the nations of the world (Saturn in Libra, 9H). A problem if it

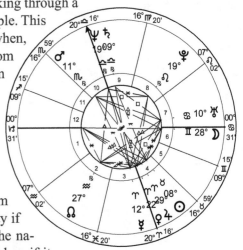

Japan 1952 natal

1   13 Jan 2021: the 102nd ranked nation in the world for deaths per capita.
2   Bailey, Alice A. The Destiny of the Nations, 99.

reverted to its fanatical warlike ways of old (Mars in Scorpio). Fortunately, Japan's leaders since the war have responded to the forces of the soul and the higher 6th ray force via Neptune. Consequently, it has become a trusted friend and ally in the western world of democratic nations. This is important because of the role the nation has to play in the future.

The soul of Japan is ruled by Scorpio; and Ray 1 of Will & Power. [1]

• In the post-war constitution, Japan's military was restricted to self-defence. But since 9/11, there has been a change. Its forces have been deployed to Afghanistan and Iraq. Although in a support-base role, this is seen as a symbolic change in attitude and a challenge to its constitution restrictions. Further, in light of China's aggressive claims to foreign sea-lanes and territories in the Asia-Pacific region, Japan, Australia and South Korea have drawn closer together for mutual protection and are increasing their defence forces and strategies. These are the first steps in Japan's warrior-role rehabilitation.

This is important, because - ruled by the 1st ray, Japan is a mental-masculine nation that is political and governing - and, is the only major nation with a Scorpio warrior soul (according to the 'Destiny of the Nations'). The aggression that caused so much trouble in the 20th Century is now being turned to world good.

In time, Japan will become renowned as the warrior soul of the world community, fighting for the freedoms and human-rights of all peoples. It will lead the fight to destroy world glamour and illusion by standing steadfastly for the truth and right-action in the world.

> Japan's spiritual keynote is: "Warrior I am, and from the battle I emerge triumphant." [2]

• Today Japan is the most advanced Asian nation in terms of its standard of living, its democratic government and the mature way it engages with the world. With Mars - the esoteric ruler of Scorpio, in the 10H, one of its tasks is to be a role model for other Asian nations.

• Mars is on *Acrux* (11 Scorpio), a blue star at the bottom of Crux, the Southern Cross constellation. It represents the suffering experienced by Japan's people, but also represents its rehabilitation and the important role Japan has to play as a warrior-protector for southern-hemisphere Asian nations.

---

1 Ibid. "its link with Germany through the soul ray of both nations." Germany has a 1st ray soul.
2 Bailey, Alice A. Esoteric Astrology, 654.

Netherlands

Netherland's personality is ruled by Cancer, its soul by Aquarius. [1]

The Cancer - Aquarius ruling signs are very different. Cancer is a watery, emotional sign and air-element Aquarius represents the advanced intellect. The Netherland's challenge is to transform the psychology of the nation from a state that is introspective, defensive and clannish (Cancer), to one that takes a lead in the world in intellectual debates that fight for human rights. The Netherlands is one of a handful of nations that has Aquarius prominent in their destinies (others are Russia, the United States and Switzerland), and they are all future potential agents for the implementation of Aquarian Age principles.

1. The St. Felix Flood, 5 November 1530.

Natural disasters, famine and plagues were a constant threat in these nation-developing centuries. In this low lying country, the danger came primarily from flooding. This one in 1530 was catastrophic. It was called the St. Felix [2] flood because it happened during the period when the saint is celebrated. Large parts of Flanders and Zeeland were washed away, including 18 villages. More than 100,000 people were killed in the Netherlands, [3] plus many more thousands of livestock.

Blood Moon eclipse for St. Felix Flood: 6 Oct 1530, 23:06, Reimerswaal.

• Nature's forces were powerful and very destructive (the eclipse spanned the MC/IC axis and was in a t-square with Pluto - that is aligned with the star *Giedi Prima* (27 Capricorn). The Capricornus constellation when it is unfavourably situated with lunar eclipses, indicates major storms, especially at sea. [4]

• Neptune, God of the Oceans, is aligned with stormy star *Scheat* (22 Pisces 50) that brings danger through water and drowning. These powerful and stormy stars in conjunction with the eclipse and Pluto, were behind the flood.

• The flood occurred a month later at the full-moon, when tidal surges are at their highest. At that time, the Moon was moving over the *Pleiades* (23 Taurus), "rainy stars" which Allen said were "intimately connected with traditions of the Flood." [5]

What was happening in nature was a reflection of what was happening in humanity. The power of the Reformation and the Protestantism movement was increasing and this new wave of thought was flooding Europe. Under threat, the might of the Catholic Church was gathering its forces and fighting back. Many would die in the religious war tsunamis that were about to engulf Europe.

---

1   Bailey, Alice A. The Destiny of the Nations, 68.
2   Saint Felix of Valois (1127-1212), religious hermit, cofounder of Trinitarians, a Roman Catholic religious order. Britannica
3   "Sint Felixvloed treft Zeeland". www.isgeschiedenis.nl.
4   Noonan, George; Fixed Stars and Judicial Astrology, 51.
5   Hinckley Allen, Richard; Star Names, 398.

2. Birth of Independent Netherlands: 26 Jul 1581, 12:00, the Hague.

In the early 16th Century, the Dutch fought for eighty years to free the nation from Spain and Catholic domination. A powerful motivating force was its new religion - Calvinism. It arrived in the Netherlands in the 1540s and both nobles and the common people converted. Pure Calvinist theology avers that 'God predestined some people to be saved and others to eternal damnation, a destiny that is unconditional and cannot be changed no matter how good or bad one is'. Some report that Calvinism contributed greatly to the growth of capitalism, and the notion that some people are destined to be wealthy and others are not.

In the 1580s, the nation achieved its goal and the Spanish yolk was thrown off. On 26 Jul 1581, in the Hague, independence was proclaimed. The time is unknown so 12-noon is used. The natal chart stemming from that date is still used today.

• The 12-noon Sun on the MC truly reflects the pride and exaltation the Dutch felt when they gained their freedom from foreign control after so many years (Sun opposite Uranus in Aquarius).

• The Sun - Uranus opposition is foundational in the psyche of the people. It indicates a nation that is perpetually being challenged to keep moving ahead, into the future. There is always something new ahead which needs to be discovered, found, or uncovered.

3. The Netherlands in World War I and Spanish Flu.

Blood Moon eclipse for WWI: 15 Sep 1913, 13:03, The Hague; around the Netherlands natal.

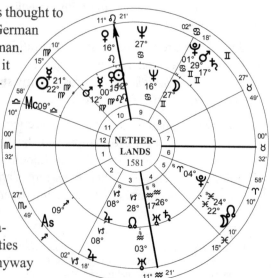

• As WWII opened, Queen Wilhelmina was thought to be sympathetic towards France while her German husband, Duke Henry was openly pro-German. The Netherlands declared its neutrality but it struggled to maintain this under the bullying tactics by the fighting nations. Its attempt to remain neutral later in WWII as it had in the Great War, did not work. It was quickly annexed by the Germans.

• The Netherlands was fortunate to have stayed neutral and to try to work with the invaders. Otherwise, with eclipse Mars-Pluto falling in the 8H of death, square natal Pluto and conjunct natal Moon; casualties would have been massive. They were anyway when Spanish Flu hit.

Lunar eclipse, Spanish Flu: 15 Jul 1916, 06:00, The Hague; around Netherlands natal.

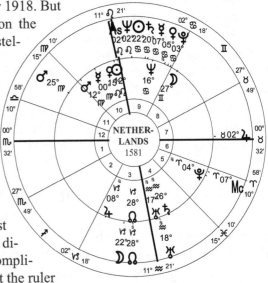

• The virus reached the Netherlands in early 1918. But it had been circulating amongst soldiers on the battlefields of Europe since 1916 (eclipse stellium in 9H of foreign lands).

• Until people began to die in droves, the government underestimated the virus. An astrologer should have been consulted. Eclipse Neptune - the virus: it is on the Sabian Symbol 2 Leo epidemic degree: conjunct the natal MC/IC axis, and it squares eclipse Jupiter on the DC/ Asc axis, expanding the virus' lethal reach.

• October and November 1918 were most deadly. More than 60,000 people died as a direct result of the flu or indirectly through complications - a huge toll (eclipse Pluto, conjunct the ruler of the 8H of death, Venus, and semi-square natal Venus).

4. Netherlands in World War II.

When war broke out, the Netherlands tried to remain neutral - as it did in WWI. But Germany attacked on 10 May 1940, and within 5 days it was under German control. Queen Wilhelmina and the Dutch government fled to London to establish a government-in-exile.

Blood Moon eclipse for WWII: 3 May 1939, 15:35,
The Hague; around Netherlands natal.

• The eclipse planets formed two crucifixes, (Sun-Moon in a grand-cross with the MC/IC axis and natal Sun; and the war t-square of Mars-Pluto-Saturn in a wide grand-cross with the Asc/DC). This portended years of suffering for the nation About 6 million Dutch Jews were deported and killed in concentration camps and 5 million others lost their lives under Nazi brutality.

• Another symbol of suffering was the eclipse north-node conjunct to *Gacrux* (6 Scorpio) in the Crux (Southern Cross) constellation. Since Biblical times, this Cross has been associated with sacrifice and perseverance. [1] Since the north-node is associated with spiritual progression, it seems this was a necessary experience for the nation. It helped to soften any residue of arrogance still hanging around due to the Leo Sun.

---

1 Hinckley Allen, Richard; Star Names, 185-186.

• The evil of Nazism may have obscured the light of the Netherlands for a period (eclipse Moon in the 1H), but the invaders were soon gone and the light of its soul re-emerged.

• In this period, the Netherlands turned 365 years old - one solar-arc cycle [1] was completed. Its age makes it a stable, wise, elder nation in the global family. After the horrors of WWII, and at the beginning of the new solar-arc cycle, the Netherlands gave up its neutral identity and became a charter member of both the United Nations and NATO, [2] and has been actively involved in U.N. peacekeeping forces. Uranus helps it to keep moving forwards.

• The Netherlands's ability to adapt itself and make fortunate new beginnings is assisted by magical Uranus conjunct Saturn, in the 4H of the people. They are a channel for the forces of *Sadalsuud* (23 Aquarius), a star called the "Luckiest of the Lucky," which lies between them.

Anne Frank, 12 Jun 1929, 07:30, Frankfurt am Main, Germany

There were approximately 6 million Jews killed by the Nazis. In 1939, there were about 140,000 Dutch Jews living in the Netherlands and among them were some 24,000 to 25,000 German-Jewish refugees who had fled from Germany in the 1930s. One of these was Anne Frank (1929-1945). She was a young Jewish girl, a member of the Frank family who hid above a warehouse for 2 years during Nazi occupation of the Netherlands. Life for the family of eight people was tense. They were in constant fear of discovery, had to remain quiet and could never go outside. Eventually, someone betrayed the family and they all died in a concentration camp.

<u>Blood Moon eclipse for WWII; around Anne Frank natal.</u>

• Frank was born in Gemini, the sign of the messenger. She kept a diary of her experiences and it became a classic of war literature (Anne Frank, 'The Diary of a Young Girl'). It gave a glimpse of life under the oppression of the Nazis. Here is an excerpt.

I looked out of the open window, over a large area of Amsterdam, over all the roofs and on to the horizon, which was such a pale blue that it was hard to see the dividing line. As long as this exists, I thought, and I may live to see it, this sunshine, these cloudless skies, while this lasts I cannot be unhappy.

• The eclipse effect on Frank's chart shows the shattering of the foundations of her life (Sun-Uranus, Moon 10th-4th houses; Saturn-Pluto on the angles), and her untimely death with eclipse Pluto on her ascendant.

---

1   The solar-arc cycle was exact at the end of the war in 1946. In solar-arc charts or primary directions, the entire chart progresses forward through the signs at the same rate of the Sun, 59 minutes per year. It is based on the notion that "one day equals a year," - each day after birth, symbolises a year in time.

2   NATO - North Atlantic Treaty Organization; UN - United Nations.

5. Netherlands and Covid-19.

Lunar eclipse for Covid-19: 16 Jul 2019, 23:39; around Netherlands natal.

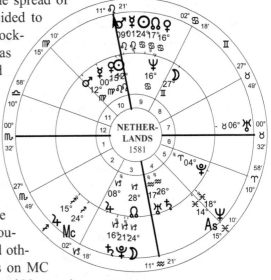

• While taking some measures to avoid the spread of Covid, in early 2020 the government decided to support the economy by avoiding hard lock-downs. But by the end of the year the toll was rising (1.6 thousand dead and 821 thousand infected, in a population of 11 million), and lock-downs were being introduced. By mid-January 2021, the Netherlands was ranked 34th in the world for deaths per capita.

• The Netherland's appeared to barter lives against commercial interests (eclipse Moon in 3H, conjunct Pluto that rules the 2H of money). In the future there will be trouble for the government because of this and other moral scandals emerging (eclipse Mars on MC square Uranus; and 9H stellium conjunct natal Neptune).

6. The Spiritual Destiny of the Netherlands.

The personality of the Netherlands is ruled by Cancer.

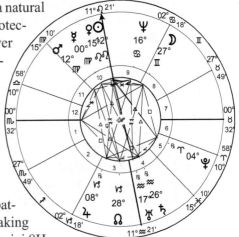

• In the past, self-concern for its own affairs was a natural expression of the Netherland's defensive and protective Cancer personality. But this has changed over the centuries, especially since WWII. The brutality of the Nazi regime was a huge wake-up call for it and other small European nations who fell under the German jackboot.

Since 1945, the Netherlands has joined many other international organizations - evidence of the increasing influence of its egalitarian Aquarius soul.

• *Problem*: the Netherland's inherited, limiting pattern in 1581, was a fear a speaking out and making trouble in case one was annihilated (Moon in Gemini 8H, square Pluto). This was the situation for all small, peace-seeking nations in the Middle Ages. But since then, it has

Netherlands 1581 natal

moved on and today the Dutch value honesty and sincerity. They are blunt in speech and are not afraid to debate controversial issues (Mercury in the prominent 10H, sextile the: "let's get straight down to it" Scorpio Asc). Another influence that contributes to this trait is *Alula Boreale*, a small star in Ursa Major. Located at 1 Virgo when the nation was born, it is conjunct Mercury. A name given to this star is 'The Leaps of the Gazelle' (leaping ideas and thoughts).

But there is another darker side to the Moon's pattern. Destructive far-right groups have risen in the nation with people who speak words of vitriol and hate. They would destroy the Netherland's modern multicultural status if they could (Pluto 5H). Human-rights groups need to oppose this trend.

• *Changes indicated by the Covid eclipse:* the 9H morals and beliefs area was emphasised by the Covid eclipse, with the vitalising Sun and north-node falling there. This indicates a change of attitude in important key areas. One of these obviously will be how to handle a future pandemic so that the lives of people are not traded off against the economy (opposite the Moon and Pluto that rules the 2H of the economy). These changes could involve the courts (9H). But it also indicates the battle to be fought over the soul of the nation and which way it should go - striking the right balance between the progressive left and conservative right.

• The Sun in Leo adds pride and bravery to Cancerian timidity and a willingness to fight against bullying nations no matter how powerful (Sun trine Pluto in Aries). This was aptly demonstrated under Nazi domination.

The soul of the Netherlands is ruled by Aquarius.

• The opening paragraph for the Netherlands included the statement, "The Netherlands is one of a handful of nations that has Aquarius prominent in their destinies - they are all future potential agents for the implementation of Aquarian Age principles."

That time has arrived for the Netherlands. Since WWII, its advanced leaders have sensed this higher destiny and have been increasingly steering the nation down a more inclusive and liberal path. Its foreign policy is based on four basic commitments: "to the Atlantic co-operation, to European integration, to international development and to international law." These policies are very much in line with Aquarian Age development.

Aquarius rules the 4H in the noon chart, and Uranus is located there. This means that the influencing power of the nation's soul is trying to express itself through "the people." Progressives who argue for instance, for a more humanitarian approach to the refugee crisis are being energised by this impulse.

• Another area of importance for soul growth is represented by Jupiter, the esoteric ruler of Aquarius. It guides the nation's spiritual destiny through all its various incarnations. It is in Capricorn in the 3H. A very vital manifestation of this placement is the International Criminal Court that moved its first permanent premises to The Hague, in 2015. Jupiter rules the 9H of the high court and its moral pondering. The Court presides over crimes of genocide, crimes against humanity and war crimes. Although its powers are currently limited it is an important beginning and part of the appearance of the Aquarian Age influence through the judicial system.

• Jupiter's task is to prepare those in the nation who are ready to become water-bearers for the world. "Water" in this context is a synonym for the expression of wisdom and love. Through the hearts and minds of the Netherland's water-bearers, Jupiter will radiate the vitalising and healing waters of love and wisdom.

> The Netherland's spiritual keynote is: "Water of life am I, poured forth for thirsty men." [1]

---

1   Bailey, Alice A. Esoteric Astrology, 654.

New Zealand

New Zealand's personality is ruled by Virgo, its soul by Gemini. [1]

The Virgo - Gemini combination indicates a shift from the practical pioneering approach that the settlers in New Zealand (NZ) had to take to survive (Virgo), to an intellectual and wise understanding of life and how to live its so that all peoples benefit.

Because it shares a Virgo connection with Australia (soul), the two nations will always have very close ties. They consider themselves a family. On a deeper level, New Zealand will always remain very close psychologically and spiritually with its mother-country - Great Britain. They both have Gemini souls. New Zealand also has a strong rapport with the United States, which has a Gemini personality.

1. Captain Cook lands in New Zealand, 6 October 1769.

Captain James Cook was a British explorer, navigator, cartographer and captain in the British Royal Navy. He sighted Aotearoa, "land of the long white cloud" [2] on 6 October 1769, landing at Poverty Bay [3] on the North Island eastern coast. This is where he first encountered the indigenous Maori people. The interaction was aggressive - about 9 Maori were killed. This set the tone for Maori-English relations in the coming decades. Cook claimed NZ for England and a stream of British settlers followed.

<u>Total Solar eclipse for Discovery: 19 June 1769, 20:10, Gisborne.</u>

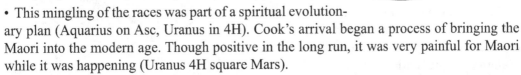

• The evolutionary pattern is Saturn opposite Pluto, in effect from mid-1767 to early 1770. This combination brings death to the old so that new structures can arise. With Cook's arrival, Maori way of life was about to undergo a radical transformation.

• Maori governance over the land and the foundations of their way of life would radically change (Uranus 4H).

• Due to normal life-interaction as the two races settled down together creating a new race through mixed-blood children; the religious, cultural and social lives of Maori and settlers would change forever (eclipse in 5H square Neptune 8H).

• This mingling of the races was part of a spiritual evolutionary plan (Aquarius on Asc, Uranus in 4H). Cook's arrival began a process of bringing the Maori into the modern age. Though positive in the long run, it was very painful for Maori while it was happening (Uranus 4H square Mars).

• On the IC, the legacy point of the chart, is *Alphirk* (2 Taurus), a star under the belt of the Ethiopian King, Cepheus. Its Arabic name is "the Flock." In the 20th Century, there were so many sheep flocks in NZ, it became known as the "sheep country."

---

1 Bailey, Alice A. The Destiny of the Nations, 68.
2 Maori name for New Zealand.
3 The author, Hodgson, was born in Poverty Bay, Gisborne - with a Ngati Porou and Ngati Pu lineage.

2. The Treaty of Waitangi: 6 Feb 1840.

Lunar eclipse for Treaty: 18 February 1840, 01:31, Waitangi.

• The Treaty (3H) is an agreement made between the British Crown (Moon in Leo 9H) and more than 500 Maori chiefs (Sun 3H). The first signing was on 6 February 1840, followed by further signatures as the governor travelled around NZ negotiating with Chiefs to sign (3H emphasis). The evolutionary pattern is Saturn square Uranus. Maori life was being radically restructured.

• Maori and English had different perceptions of the treaty. The English thought it gave them the right to buy Maori lands. Maori believed they retained ownership. (The star *Facies* at 6 Capricorn, on the Asc brings blindness and defective sight). These disagreeing views led to the 1845-1872 Maori Wars. Resentment over the deal and subsequent loss of land ownership (Uranus-Mars opposition MC), continues amongst some Maori today.

• The Sabian Symbol for the IC degree 19 Pisces, is "A master instructing his pupil." By the mid-20th Century, Maori - having taking full advantage of English culture and education; were becoming modern and sophisticated. This, the eclipse promised.

3. Birth of the Dominion of New Zealand: 26 Sep 1907, 00:00, Wellington.

The colonists became self-governing on 17 January 1885. The official change of status to the Dominion of New Zealand, occurred on 26 September 1907, at 00:00 hours.

The Dominion was proclaimed the next day in parliament, seated in Wellington.

• NZ was born under a Saturn - Pluto square. Saturn in Pisces, in the 9H, was the most exalted planet in the chart. In 1907, this clearly represented the structured power of Great Britain, exerting its authority from across the seas. It impressed its traditions, customs and cultural institutions on the new nation (Saturn opposite Sun).

• Pluto rising is the strongest influence. It is the planet of death and rebirth. In 1907, it represented the dramatic changes taking place in the nation and people.

Rising towards the Asc (the soul-purpose point of the chart), and in NZ's soul-sign Gemini, it represents transformations that the nation will be taken through so that it can fulfill its spiritual potential.

4. New Zealand in World War I and the Spanish Flu.

Blood Moon eclipse for WWI: 16 Sep 1913, 00:16, Wellington; around NZ natal.

• NZ was only 7 years old when Britain declared war, which meant that NZ (a British Dominion), was also at war. The conflict had a significant impact on the tiny nation (just over 1 million people). The angles of the eclipse chart fall on NZs angles. 120,000 NZers enlisted - 16,697 were killed and 41,317 wounded – a 58 % casualty rate.

• The more significant impact was upon race relations. The chart shows that any type of structured Mars' activity (pioneering the land, war, sport), would be helpful in racial-integration. It would also help build up the nation's moral fibre and lay down a stable foundation for the nation's roots (natal Saturn 9H, sextile Mars 8H of transformation; Saturn opposite natal and eclipse Sun).

• Before the war, white settler attitude towards Maori was imperious and Imperial policy excluded Maori "from the battlefields of Europeans." [1] That policy was thrown out when more soldiers were needed. 2,200 Maori signed up to fight. White and brown travelling, fighting and living together helped to forge a mate-ship, friendship bond that improved race relations back home. (Eclipse Sun-Moon fall in the 3rd-9th communication/ travel houses; Sun on Venus, ruler of 4H of home and 11H of friendship).

Lunar eclipse for Spanish Flu: 15 Jul 1916, 16:10, Wellington; around NZ natal chart.

• Returning soldiers (eclipse Mars 3H) from the war brought with them a dangerous hitch-hiker - the Spanish Flu. People died quickly from the disease that attacked the lungs and breathing mechanism (eclipse Moon conjunct natal Mars 8H, square Mercury).

• No other event has killed so many NZers in such a short a time. In only two months, about 9,000 died - about half as many as in the whole of WWI (Moon 8H opposite eclipse stellium 1H, including Pluto).

• The indigenous Maori were 7 times more likely to succumb - 2,500 died (eclipse Mars/ MC conjunct natal 4H cusp, representing the people of the land.

1   New Zealand Ministry for Culture and Heritage, 2016.

5. New Zealand in World War II.

Blood Moon eclipse for WWII: 4 May 1939, 02:46, Wellington; around NZ natal.

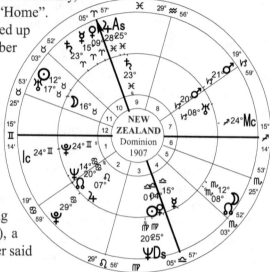

Again, NZ entered the war when Britain did. To many, England was still the "mother country" or "Home". The Prime Minister Michael Savage summed up local sentiment in a broadcast on 5 September 1939, when he said:

> We range ourselves without fear beside Britain, where she goes, we go! Where she stands, we stand! [1]

140,000 service-men out of a total population of 1,600,000 people served in the NZ forces. Shared pride over feats of bravery on the battlefield again helped to unite New Zealanders. But there was still a long way to go. Sir Apirana Ngata (1874-1950), a pragmatic cultural and political Maori leader said cynically in 1940:

> Fighting on faraway battlefields was the price Maori had to pay to be accepted as citizens of New Zealand. [2]

This gives insight into the unequal state of race relations that still existed in the country at the time and the desire by Maori to be accepted as equals. Ngata helped recruit men for the 28th Maori Battalion - around 3600 Maori from various tribes. The Battalion distinguished itself in the war for bravery.

• NZ's death toll was the highest in the Commonwealth per capita (eclipse Mars conjunct natal Mars in the 8H of death, opposite Pluto). One in every 150 New Zealanders serving, died.

• This is why, when Britain joined the European Community in 1973, cutting its trade ties to New Zealand; people looked at this sacrifice and felt bitter. The loss in trade was a severe setback for the local economy. Many NZers saw it as a gross betrayal. NZ (and Australia), had sacrificed their sons and daughters to fight in the wars on Britain's behalf and now it "went off" with the enemy - Germany and Italy.

Positively, Britain's "treacherous" act cut the imaginary umbilical cord binding the countries and NZ began to develop its independence.

• The legacy of the war is indicated by the eclipse IC (at 24 Gemini). It is conjunct natal Pluto and *Wazn* (25 Gemini 34). *Wazn* is a star on the back of the Dove constellation. In the Bible we read, Noah sent a dove from the Ark to seek land after the great deluge, which it did (find dry land). For NZ, this land located at the farthermost reaches of the known world, across the stretches of one of the largest oceans; it seems prophetic. It is a symbol for the NZ people and their future. That the soul of the nation will survive come what may, including catastrophes such as this war, the bloodiest in modern memory.

1   The Empire and the Second World War Radio 4, episode 88.
2   https://www.nzherald.co.nz/northland-age/news/article.cfm?c_id=1503402&objectid=12307826

6. Tangiwai Bridge Disaster: 24 December 1953.

Blood Moon eclipse for Tangiwai: 26 Jul 1953, 23:51, Tangiwai; around NZ.

On Christmas eve 1953, a dam on Mount Ruapehu's crater lake collapsed, creating a mudflow that destroyed a support on the nearby Tangiwai bridge. At 22:21 that night, a passenger train carrying 285 people going home for Christmas, plunged off the bridge into the mudflow. 151 people died.

Maori people said their land was venting its anger at Queen Elizabeth II, who had just arrived in NZ, because of violations of the "Treaty of Waitangi." The connection was made between "Tangiwai" and "Waitangi" both of which, in Maori, mean "weeping waters." Maori were still grieving over the loss of their lands.

• In this period of NZs history, Maori were struggling to find their identity in the 'pakeha' [1] world. Disasters such as this and shared community grief helped bring the races together.

The pattern shaping events was Neptune-Saturn, square Uranus - shattering outdated beliefs so new ones can grow. These planets also represent the disaster: Uranus the railcar, Neptune (water and grief) and Saturn (earth) the river mudflow. The latter are on the star *Foramen*, (22 Libra), which warns of the danger of shipwreck. A rail-wreck in this instance.

7. The Christchurch Earthquake: 22 February 2011.

Solar eclipse for the Earthquake: 4 Jan 2011, 22:02, Christchurch; around NZ.

On 22 February 2011 at 12:51, a magnitude 6.3 earthquake severely damaged Christchurch and Lyttleton, killing 185 people and injuring several thousand. The epicentre was near Lyttleton, 10 km south-east of Christchurch business district. Fortunately, the earthquake struck at lunchtime, when many people were on the city streets and managed to avoid collapsing buildings.

• *The earthquake:* eclipse Mars is the key. It was conjunct its natal position at 20 Capricorn. As the end planet of the stellium - it/ the earthquake, was the end result of the violent cocktail of forces that had assembled at the eclipse (Sun, Moon, Pluto - square Saturn in the 4H of the land and people).

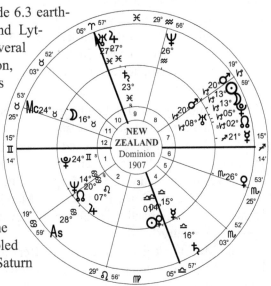

---

1 Maori word for Europeans.

Saturn was separating from its 3/4 square to Pluto when the tectonic plates in the earth released their screaming tension and the earthquake struck. The pattern portends reconstruction from demolition, a process that began in the early 1980s at their conjunction. That was when the Baby-Boomer generation took over power with their progressive ideas and changes. Now, in the 21st Century, the next generation is taking over.

• As for the esoteric cause behind it all? The most important building that was flattened, was the Christchurch Cathedral, which was built between 1864 and 1904. This was just prior to New Zealand becoming a Commonwealth Dominion, in 1907. With eclipse Uranus on the MC in the religious sign Pisces, it seems the event was portending the demise of old beliefs linking the nation to the past and new and more progressive attitudes flooding in.

8. Massacre in a Christchurch Mosque: 15 March 2019.

Grief again played a role with this disaster. At 13:40, on 15 March of 2019, a White Supremacist born in Australia, massacred 51 Muslim worshippers in a Christchurch mosque (eclipse Sun and Pluto in the 8H, conjunct natal Mars in the 8H of death). The attacker called himself a revolutionary (Uranus in Aries, t-square with eclipse), in the White Supremacy cause, which is based upon warped values (Moon in Leo 2H).

Blood Moon eclipse for the Massacre: 21 Jan 2019, 18:16, Christchurch; around NZ.

• Violent eclipse Mars dominated the event (10H, forming a t-square with natal Mars and Neptune). Mars is on *Alpheratz* (14 Aries), portending death by a fiery cutting weapon, a gun in modern times. The event was fast and brutal and broadcast around the world (Mars 10H, trine Jupiter, sextile natal Mercury). It brought grief and sorrow to the nation (Mars square natal Neptune 1H). The gunman wanted and got international attention. But in NZ people avoid using his name. He pled guilty to the murders and will never be released from jail. In the words of PM Jacinda Ardern, he "deserves a lifetime of complete silence."

• The evolutionary pattern shaping events is Saturn conjunct Pluto, which destroys crystallisations binding the soul. In NZ, the massacre awakened the people to the need to be more vigilant, to ensure that extremists with their evil values and ideas do not take root in NZ. Where the gunman was fuelled by hate and wanted to perpetuate this, it had an opposite effect. In March 2020, Police Commissioner Mike Bush said 15 March had changed New Zealand forever. "The victims, their families and the community, they have inspired all of us to be a kind and more tolerant community." [1]

Prime Minister Jacinda Ardern, led NZers in their support of the traumatised community. This helped develop NZ's higher function of becoming a world messenger of goodwill (Gemini rising).

1 https://www.theguardian.com/world/2020/mar/26.

Jacinda Ardern natal chart: 26 Jul 1980, 13:59 [1] Hamilton, NZ.

• NZ's/ Jacinda Ardern's handling of the massacre gained world attention. She is NZ's youngest ever Prime Minister. She was born in Generation X (1971-1983). Those in this group with Pluto in Libra, are tasked with bringing fairness and justice to the world.

• With idealistic Neptune in Sagittarius rising, Ardern's higher task is to inspire people to higher moral and spiritual heights. She is doing this and it has caught the attention of people across the world who admire how she does her job.

• NZ has a Gemini Asc, which means its soul-purpose is to be a messenger of goodwill. Ardern has Venus at 22 Gemini, which is stationed on NZ's Asc. She was born to be a spokes-person for NZ's spiritual expression.

This is accentuated by planet Earth (the esoteric ruler of Sagittarius), in the 3H of communications. Its location in Aquarius places her into that special group of people and nations whose task is to guide the masses into the humanitarian Aquarius Age. The Sabian Symbol for 4 Aquarius (where the Earth is located) is, "A Hindu healer, with magical powers." Ardern carries the power to heal.

9. New Zealand and Covid-19.

Lunar eclipse for Covid-19: 17 Jul 2019, 10:39, Wellington; around NZ natal.

• Being an isolated island nation and by "going in early and going in hard" (the policy implemented by PM Ardern) Covid was contained. By 2021, there were 25 dead and 2.2 thousand infected. NZ was lucky to have Ardern guiding its direction. With the toxic forces of the eclipse Moon, Saturn and Pluto threatening in the 8H of death, the toll could have been much higher - and still could. By January 2021 the virus was accelerating its lethal effect across the world.

• *Changes indicated by the Covid eclipse:* After the Covid-recession is over, with the vitalising eclipse Sun in the 2H, NZ's economy will be vitalised by foreign investments (Sun trine natal Saturn, ruler of the 8H).

Since Covid, polls taken indicate that NZers have re-assessed their values and that good health is now the most highly valued life-factor. Other values that have increased include kindness, relationships and spirituality.

1 Birth time unknown. Rectified by NZ astrologer Graham Bell.

10. The Spiritual Destiny of New Zealand.

The personality of New Zealand is ruled by Virgo.

• New Zealand in its personality aspect is ruled by clever and thoughtful Mercury - both of its signs (Gemini and Virgo), rule the nation. This emphasises NZ's role as a communicator nation and also the cleverness of its people. Skill in detailed work, craftsmanship and technical and mechanical ingenuity; these Virgo qualities helped early settlers become self-sufficient in their remote land. The people are modest and shy (Virgo and Sun on the IC). The national symbol - the kiwi, a flightless bird that only ventures out at night seems apt.

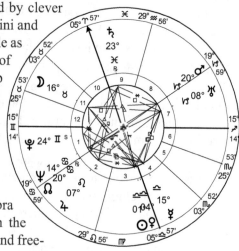

New Zealand 1907 natal

• NZ's Virgo personality works through a Libra Sun, which adds balance and diplomacy. With the Sun in the 3H, education, good communication and freedom of speech will always be important.

• *Problems:* NZ's limiting pattern is materialism (Moon in Taurus) of those politicians (11H), ultra-wealthy individuals and business corporations (Cancer rules the 2H), who put profit before the people. In the 21st Century, the imbalance between the super-rich and "the rest," is widening and this is an impediment to soul growth (Moon sesquiquadrate Mercury-Venus).

• Pluto (rising) square to Saturn, this aspect means that NZers will always be urged to challenge and confront in a major way, bad things or people that threaten them from within or from other parts of the world.

The soul of New Zealand is ruled by Gemini.

• New Zealand's Gemini soul expresses through a Gemini ascendant, making it easier for the altruism of the soul to demonstrate through the people. Though young in years, its progressive policies and inclusive nature show the evidence of that. This influence enables the advanced people in the nation to see past surface appearances of what is going on in the world to the heart of things; to draw out the very best from people.

> The spiritual keynote of New Zealand is: "I recognise my other self and in the waning of that self I grow and glow." [1]

• NZ's spiritual task is to be a Messenger of goodwill that creates harmonious relations between nations. It shares this task with the United Kingdom, which also has a Gemini soul. Venus as the esoteric ruler of Gemini, guides NZ through all its incarnations. In the 3H of communications, it emphasises its role as a messenger of beauty, wisdom and love.

• The great star *Rigel* (16 Gemini), is on the ascendant. It represents Orion's left foot - "the foot of the Pharaoh." To be under such a foot was considered a blessing. *Rigel* is "the educator, the one who brings knowledge." [2] This fits completely with Gemini's purpose and is *Rigel's* blessing to New Zealand.

---

1   Bailey, Alice A. Esoteric Astrology, 654
2   Brady, Bernadette. Solar Fire software commentary, 2012.

Norway

Scandinavia-Norway's personality is ruled by Cancer, its soul by Libra. [1]

The Cancer part of Scandinavia's rulership gives these nations (Norway, Denmark, Sweden and Iceland), the sense of being a family. The communities are very closely linked with common roots. In the 14th Century Norway unified with Denmark and after the Napoleonic wars it was controlled by Sweden. It was only in 1905 that Norway managed to emerge with its own individual identity. Libra is a mental sign and the soul of the nation was encouraging Norwegians to be independent, to think for themselves and to have their own voice.

1. The Storofsen Flood disaster, July 1789.

Natural disasters reflect what is happening in humanity and this eclipse also portended the French Revolution. After a cold winter with heavy rainstorms and numerous landslides that filled river beds, watercourses flooded the land, claiming 72 lives, thousands of livestock and destroying more than 1500 farms. It was a dire weather event.

<u>Lunar eclipse for the Flood: 9 May 1789, 09:55, Vagamo.</u>

• The strength of the lunar eclipse was greatly magnified when it formed a grand-cross with the Asc, DC-Pluto and stars in constellations associated with storms and floods.

- The Sun was on *Zaurak* (21 Taurus), a star in the river constellation Eridanus, that is associated with floods and drowning.

- The Asc was on *Naos* (16 Leo), that is in the constellation Argo, also associated with storms.

- Pluto and the DC were on *Castra* (17 Aquarius), in the constellation Capricorn. The latter is unfavorable with lunar eclipses, indicating major storms. [2]

• Neptune, that rules all water-ways, is on *Arcturus* (21 Libra), a star that has a stormy reputation. [3] On the 4H cusp, it emphasises the danger to people and villages from the flood. Neptune also corules the 8H of death with Pisces sharing that region.

• Neptune is in a t-square with Mars on *Baten Kaitos* (19 Aries), a stormy star, known for shipwrecks and drowning. [4]

• The chart is filled with stars warning of an impending water (and human) disaster. Floods like these resulted in actions being taken to protect the people against rogue water events through means such as building dikes and reservoirs. Norway's attempts to protect itself against the destructiveness of nature is symbolic of what it was trying to do to avoid being swept along with the flood of destructive politics in Europe at the time.

1   Bailey, Alice A. The Destiny of the Nations, 68.
2   Noonan, George; Fixed Stars and Judicial Astrology, 51.
3   Hinckley Allen, Richard; Star Names, 99.
4   Rosenberg, Diana. interview with Edith Hathaway, 2010. http://edithhathaway.com/pdf/DianaKRosenbergInterview.pdf

2. Birth of Independent Norway: 7 June 1905, 11:00, Oslo.

After being on the losing side of the Napoleonic Wars with Denmark, in 1814 Norway was ceded to the king of Sweden. But in the early 20th Century, tension grew between the neighbouring territories and the dissolution of the union was set in motion.

Secession was declared in the Norwegian Parliament around 11:00, on 7 June 1905. This chart is still used today.

• Norway's deep and determined resolve to achieve independent status is shown by the Sun conjunct Pluto in the 10H. They are in Gemini and the ruler of that sign - Mercury, is conjunct Jupiter on the MC point of higher goals and aspirations. Fuelled by the vitality streaming in from *Miram* (27 Taurus), an orange-blue star on the right arm of the champion Perseus, Norwegians wanted to fly free. Perseus rode the winged horse Pegasus.

3. Norway in World War II.

In WWI, Norway remained neutral, but because it kept trading with both combatant powers, its ships were attacked and about half its merchant shipping destroyed. But it lost more people to Spanish Flu than it did to the war. From the middle of June 1918, the virus swept across the country in three waves - 13,000-15,000 died. Statisticians today say the mortality rate of around 1.3 per cent then is quite similar to the 2020 Covid-19 outbreak.

Blood Moon eclipse for WWII: 3 May 1939, 16:16, Oslo; around Norway natal.

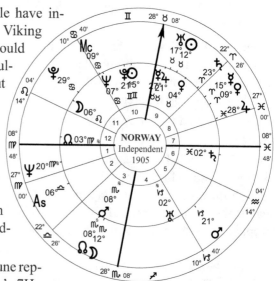

• But Norway fought in WWII. Its people have inherited all the courage and pride of their Viking forebears (natal Moon in Leo). They would rather die fighting than acquiesce to a bullying invader. So, when WWII broke out and Germany launched a seaborne attack on both Denmark and Norway early on 9 April, they fought. Germany was vastly superior and beat both countries to a surrender within 2 months.

• King Haakon fled to the UK to set up an in-exile government (the eclipse Sun is in the 9H of foreign countries, conjunct friendly Uranus, trine Norway's ascendant).

• Norway suffered in the war. Eclipse Neptune represents the enemy, with Pisces on Norway's 7H cusp of open enemies. It is in the 1H, showing its domination over

Norway as a nation. Many towns and settlements were damaged or destroyed by bombing and fighting and large areas were destroyed by the scorched earth policy Germans used as they retreated (Neptune square natal Sun and Pluto that rules the 4H of the people and land).

Norway's Moon also represents the people and land. It is conjunct the dangerous star cluster *Praesepe* at 6 Leo (brutality, injuries, violent death), and forms a t-square with the eclipse Sun and Moon. Over 10,000 Norwegians lost their lives in the conflict or while imprisoned, while approximately 50,000 were arrested by Germans during the occupation.

• German soldiers were encouraged to have children with Norwegian women to help promote the Nazi concept of seeding an Aryan master race (Neptune trine Mars in 5H of children). Many had intimate relationships with German soldiers and had babies.

• Norway has several stars clustered on its ascendant. The most spiritually appropriate is *Alsuhail* (10 Virgo), a star in the sails of Argo Navis, the great ship of the Argonauts. A most appropriate star to represent the spiritual destiny of this sea-going nation. The full name of the star is 'Al Suhail al Wazn', 'The Bright Star of the Weight,' because the star seems to rise with difficulty from the horizon, as if weighted. This can be interpreted as - no matter what heavy troubles come Norway's way, it will always rise above them.

4. The Norway Attacks on 22 July 2011.

White Supremacist terrorist, Anders Breivik bombed an executive government block, killing eight people and injuring at least 209. Then two hours later at a summer camp on the island of Utøya, he shot and killed 77 mostly young people and injured over a 100 more. The attack was the deadliest in Norway since WWII.

Blood Moon eclipse for the Attacks: 15 Jun 2011, 22:14, Oslo; around Norway natal.

• The attack was sudden, shocking and grabbed headlines around the world (eclipse Mars on the MC and Mercury-Jupiter). The horror and evil of the act traumatised the nation (eclipse Sun, Moon and Pluto impact the natal Sun; Mars on MC). Norwegians are very sensitive (Cancer influence).

• The star-group, the *Pleiades* (at 0 Gemini), is near the MC of Norway's chart. One of its names is the 'Seven Weeping Sisters'. The message implied, is that the people are taken through traumas such as this to develop compassion for others. This is very relevant today. Because, although Norway generally is a benevolent society, far-right nationalist movements, groups and politics are gaining a foothold in the country. Murderous Breivik belonged to this group.

• True to its values and legal system, leaders did not react retributively. Norway's justice system operates on the basis of "restorative justice" that emphasizes healing for all involved - for the victims of crimes, for society and also for the criminal. The murderer received 21 years in prison for the attacks, although experts say his term can be permanently extended. It will be interesting to see if Norway's system can rehabilitate him, because from the point of view of Esoteric Psychology, freeing violent partisans from the ideas that control them is exceedingly difficult.

• Norwegians have great reserves of inner-strength to draw on and in time will heal the trauma (Sun conjunct Pluto). Meanwhile, law and order measures have been stepped up to help keep the people safe (trine Saturn).

5. Norway and Covid-19.

Lunar eclipse for Covid-19: 16 Jul 2019, 23:39, Oslo; around Norway natal.

• Norway benefited by the fact that the eclipse missed the health and death houses. With a population of 5.3 million, it applied strong containment measures for Covid with an emphasis on contact tracing. With the virus under relative control, by 2021 there were about 400 dead and 50 thousand infected. By January 2021, Norway was the 81st ranked nation in the world for deaths per capita. Compare this to neighbouring Sweden's 9000 dead and its rank of 21st in the world.

• The nation benefits because of the wisdom of its elected officials (Gemini corules the 10H), and how they make decisions when important matters are pondered (natal Mercury, ruler of the 2H, is at the hub of a Yod pattern). Decision-making in relation to Covid-19 could have gone like this:

- Option 1 (Mercury inconjunct Uranus 4H): put people and their health first (Uranus rules the 6H of health, sextile Saturn).

- Option 2 (Mercury inconjunct Mars 3H): put trade and travel first, local and international.

We know the Uranus option was selected and the precautions taken as a consequence of that helped the nation avoid a catastrophe (Neptune, the virus, ruling the 8H of death, square natal Sun-Pluto).

• *Changes indicated by the Covid eclipse:* the location of the eclipse Moon, Saturn, Pluto in the 5H indicates there are certain attitudes that are rising (nationalistic and far-right), and that these need to be addressed. They are the down-side of Norway's defensive, protective Cancer nature. There are retrogressive people who resent multiculturalism, refugees and asylum seekers (natal Moon square Venus 9H), who are responding emotionally and violently (Mars opposite Venus). These attitudes are contagious and they must be resisted by the rest of the community.

• With the vitalising eclipse Sun in the 11H, the goal of the eclipse is to adjust the political narrative so that it better reflects the higher values and goals of the nation (eclipse Sun and Mercury sextile the MC).

6. The Spiritual Destiny of Norway.

The personality of Norway is ruled by Cancer.

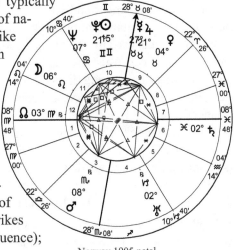

Norway 1905 natal

• Due to the Cancer influence, Norwegians are typically home-bodies, and the family unit is the bedrock of national life. People are proud of their families and like them to shine socially (Moon in Leo 5H). With their Cancer-Viking forces and background, Norwegians will fight to the death to protect the family if it is in danger (Moon square Mars).

• Though the people are friendly (Sun in Gemini), people like their personal space (Sun conjunct Pluto, square Asc).

• Norwegians also trust each other implicitly - perhaps an inheritance from the honour system of the Viking age. However, if trust is broken, it strikes at the heart of a relationship (the Pluto death influence); which may never recover.

The soul of Norway is ruled by Libra.

• Norway has an amazing 6-pointed star in its chart. It is marked out by Neptune, Mars and Saturn - the upturned triangle; and Uranus, Venus and the ascendant/ north-node - the down-turned triangle. Esoterically and in general, the upturned triangle represents God or the soul; while the down-turned triangle represents humanity - a mirror of its spiritual source, but embedded in a body. What could this mean for Norway?

The nation shares with all Scandinavian countries, a solid spiritual foundation based on the Libra values of equality, justice and fairness for all - the upturned triangle. This is evident in the generous and humanitarian social policies that these nations have and the care and concern (Cancer) they give to their people - the down-turned triangle.

• Uranus' creative force motivates those who are in touch with the soul of the nation to rise above all physical and psychological limitations; to be free and fly. The Sabian Symbol for Uranus' zodiac degree of 3 Capricorn, is "The Soul, as a hovering spirit eagle to gain experience." [1]

• In the future, Norway and the other Scandinavian nation's will play a powerful international role in advocating for human-rights and negotiating peace between warring nations - the influence of their Libra soul and the up-turned triangle. Their collective higher goal is to become a reconciliating force in world affairs - the down-turned triangle.

Norway's spiritual keynote is: "I choose the way which leads between the two great lines of force." [2]

---

1   Rudhyar, Dane. The Astrology of Personality, 297.
2   Bailey, Alice A. Esoteric Astrology, 654.

Poland

Poland's personality is ruled by Gemini, its soul by Taurus. [1]

Gemini is the messenger and when the lower forces in a nation are in control, incendiary messages that demonise minority groups or those with opposing views are used to gain power. When it is used for the greater good then positive things happen. Such as when Pope John Paul and Lech Walsea argued the case for greater freedoms. In the 21st Century, populist nationalists are causing division in the nation with incendiary attacks on minorities. As the Taurus soul becomes more influential, gradually the people will look for more stable, grounded leaders (Taurus), who care more for the people than their own interests.

Poland has a deep resonance with Great Britain and the United States, because they are also ruled by Gemini. The nation fought heroically against the Nazis in WWII and many of its nationals fought alongside the British and Americans.

1. Massacre of Praga: 4 Nov 1794.

In 1569, the Polish–Lithuanian Commonwealth (the 1st Republic) formed. But it was a small player on the European chessboard of politics and during the late 18th Century as its power declined, its territories began to be gobbled up by its stronger neighbours - Austria, Prussia and Russia. Still, Poland fought for its freedoms and this massacre committed by Russia was the consequence of one effort.

Blood Moon eclipse for the Praga massacre: 11 Aug 1794, 08:54, Praga.

Praga was the easternmost suburb of Warsaw. The Praga massacre occurred during the "Kościuszko Uprising" in March 1794, a failed attempt to free the nation from Russian control.

• The uprising was a fight for power and control (Sun-Uranus, 11H); Poland against its powerful neighbour Russia (Sun opposite Pluto, ruling 3H of neighbours).

• The omens for the period in which the massacre occurred were very bad. A terrible retribution in the form of a brutal massacre is being threatened:

a. *Edasich*, 2 Libra, a star in the dangerous Dragon / Draco constellation (Russia), is on the Asc, dominating the angles of the chart (the corner-stones of the Commonwealth).

b. The Sun and Moon are in a grand-cross with the rulers of the 8H of death, portending brutal (Mars), mass deaths (Pluto). The 4th point of the grand-cross is marked by *Botein* (18 Taurus), a star in Aries in the 8H. Aries's stars when afflicted, presage large-scale aggression and barbaric raiding - traits that fit Russia.

The Russians attacked Praga and killed around 6,000 civilians. Independent Poland disappeared.

---

1   Bailey, Alice A. The Destiny of the Nations, 68.

2. Birth of Poland 2nd Republic: 11 Nov 1918, 12:00, Warsaw.

After the massacre, the resilient Poles persevered in their efforts to be free, with Germany and Russia bullying them and at times controlling the region. Its successful effort came when Germany was defeated in WWI.

On the 3rd of November 1918, Warsaw proclaimed itself a republic. True independence came when Germany accepted defeat on 11 November 1918. This date, "armistice day," was the birth date for the 2nd Polish Republic. This was confirmed by the Allies at the Treaty of Versailles in June 1919. A 12-noon time is used.

• Poland was born fighting for its very survival (Sun in Scorpio). It was a very painful birth - Mars, God of War is conjunct its ascendant. The first months and years for this fledgling nation were extremely harsh. The Soviets attacked again in 1920. But this time the Poles repulsed them. But by then, Spanish Flu was on the rampage and Poland was hit hard.

• This incarnation for Poland would last until 1945, when it was gobbled up again by Russia. In the 7H of open enemies is formidable Pluto (Russia). On the IC, the legacy of the chart, is malevolent *Menkar* (13 Taurus), an orange star in the open jaw of the Sea-Monster, *Cetus*. It portends danger from great beasts.

3. Poland and the Spanish Flu: 1918 to 1920.

Lunar eclipse for the Spanish Flu: 15 Jul 1916, 06:40;
around Poland 1918 natal.

• The virus began its circulation in France in 1916. It appeared in Poland in mid-1918, by which time it was beginning to accelerate. Because the economic situation was dire there were shortages of doctors and medicine. To make matters worse, two other serious epidemics - typhus and dysentery were sweeping the country. Preventive measures for the virus were ineffective and consequently, it took a terrible toll. It is estimated that between 200,000 to 300,000 people died from the virus (eclipse Sun rules the 8H of death - conjunct Neptune that represents the virus). Due to poverty, Soviet aggression and continuing border wars, a significant part of its existing infrastructure was also destroyed.

4. Poland in World War II.

<u>Blood Moon eclipse for WWI: 3 Mar 1939, 16:16, Warsaw;
around Poland 1918 natal.</u>

• Germany's attack on Poland on 1 Sep 1939, started
WWII. The Polish Army was defeated within a
month (eclipse Pluto 7H - the Germans; inconjunct natal Mars on Poland's Asc).

But Poland never officially capitulated.
A government-in-exile was established in
the United Kingdom.

• Poles are famous for their bold, fighting
spirit. This is shown by Sun in Scorpio in
the 10H conjunct the MC of higher goals.
Its people will stand up to bullies and fight
for their values (Sun conjunct Venus, semi-
square Mars).

• Poland's heroism is shown again with *Kaus
Borealis* (5 Capricorn), on the Asc. A yellow
star in the Bow of the Archer (Sagittarius). It gives
strength, an ability to put force behind reasoning, and produces heroes. Many Pole heroes fought in the war.

• Many Poles contributed to the Allied effort and some found their way into various allied
Air Forces, including the Royal Air Force in Britain. Not many know or remember this, but
Polish squadrons fought in the Battle of Britain and greatly distinguished themselves and
their countrymen. Here is an account.

> Polish pilots distinguished themselves in the Battle of Britain which lasted
> from 10 July 1940 until 31 October 1940. This was the decisive battle that
> prevented the Nazis from invading the British Isles. A total of 145 experi-
> enced and battle-hardened Polish pilots participated - 79 in various RAF
> squadrons, and 56 in Polish Fighter Squadrons 302 and 303. The feats of
> the latter 303 Squadron were amazing. They achieved an astonishing score
> of 126 enemy planes, as well as 13 probable's and 9 damaged, claiming the
> title of the best scoring unit of the Battle of Britain.

• Valiant resistance forces fought undercover in Poland and a substantial number of citizens
risked their lives to save Jews. In retaliation, Germans killed an estimated 6 million Poles
and razed over a thousand villages. The nation's suffering did not end when the Red Army
drove out the German occupiers in 1945. It was then subjugated to repressive Soviet Union
control.

• With dangerous *Menkar* (13 Taurus) on the IC, which symbolises the "beast", first Poland
was consumed by the German Nazis, then it was swallowed by the Soviet Bear. Though it
was a dark period for the nation, it ended that unfortunate incarnation that was poisoned by
Menkar. This is because Poland went through a rebirth and got a new chart.

5. Birth of Communist Poland: 28 June 1945, 16:00, Lublin.

After WWII, the "liberating" Russian forces never left and on 28 June 1945, at 16:00 hours in Lublin, a joint government of national unity was set up. This date and time marks the official birth of Communist Poland. In 1947, Poland was renamed the Communist People's Republic of Poland.

• The Russian's are represented in the chart by Pluto in Leo, 9H. A foreign people repressing and controlling Poles and its land (Pluto opposite the Moon and square the Asc).

• The planet pattern is a "Bucket chart." Most planets are above the horizon, representing the outer state of the people and nation as they adjusted to living under foreign control. The singleton Moon is the handle of the bucket. It represents the coordinating force within the people - hidden out of sight; which kept them anchored. The powerful and burning desire for independence and freedom (Moon opposite Pluto in Leo). By the 1950s and 60s, this force erupted and people started rioting.

6. The Fall of the Iron Curtain, May 1988 into 1989.

The Iron Curtain was the political, military and ideological barrier erected by the Soviet Union after WWII to seal off itself and annexed nations from contact with the West. In May 1988, Secretary-General of the Communist Party, Mikhail Gorbachev introduced reforms that loosened Soviet control. The oppressed nations broke free and Poland was the first.

Solar eclipse for the Iron Curtain fall: 11 Sep 1988, 08:50, Moscow; around Poland 1945 natal.

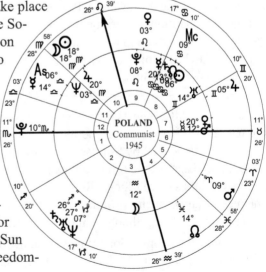

• The absolute transformation that was to take place in Poland as a consequence of the fall of the Soviet Union is shown by eclipse Pluto falling on the natal ascendant. The nation was about to go through a death/ rebirth experience.

• Poland was the force that finally rent the Iron Curtain. The wedge was the "Solidarity" movement that had its roots in Polish, non-Communist, trade unionism.

Solidarity/ Poland rejected the identity forced on them by the Soviets (eclipse Mars ruling the 6H of workers-unions, inconjunct Asc, square Sun). They fought for and got freedom and autonomy (eclipse Sun and Moon 10H, conjunct beneficial and freedom-giving natal Jupiter).

Lech Walsea: 29 Sep 1943, 03:30, Popowo, Poland.

• The "Solidarity" movement that split the Soviet Union apart was led by a granite-jawed Lech Walesa. Visionary and highly idealistic (Sun-Moon conjunct Neptune), he embodied the movement's force. There is little doubt that the force of Poland's enduring and powerful Taurus soul worked through him.

• Walsea radiated a natural and powerful authority. On the Asc was the star *Megrez* at 0 Virgo. In China, its name was 'Tien Kuen' - 'Heavenly Authority'. He expressed this authority intelligently and discriminatively (Venus on Virgo Asc).

• Walsea led a peaceful but forceful revolution to attain Poland's independence (Sun in Libra, trine Uranus 10H; Venus-Asc square Uranus). A charismatic "military" leader (his Uranus was conjunct the military star *Aldebaran* - 9 Gemini), people rallied behind him. Notably Pope John Paul II. His visits to Poland and speeches around the country attracted and motivated millions of Poles to unify their forces and to get behind Walsea and Solidarity.

• Finally, on 6 February to 5 April 1989, the Soviets entered into negotiations with Solidarity and free elections were held on 27 October 1991. Walsea, Solidarity and Poland at this moment in history, represent all subjugated people in the world who cry out for freedom. Walsea won the Nobel Peace Prize and served as the first democratically elected president of Poland from 1990 to 1995.

7. Birth of Democratic Poland: 24 August 1989, 13:05, Warsaw.

On 24 August 1989 in Warsaw, Tadeus Mazowiecki became the Prime Minister in Poland's Solidarity dominated coalition government. This occurred "a few minutes after 1 pm," which is generally considered to be the birth of Democratic Poland. The chart is set for 13:05.

• Mars on the MC, reflects the forces at work in the nation at this momentous period - the military-like battle waged by Solidarity and the people of Poland against the Soviet annexation of their territory (Mars square Moon - Russia, in 7H of open enemies). Mars in such a prominent position endows the nation with a fighting, though impulsive spirit.

• It will take the people a long time to heal the damage inflicted on them by Russia and they will never forget (Pluto 12H, conjunct Asc, inconjunct Moon).

8. Poland and Covid-19.

Lunar eclipse for Covid-19: 16 Jul 2019, 23:39, Warsaw; around Democratic Poland 1989 natal.

• In January 2021, hospitals reported they were running out of oxygen, so could not use ventilators to assist critically ill Covid patients. By 2021 there were over 29 thousand dead and 1.3 million infected.[1] With new waves of the virus ramping up in 2021, Poland needed to be very careful (eclipse Sun in the 8H of death, afflicted Uranus in the 6H of health).

• *Problems*: the areas targeted for change by the eclipse's cathartic forces are politics and the nation's values (eclipse Moon, Saturn and Pluto in the 2H, square Venus that rules the 11th political house).

In recent years, the rightwing Law and Justice party (PiS) gained power. It did this by using destructive Gemini messaging to stir up hatred and fear (that liberals, homosexuals, and Communists are a threat to the nation). The message is popular with older, religious and fear-filled conservatives who feel that European integration and economic liberalisation has left them worse off.

• *Changes indicated by the Covid eclipse:* transformation of the nation's values will occur during the coming 33-year cycle of Saturn-Pluto, with cathartic Pluto in the 2H of values. Crystallisations that blight the nation's consciousness such as racial hatreds, greed and ambition for territorial gain are ear-marked for elimination.

This is emphasised with the vitalising Sun in the 8H, on the 9H cusp. The nation will go through a purging process that will be healing and transformational. A greater alignment with the higher moral compass of the soul will occur and a resurgence of spiritual giving.

9. The Spiritual Destiny of Poland.

The personality of Poland is ruled by Gemini.

• Generally, Poland's prime difficulty through its history has been a lack of integration. Negative Gemini imbues the nation with too many ideas, too many voices, too many opinions and too many would-be leaders trying to argue their way into prominent positions. This has led to a state of constant disunion and friction and bred a nation that was weaker in its warp and weft than it should have been. Poles are valorous people and greater cohesion may have helped avoid being dominated by other nations and cultures for as long as it was.

• Moon in Gemini in the 1989 chart, indicated this lack of internal coordination still existed. If people ruled by this force gain control again, the nation will go backwards in its evolution (Gemini on the 8H cusp). There is a warning here about the PiS party.

---

[1]   13 Jan 2021: the 26th ranked nation in the world for deaths per capita.

The soul of Poland is ruled by Taurus.

• The Solidarity movement was the first real evidence in modern times that the cohesive and enduring power of the nation's Taurus soul was becoming influential in a group rather than individual sense. The world "solidarity" carries the Taurus vibration.

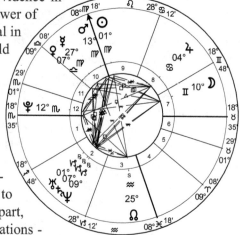

Poland 1989 natal

• Taurus governs two houses. First the 6H of work and health. This confirms that the soul of the nation is working through the working class - as it was through the Solidarity movement during the struggle to be free of Russia domination.

Taurus also rules the 7H of important relationships. This indicates that not only is it important to heal the internal bickering that rips the nation apart, but to build healthy alliances with other world nations - including with its former enemy Russia. In relation to this, it is interesting that aligned with, or close to the Sun, are several stars in the Great Bear (Ursa Major) constellation (1 to 4 degrees Virgo). Meaning, a closer relationship with Russia, one that is supportive and mutually beneficial will be helpful for Poland's growth.

• Warrior sign Scorpio is on the ascendant of the 1989 rebirth chart, representing the valorous fight this nation's people put up against the controls of the Russian Bear. It also indicates that the spiritual forces were supporting this battle (the Asc represents soul purpose). Victory is shown by ruler Mars on the MC. But also, that the battle against insidious forces within the nation that would tear the people apart continues (Mars square Moon, 7H).

• Poland has a beautiful pale emerald star energising its ascendant and spiritual direction. *Zuben Elschemali* or North Scale (19 Scorpio), in balancing Libra. This is symbolic for Poland's destiny, which is to stand solidly for world peace and justice. As the nation gradually grows in wisdom, this destiny will unfold.

> When the mind has become a vessel for the light of wisdom, then right-action in the world follows. Poland's spiritual keynote is: "I see and when the Eye is opened, all is light." [1]

---

1 Bailey, Alice A. *Esoteric Astrology*, 654.

Romania

Romania's personality is ruled by Aries, its soul is ruled by Leo. [1]

Romania's ruling signs Aries and Leo, are quite similar to those of Italy (Leo and Sagittarius). This is no accident. Its early tribes - the Vlachs, were Latinised by the Romans, their language has Latin roots and the name Romania is designed to reflect this connection. The Romanian people derive much of their ethnic and cultural character from Roman influence. In the future, because they both have Leo in common, Romanians will be drawn more closely to the country that helped shape their roots and be greatly influenced by the wisdom and guidance Italy has to offer.

Through the centuries the nation has been continuously over-run by foreign powers who rarely left them in peace. They have been invaded and controlled by Hungarian and German tribes, then the Ottoman Empire in the 15th Century. This led to a loss of identity. The current period is an important healing and integration period. Romania's place in the sun lies ahead - Leo, the sign that rules its soul, is a dominant, political ruling sign.

1. Birth of Independent Romania: 13 July 1878, 15:22, Bucharest.

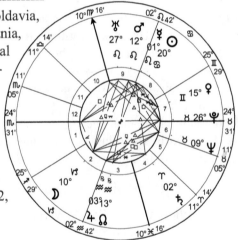

In 1859, the principalities of Walachia and Moldavia, the geographical and historical regions of Romania, united. By 1866, the nation had a constitutional government and ties to the powerful and protective Hohenzollern German dynasty. But it was still at that stage a vassal state of the Ottoman Empire.

On 21 May in 1877, the union proclaimed its independence from the Ottoman Empire. Its Independence was officially recognised by international powers on the 13th of July 1878, at 15:22, Bucharest time.

This incarnation lasted until 1947.

• Freedom seeking planet - Uranus, is the most exalted planet in the chart, in recognition of the drive to gain an independent status. Uranus is in Leo, the fiercely independent sign of individuality and that rules the nation's soul.

• Uranus square Pluto represents the cutting of the link between the newly resurrected nation and its Ottoman overlords (Pluto on 7H cusp). But this placement also warned of danger in the future from a tremendously powerful enemy. This came true when Russia annexed the country.

• Scorpio on the ascendant represented the fight it took for the people to gain their independence. It would also give them the power to fight their way through the coming years of Soviet Union oppression.

---

1 Bailey, Alice A. The Destiny of the Nations, 68.

2. Romania in World War I.

<u>Blood Moon eclipse for WWI: 15 Sep 1913, 14:30, Bucharest; around Romania natal</u>

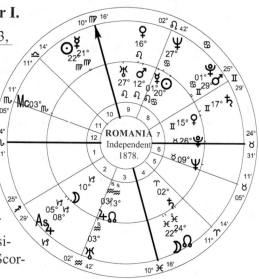

• Romania entered the war one day before it ended (allied with the UK, France and Russia) with the goal of gaining control of a part of Austria-Hungary that was occupied by Romanian speaking people; and gained its objective.

• This fortunate gain can be seen by the eclipse Sun located in the 10H of government and power, and the Moon in the 4H of the land and its people; forming an easy opposition with natal Pluto that rules the chart with Scorpio on the ascendant.

3. Rebirth of Constitutional Romania: 29 March 1923, 12:00, Bucharest.

Romania united with Transylvania in 1918, and a new Constitution of Union was ratified on 29 March 1923. It gave all adult male citizens the right to vote.

The new constitution was a hope for democracy. But when the economy collapsed in the 1929 Great Depression, Romania became a dictatorship (in 1938). Then in 1940, just before Romania entered the war, the 1938 constitution was suspended.

4. Romania in World War II.

<u>Lunar eclipse for WWII: 3 May 1939, 18:16, Bucharest; around Romania natal.</u>

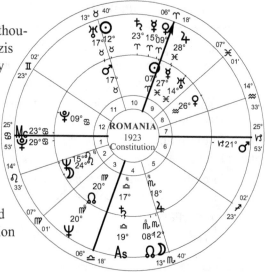

• Romania allied with Germany and sent thousands of troops to fight for it. But the Nazis simply took control of the country anyway and its oil and food supplies.

• Overall, the war was brutal on Romania. It lost control of its affairs, its identity was extinguished, it was bombed by the Allies and invaded by the Soviets. Around Romanians 800,000 died during the war (eclipse Pluto-Mars hit Romania's angles).

• Romania's war-government did very bad things. It was responsible for the persecution and massacre of up to 260,000 Jews.

5. The 1940 Vrancea Earthquake: 10 Nov 1940.

Total Solar eclipse for Earthquake: 1 Oct 1940, 14:40, Bucharest; around Romania natal.

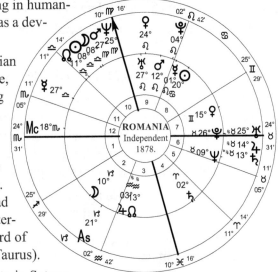

Nature's disasters mirror what is happening in humanity. As the world erupted into war, there was a devastating earthquake in Romania.

• The Vrancea region in the Carpathian Mountains, a highly active seismic zone, lies 480 klm north of Bucharest. During WWII, a massive 7.7 earthquake struck, the most powerful registered in the 20th Century. Because it struck early on a Sunday morning at 03:39 when most people were asleep, its effects were devastating. Casualties were estimated at 1,000 dead and 4,000 injured (Uranus, with its shattering power, is conjunct natal Pluto, the Lord of Death, and also the evil star *Algol*, at 25 Taurus).

• The evolutionary pattern shaping events is Saturn square Pluto, formidable forces fighting each other - nature mirroring what was happening in the war. They were separating, releasing tension when the earthquake struck - the earth's tectonic plates smashing their way to freedom.

6. Birth of Communist Romania: 30 Dec 1947, 12:00, Bucharest.

But freedom was not to be for Romania after the war. It was annexed by Russia and turned into a communist state on 30 Dec 1947, using the time of 12-noon.

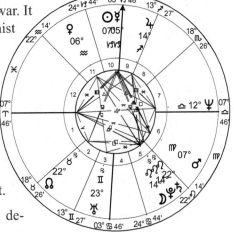

• The Romanian people persevered throughout these difficult decades. The soul of the nation is forged from fire. It has a Leo-ruled soul and an Aries-ruled personality. Fire is the element that allows for a rapid transformation into a new state when that is required. The new incarnation at 12-noon gave the nation a fiery Aries ascendant.

German author Countess Waldeck (1898-1982), described how she saw the Romanians:

> Two thousand years of severe foreign masters, barbarian invasions, rapacious conquers, wicked princes, cholera, and earthquakes have given Rumanians a superb sense of the temporary and transitory quality of everything. Experience in survival has taught them that each fall may result in unforeseen opportunities and that somehow they always get on their feet again. [1]

---

1   Encyclopaedia Britannica.

• In this chart, the Capricorn Sun represents the new identity the Soviet Union overlords forced onto the nation. It locked them into controlled and rigid rules.

• The subjugated state of the people and their culture is represented again by the Moon, oppressed by Pluto and Saturn in Leo in the 5H (oppressing their Leo soul).

• But the people retained their independent spirit and the driving desire for autonomy (Aries ascendant).

7. The 1977 Vrancea Earthquake: 4 March 1977.

In 1971, Nicolae Ceausescu, the Communist official who had led the country since 1965, instigated tighter and more intrusive controls into the daily lives of its citizens. His life of luxury, his nepotism (he placed his wife Elena into a key government position), and mishandling of the economy; resulted in extreme shortages of the basic necessities. This intensified civil unrest and hatred towards him from the nation's citizens.

Total Solar eclipse for Earthquake: 23 Oct 1976, 07:09, Bucharest: around Communist Romania natal.

• A powerful 6 planet stellium that included the ascendant, fell in Communist Romania's 7H of open enemies.

Because Romania was not at war, the stellium can be seen to represent the collective enmity of the free-world community directed towards the hard Communist rulership's in nations such as Romania.

The stellium also represents the collective enmity of Romania's people towards Ceausescu and his government (rulers of the 1H of the nation and the 4H of the people, are in the stellium).

Generated, collective hatred does not just dissipate harmlessly into the atmosphere. It is too powerful. There is truth in the ancient aphorism: "Curses, like chickens, come home to roost." Karma or nature returns the malevolent force to those who generate it. In this case, the malevolence of the earthquake mirrored the intensity of people's feelings.

• Powerful eclipse Pluto - driving the stellium, hit the angles of the chart, shaking up the foundations of the nation and causing major physical and psychological damage. The quake did not occur until 6 months after the eclipse - on 4 March 1977. Transit Mars had moved from Scorpio into the inharmonious force (to it) of Aquarius and began moving opposite natal Pluto and Saturn. The tension generated the explosion.

• The earthquake was of magnitude 7.2. making it the second most powerful earthquake in Romania - after the 1940 quake. It killed about 1,578 people and wounded more than 11,300.

• Ceausescu held power until 1989, increasing all the time, the brutality of his reign.

8. The Romania Revolution of 1989 and Restoration of Self-Rule.

Ceausescu's brutal rule came to a rapid end in the course of a single week. It was inevitable, the conclusion of a tidal change when Soviet premier Mikhail Gorbachev loosened the reins of Communism and former Iron Curtain states began to gain their freedom.

<u>Blood Moon eclipse for Revolution: 17 Aug 1989, 06:06, Bucharest:</u>
around Communist Romania natal.

• Ceausescu had his forces fire on anti-government demonstrators just before Christmas (in 1989). Civil unrest exploded and on 22 December, when the Romanian army joined the demonstrators, it was all over. Romania was the only Communist state to overthrow its government violently. Ceausescu and his wife fled but were captured and shot (on December 25). A brutal end to a brutal regime.

• The Saturn-Uranus-Neptune conjunction in Capricorn was shaping events. Uranus was a lord of the eclipse due to the Moon being in its sign - Aquarius. It was also conjunct *Alnasl* (1 Capricorn) "the Point" or "Arrowhead", a star in warlike Sagittarius.

• The triple conjunction hit the natal MC and all angles of the chart. Under the impact of the prevailing forces, the seat of Communist rule in Romania shattered. There was no formal dissolution - it simply ended with events like these.

9. Birth of Democratic Romania: 22 Dec 1989, 13:00, Bucharest.

The date and time used for the birth of the arisen nation is set for when Ceausescu and his wife fled - on 22 December 1989 at 13:00. [1]

Since then, Romania has thrived. But there is instability. The nation has one of the widest gaps between rich and poor in Europe and many are leaving the country to live elsewhere. Many believe their politicians are still corrupt ("like Ceausescu"). According to a 2019 poll, if he were still alive today, many Romanians would like to hand the country over to the cruel medieval prince Vlad the Impaler, because: "We need a tough leader now more than ever, as Romania is still plagued by corruption and insecurity." [2]

1 Campion, Nicholas. The Book of World Horoscopes, 253.
2 https://balkaninsight.com/2016/02/12/romanians-would-welcome-authoritarian-leadership-02-11-2016/

10. Romania and Covid-19.

Lunar eclipse for Covid-19: 16 July 2019, 23:39, Bucharest; around Democratic Romania natal.

• In 2020, Romania was reported as having the worst healthcare system in the EU and the lack of protective equipment for its healthcare workers resulted in hundreds of them becoming infected with many deaths. By 2021, almost 16 thousand people had died and 640 thousand infected. (Population 19.4 million). On 13 Jan 2021, Romania was ranked number 25 in the world for deaths per capita.

• *Changes indicated by the Covid eclipse:* In the aftermath, the people will not be happy and will look for a scapegoat. This will likely be the government with the eclipse Moon, Saturn, Pluto in the 10H and Uranus rising trine the MC. In the short term, this discontent could propel the populist right-wing AUR party into power. It ran on a nationalistic, anti-establishment and anti-homosexual platform. If so, there will be further trouble ahead.

• With the vitalising eclipse Sun in the 4H, in the years ahead the people will be inspired to think for themselves (conjunct Mercury), and to fight for their best interests (conjunct Mars), just like they did when they overthrew the hard-line Ceausescu government. This time through the ballot box. Even if mistakes are made and corrections are required downtrack, people fighting for their freedom against dictators is a positive step forward.

11. The Spiritual Destiny of Romania.

The personality of Romania is ruled by Aries.

• Romania's personality is ruled by Aries and Mars - proud and warlike signs. But constant defeat and bullying over the centuries has suppressed the spirit of these proud people. This is represented by the Capricorn Sun, which is restrictive to the people's spirits and the nation's soul. [1] However, in the meantime, Capricorn is a maturing sign and it is helping the nation to make its transition into a modern, democratic European state. Building links with the western world through the European Union and North Atlantic Treaty Organisation, and having to conform to the standards and rules that this membership requires, is tremendously maturing. Though it is lagging behind other former Communist states in this regard, this is temporary. Capricorn is helping the nation to lay down a new democratic foundation from which to operate.

• *Problem*: the nation is relatively poor and poverty is being exploited by Romanian criminal gangs (sex-slavery, drugs, paedophilia, theft, begging, etc). This has given the nation and its people a bad reputation in Europe (Capricorn stellium - organized crime; square

---

1 Romania would be advised to take steps to change this chart - peacefully, such as through a change of constitution, and to set the time so that Leo is either the Sun or rising sign.

Moon in Libra). Associated with this side of the nation's character are the myths surrounding blood-thirsty vampires preying on people in the countryside. Transylvania has long been associated with the land of Dracula.

• Positively, Romanians are a warm and passionate people, vibrant and talkative, who value family and friendships (Mars in Sagittarius sextile Venus). The younger generation generally align with Western culture, while some in the older generation remain nostalgic for the communist era and the job security it provided.

• The stellium on the MC in Capricorn indicates the importance for Romania's leaders to build a stable, well governed and progressive Romanian nation (Sun-Uranus in Capricorn).

The soul of Romania is ruled by Leo.

• Since 1989, Romania's Leo soul has been expressing through an Aries ascendant, the sign that rules its personality. This can be interpreted as the need for the nation to continue with its integrative process, a prerequisite for higher advancement. The need for integration and grounding is shown again with Jupiter, the sole planet under the horizon, on the IC or 'roots' position of the chart.

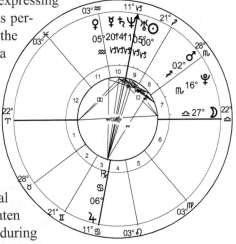

Romania 1989 natal

• A star Jupiter is aligned with is meaningful for Romania. This is *Dirah,* a beautiful crocus yellow star in the Gemini constellation at 5 Cancer. This star is in the right heel of Castor, the mortal Twin and one of its names is "The Abused or Beaten One." This fits what the nation has been through during its history. *Dirah* gives power and protection to those who have been abused and this Jupiter promises for Romania in the future. The IC is the legacy point of the chart.

• At the higher level, the Sun also carries the power of Romania's Leo soul, and its location in the 9H of the higher way carries a message for Romanians - to reorient themselves to a higher way of living and believing. The people are at ease with their spirituality, whether this is an orthodox religion, or a new-age type of spiritual expression. This will be taken to a new and higher level with Uranus' conjunction to the Sun.

> The loving, self-conscious Leo soul, identifies both with God and with the beating heart of humanity as a whole. Romania's spiritual keynote is: "I am That and That am I". [1]

• Aries and Leo are leadership signs. In the future, as integration proceeds and the intellectual and scientific brilliance of its people develops, Romania will shine its light across Europe and the world. It is not clear in what particular direction this may be at the moment. But, in time, Romania will deservedly find its place in the sun.

---

1 Bailey, Alice A. Esoteric Astrology, 654.

Russia

Russia's personality is ruled by Leo and its soul by Aquarius. [1]

Much of Russia's history has been a grim tale of the very wealthy and powerful few (Leo), ruling over the poor masses (Aquarius). Serfdom - a modified form of slavery, was only abolished in 1861. This is a hundred years after the beginning of the Industrial Age. In this system, the landowners owned the serfs who could be sold off without the serf's personal property and family. Serfs were given a small plot of land to work for their food, but could only do so after the master's massive fields had been tended. Because they had "their plot of land," serfs mistakenly thought they owned the land.

In early centuries, the region was dominated by Kievan Rus, a powerful East Slavic state and the roots of modern Russia - and its name; stem from this nation. In the 13th century, the Tatars invaded and ruled but were thrown out in the 16th Century by Ivan the Terrible (1530-1584). Ivan extended the country's borders into Siberia. Following the example of imperial houses in Europe, he crowned himself as ruler - the first Czar. His marriage to Anastasia Romanov (the first of his seven wives), was for love. After her death, which removed her moderating influence, he became known as "Ivan the Terrible" because of the terrible things he did.

1. Birth of Romanov Russia: 3 Mar 1613, 12:00, Moscow.

The first Romanov czar - Mikhail Romanov (1596–1645), assumed the throne on 3 March 1613, setting the date for the Romanov Dynasty chart. Because the time is unknown, a 12-noon chart is used. Mikhail reigned from 1613 until 1645.

This glittering Romanov Dynasty reigned from 1612 to 1917. It was the last imperial house to rule Russia.

• Although this is a noon chart, Sun conjunct Saturn on the MC suits the period - a story of the control wielded by the very wealthy aristocratic class over the poor and struggling masses (Pisces).

• A symbol of serfdom in the chart is the Moon in Cancer in the 1H (the people of the land), square Pluto (their over-lords, who had complete control over them and their lives).

• A second symbol is Jupiter conjunct Neptune in Virgo - which is the sign of service and servants; opposite Saturn conjunct the Sun in the 10H, representing the dynasty.

• When serfdom was abolished, it freed these workers to move to the cities to find employment in factories if they chose to. But poverty was widespread and when the 1891 famine hit, many died.

---

1   Bailey, Alice A. The Destiny of the Nations, 67.

2. The Russian Famine: 1891-1892.

Blood Moon eclipse for the Famine: 23 May 1891, 21:23, Volvograd:
around Russia - Romanov natal chart.

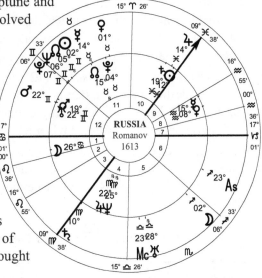

• The eclipse hit the rare conjunction of Neptune and Pluto that only happens every 492 years. Involved in an eclipse, this portended a catastrophe.

• Eclipse Neptune rules major water events. In this case, there was a severe lack of water, a drought that decimated crops. (Eclipse Neptune conjunct Pluto, square Saturn). Mercury that rules the 4H of the people, agriculture and farming, is conjunct *Menkar* (13 Taurus), a star that is often involved in famines. About 375,000 to 500,000 people starved to death.

• The eclipse Moon (afflicted by the planets opposite), was conjunct the cusp of the 6H of health. As well as starvation, the famine brought disease.

• As a result of the Czar's poor handling of the drought, the people lost faith in him and the regime (the Moon opposite Neptune that rules the 10H -the Czar; with Pisces on the cusp). This led eventually to the 1917 revolution.

3. Russia in World War I and the Russian Revolution (1917-1922).

Blood Moon eclipse for the Russian Revolution: 5 Jul 1917, 01:11, Moscow:
around Russia - Romanov natal.

When Serbia entered WWI, so did Russia, in defence of its treaty partner. Czar Nicholas was foolish to do so because there was serious trouble at home. Social unrest had been simmering since the 1891 famine. Russia was impoverished with an enormous peasantry and a growing number of poor industrial workers living in hard and often miserable conditions.

Three years of WWI exhausted the Russian economy and left its people starving. Corruption, inefficiency, unpopular czarist policies, defeats in WWI and widespread poverty; bred discontent. The first part of the Revolution was relatively mild. It started in March 1917, with riots over food shortages, mass strikes and clashes with police and troops. Czar Nicholas abdicated and a provisional Russian Republic was formed.

• The second revolution erupted on November 6. The eclipse Sun was conjunct dangerous Pluto that presides over brutal mass-upheavals; and they were on the Romanov ascendant. They portended death to the old regime and birth of a new one - the Bolsheviks. [1] Pluto's presence indicated the change would be brutal.

The eclipse Sun that represents the incoming rulership is conjunct the 1st magnitude star *Sirius* (13 Cancer), this is the Chieftain's Star that presides over floods. The Bolsheviks were like an unstoppable force of nature. At their most powerful (after WWII), they drowned great swathes of Europe with their ideological tidal surge.

• The eclipse Moon was on *Ascella* (12 Capricorn), in the 18th Hindu Moon Mansion, that portends destruction, deceit, imprisonment, beating, burning and poison - methods employed by the Bolsheviks to get and maintain power. The Communist principle of regimented sharing is easily corrupted when it is administered by a dictatorship.

• The provisional government established in 1917 went through several adjustments. Then in January and February of 1918, a civil war was fought between the Red Army Bolsheviks and White Army monarchists. The Bolsheviks won and on 16 July 1918, they executed the Romanovs.

4. Birth of the USSR: 30 December 1922, 12:00, Moscow.

On 30 December 1922, the first congress of the Soviets of the USSR (United States of Soviet Union Republic), formed. This marks the birth of the Communist USSR regime. A 12-noon time is used.

• Communism is defined as "a theory or system of social organization in which all property is owned by the community and each person contributes and receives according to their ability and needs." People generally thought that under Communism, everyone would be equal in status and have equal opportunity. But as we know, this is not true. Those at the top have power, those underneath do not.

• The USSR became a highly regimented police-state, where people were encouraged to spy on their neighbours and to report transgressors to the authorities. These unfortunate people were then picked up by officials and punished. Some were killed. (Sun in Capricorn, opposite Pluto, wide square to Saturn).

• Joseph Stalin was appointed General Secretary of the Central Committee on 3 April 1922. In control, he was ruthless and consolidated his power by initiating the "Great Purge" (1936-1938). It was a brutal campaign designed to eliminate anyone he considered a threat. At least 750,000 people were executed and more than a million were sent to forced labour camps. Pluto on the IC symbolises a nation founded on brutal murder, mayhem and terror. This all took place just before WWII, during the rise of Nazism.

---

1   The Bolshevists, were a radical, far-left, Marxist faction founded by Vladimir Lenin and Alexander Bogdanov.

5. Russia in World War II.

Blood Moon eclipse for WWII: 3 May 1939, 18:16, Moscow:
around USSR natal.

• Originally, Russia was an ally of Germany. But Hitler wanted to control Russia's natural resources and on 22 June 1941, launched the Operation Barbarossa invasion. It was the largest and most powerful force assembled in human history. Under this surprise attack, Russia became an instant ally of the Allies. (The surprise was portended with eclipse Uranus on the USSR Asc).

But Hitler did not take into account the formidable spirit of resistance embedded in Russian DNA (natal Sun in Capricorn opposite Pluto on the nation's IC).

• Russian resistance was bolstered by Stalin in 1941 when he ordered special troop units to kill any soldiers who surrendered or were captured, if they returned to the Motherland. Then in 1942, he ordered that these units should be positioned behind the front line and to "liquidate cowards on the spot." He meant, any of his own soldiers who tried to retreat. According to some estimates, these units killed as many as 150,000 service-people during the war.

• Willingness to sacrifice individuals for the good of the nation and Motherland was foundational in the USSR chart (natal Neptune in Leo, square the Moon 1H, square Jupiter, ruler of the 8H of death).

• Whatever one may think about Stalin's actions, in late 1941 the Soviets stopped the Wehrmacht some 30k from Moscow. The delay gave time for Russia's greatest ally - "General Winter" (as Russia's winter was called), to come to its aid. During the 4 years of the Eastern Front War, Winter destroyed the Wehrmacht spirit, cut its supply lines and killed its troops. It is estimated that 30 million troops on both sides died on the Eastern Front. This victory swung the tide of the war into the Allies favour, which gained momentum when the United States entered the war.

• The contribution made by Stalin and the Soviet Union's people towards the Allied victory in WWII, was immensely important and some commentators say has been vastly under-rated. Whether this is true or not, there is no doubt that the Russian people made a tremendous contribution and this should be acknowledged.

• In the aftermath of the war, Stalin extended the USSR's borders by annexing states they had "freed" from the Germans. Communist governments were created. They controlled the people there as they did in Russia - through police surveillance, spying, and harsh punishment for dissenters who rebelled again the regime. The Soviet Union became a super-power after WWII. But its moment of glory was relatively brief. It came unstuck because it could not match western economies and "free enterprise." This is an economic system where private business operates in competition and largely free of state control.

6. The Fall of the Soviet Union: 1988.

<u>Solar eclipse for "the Fall": 18 Mar 1988; 05:02, Moscow: around USSR natal.</u>

At the beginning of 1991, the Soviet Union (the "Iron Curtain)"; was the largest country in the world (1/6th of the earth's land surface, 290 million people). But it was uncompetitive economically and the subjugated countries increasingly agitated for their freedom.

Mikhail Gorbachev was the instrument that brought about the end. He was elected head of the Communist Party in 1985. In May 1988, he introduced his new *perestroika* ("restructuring") policy that allowed private enterprise, without calling it that. It effectively democratised the old system. This was the crack that eventually split the Soviet Union apart.

The March 1988 eclipse has been chosen to reflect that. It was a total solar eclipse that often portends the fall of a king or government. By the end of 1991, the Union had ceased to exist.

• The forces of dissolution and regeneration that were gathering over the Kremlin are represented by eclipse Neptune, Uranus and Saturn. They were moving over the natal Sun, opposite Pluto (death), and towards the MC, representing the power of the Kremlin.

• Pluto, the Lord of Death, because of its location on the IC of the chart (the legacy point of the USSR); correctly predicted its death on the day the nation was born.

Eclipse Pluto hit the angles, symbolising the bite of death and transformation that was implemented by largely peaceful means (sextile Neptune on MC).

• The process picked up in 1989, when Jupiter began travelling through Cancer opposite the stellium in Capricorn - inspiring progressive freedom through peaceful revolution. The Polish "Solidarity" movement of non-Communist trade unionists, was the first wedge. It successfully bargained with the Kremlin for free elections. This sparked peaceful revolutions in other nations and within 6 years of Gorbachev coming to power, the Soviet Union collapsed.

• On 25 December 25 1991, the Soviet hammer and sickle flag was lowered for the last time, symbolising the death of the former Communist behemoth and rebirth of Mother Russia. Here is how the New York Times (26 Dec 1991), described the event:

Mr. Gorbachev finished speaking at 7:12 P.M.; the Soviet flag was lowered at 7:32. Then at 7:45 the Russian flag was hoisted to fly above the illuminated dome of the Council of Ministers building, and the chimes on the Kremlin's Spassky Tower clock rang for several minutes. Several dozen people were in the huge square, but most said they had just happened through on the way home from shopping or other errands, that they had no idea they would be witnessing the ringing in of a new era.

7. Birth of the Democratic Republic of Russia: 25 Dec 1991, 19:45, Moscow.

Astrologers consider the rebirth of Russia to have taken place when the new Russian flag was raised over the Kremlin, on 25 Dec 1991. The New York Times reported that, "at 7:45 PM, the Russian flag was hoisted to fly above the Kremlin." [1]

• The chart, with all planets below the horizon, marks an introspective stage of the nation's journey. Such a process is healthy after a tremendous trauma and death - such as the rise and fall of the Soviet Union. However, having all planets in the dark (bottom) hemisphere is not helpful for bringing the nation "into the light."

• With the Sun in Capricorn and ascendant in Leo, new Russia has strong ruling signs. With autocratic and controlling Leo on the ascendant, it did not take long for another dictator to assert himself, Vladimir Putin. He has been called the new Czar.

8. Russia and Covid-19.

Lunar eclipse for Covid-19: 17 Jul 2019, 00:39, Moscow; around Russia natal:

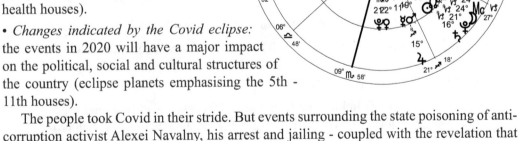

• The Russian government reported that it applied containment measures relatively early. But many of its citizens say these were woefully inadequate and that front-line staff in hospitals were treating Covid patients without proper protective masks and gowns. Consequently, by 2021, there were 58 thousand dead and 3.2 million infected. [2] (However, Russia has a large population; 144 million people).

• The eclipse indicated a dire health crisis (eclipse planets impacting the 6th - 12th health houses).

• *Changes indicated by the Covid eclipse:* the events in 2020 will have a major impact on the political, social and cultural structures of the country (eclipse planets emphasising the 5th - 11th houses).

The people took Covid in their stride. But events surrounding the state poisoning of anti-corruption activist Alexei Navalny, his arrest and jailing - coupled with the revelation that Putin owns a 1.7 billion palace on the Black Sea; have begun a revolution that will have far-reaching implications (Uranus on the MC),

---

1   NY Times, 26 December 1991.
2   13 Jan 2021: the 49th ranked nation in the world for deaths per capita.

9. The Spiritual Destiny of Russia.

The personality of Russia is ruled by Leo and Ray 6 of Idealism and Devotion.

• Governed as it is by the emotional 6th ray, Russia in its psychology is feminine, intuitive, inclusive and mystical. The nation's role is to nurture its people and it is no accident it has been given the name "Mother Russia." The people have a great warmth to them and are steeped in the urge to look after each other.

• The selfish side of Russia's Leo personality is epitomised in Vladimir Putin. He is an autocratic dictator living a lavish and extravagant lifestyle. Many Russians seem to be accepting of what he does and a reason for this is because they are attracted to the Leo power and the testosterone he radiates. (Putin has Pluto in Leo, conjunct his Leo MC at 21 Leo; trine Mars).

Russia 1991 natal

• *Problem*: the nation's limiting problem continues to be the state of ignorance that the people are kept in regarding the corruption of their leaders of which Putin is the latest example (Moon in obedient and reverential Virgo, 1H; sesquiquadrate Neptune).

The soul of Russia is ruled by Aquarius and Ray 7 of Ceremony, Order & Magic.

• The Russian people are driven by their 7th Ray - Aquarius soul, to work together in concert and rhythm for the good of the nation. Though Communism lifted the peasantry out of poverty, enforced standardization will not work in the Aquarian Age.

• An area of importance for soul growth is represented by Jupiter, the esoteric ruler of Aquarius. It is afflicted in Virgo in the 2H, indicating a corruption of the nation's values that need renewing and spiritualising. The nations' prosperity that is held in the hands of a few, must be redistributed to the nation (Jupiter trine Uranus and Neptune).

Russia's spiritual motto is, "I link two Ways." [1]

Russia's spiritual destiny is to demonstrate how a nation and its people can make the transition from being state-controlled, selfish and materialistic entity, to that of being understanding, kind, inclusive and holy. Here is the relevant quote:

> [Russia, its task of] linking the East and the West and also [the linking] of the worlds of desire and of spiritual aspiration, of the fanaticism which produces cruelty and the understanding which produces love, of a developed materialism and a perfected holiness, of the selfishness of a materialistic regime and the unselfishness of a mystically and spiritually minded people. [2]

---

1 Bailey, Alice A. Esoteric Psychology I, 383.
2 Bailey, Alice A. The Destiny of the Nations, 61.

This tremendous transition will be brought about by an impulse rising from the loving hearts and minds of spiritually advanced Russian people and not by any of its Leo type leaders.

• *A new religion.* Significantly, a new magical religion is destined to arise in Russia. This is shown in the chart with the conjunction of Uranus (that carries the 7R), Neptune and the north-node, trine Jupiter that rules religion and the world. Here is the relevant quote:

> Out of Russia - will emerge a new and magical religion. [from there] the light which ever shineth in and from the East will irradiate the West and the whole world will be flooded with the radiance of the Sun of Righteousness. [1]

The quote may be obscure to some, but it portends that a new religion or spiritual worship will pour out from the heart of Russia to nourish the world.

> Russia's spiritual keynote is: "Water of life am I, poured forth for thirsty men." [2]

1   Bailey, Alice A. The Destiny of the Nations, 61.
2   Bailey, Alice A. Esoteric Astrology, 654.

South Africa

South Africa's personality is ruled by Sagittarius, its soul by Aries. [1]

Anthropologists believe the African continent was the cradle of civilization, from where humans first evolved (Aries). The early people were nomadic hunters and gatherers, generally ruled by Sagittarius. From Africa, these nomadic tribes and people migrated to all parts of the globe. This means that every race has its roots in Africa. For a long period, its people were undisturbed by the outside world. But gradually, in the Middle Ages, explorers and travellers made contact. The heavy and cruel impact and exploitation of western civilization began in the 17th Century. A consequence of this was the speeding up of the evolution of the indigenous people. This happened to all undeveloped people in the world and caused great suffering. Still a developing nation, South Africa's higher Aries destiny lies far in the future.

1. White Colonisation of South Africa and Slavery: 17th Century.

The roots of the nation we know today stem from the Middle Ages with the establishment of the African kingdom of Mapungubwe (11th - 15th centuries). When Europeans arrived, the scattering and crushing of Africans began. The Dutch East India Company under Jan van Riebeeck began white settlement on the Cape of Good Hope on 6 April 1652. He was accompanied by 82 men and 8 women.

Solar eclipse for Dutch Arrival: 14 Oct 1651, 14:55, Cape Town.

• The evolutionary planets - Uranus, Neptune and Pluto; are in the travelling and explorative signs Gemini and Sagittarius. It was a visionary (Neptune), new beginning (Uranus), for the those coming from overseas (Jupiter and Sagittarius).

• The eclipse is in the 8H that represents major losses - for the travellers, the major loss was to leave behind the secure comfort and safety of Holland. The gain was a new life.

• The newcomers quickly assumed a position of power and dominance (10H). Within 50 years, the indigenous communities near Table Bay had been dispossessed of their lands and slavery had been implemented (Pluto in 4H). Some African rulers traded native men, women and children for guns. The Atlantic slave trade was big business for Europeans. Slaves were the most valued trade commodity in Africa and many grew rich from this degrading of human beings.

• The legacy of the invasion is represented by *Tabit* (on the IC at 7 Gemini). It is one of a number of stars on the trophy held in the left hand of the Hunter, Orion. South Africa was a trophy for the new-comers. It brought great wealth not only from slavery, but from its mineral wealth (Mars, ruler of 2H of wealth, conjunct Jupiter in the stellium, and trine the north-node in the 2H).

---

1   Bailey, Alice A. The Destiny of the Nations, 68.

2. Birth of the South African Union: 31 May 1910, 12:00, Pretoria.

English settlers to the Cape colony began to arrive in earnest from 1820. Then began a struggle with the Boers [1] to control the wealth of the land. This broke out into open hostilities in 1899 in the Boer War. It ended in 1902 with a British win.

The Union of South Africa (S.Africa) was born in Pretoria on 31 May 1910 at 12-noon when the Governor General and ministers began to take their oaths. It consisted of the various British and Boer possessions in the country.

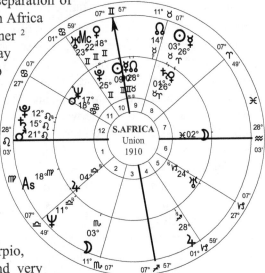

• The nation was born with the constellation Scorpius on the IC, the legacy point for the new nation. *Antares* in Scorpius was located there at 9 Sagittarius. Marcus Manilius in Astronomica (pages 239-240) said: "The Scorpion creates natures ardent for war and a spirit which rejoices in plenteous bloodshed and in carnage." So it proved to be for South Africa in the following years.

3. Apartheid (apartness) began on 6 May 1948.

Lunar eclipse for Apartheid: 23 April 1948, 15:28, Pretoria: around South Africa Union natal.

In the early decades of the 20th Century, separation of the races became widely practiced in South Africa - primarily by the Boers. When the Afrikaner [2] National Party won the election on 26 May 1948, legalised Apartheid was just a step away. They had pledged to implement a policy of strict racial segregation in all spheres of living and did so later that year. Coloured voters were no longer allowed to vote and seats for white representatives of Blacks and Coloureds were abolished. Then began a nearly 50-year period of institutionalised racism and brutal suppression of non-whites.

• The eclipse spanned Taurus and Scorpio, tough signs symbolic of the stubborn and very tough Boers who had carved out a life for themselves in the heat and dirt of burning hot Africa.

---

1 The term Boer, derived from the Afrikaans word for farmer, was used to describe the people in southern Africa who traced their ancestry to Dutch and German Huguenot settlers who arrived in the Cape of Good Hope from 1652.

2 An Afrikaans-speaking white person in South Africa, descendants of Dutch and Huguenot settlers of the 17th century.

• The evolutionary pattern shaping events is a Saturn-Pluto conjunction (in a t-square with the eclipse); which destroys crystallisations binding the soul of humanity. In a country where attitudes and values are antithetical to human rights and greater freedoms, these are solidified, making it easier for them to be destroyed in a later cycle. It took one and a quarter more cycles for this to happen, for Apartheid to end - when Saturn squared Pluto in 1994.

• It was a very brutal regime, that used its power and control to repress the people (eclipse Mars on ascendant).

• The values of the Boers (eclipse Moon 2H), were enshrined in Apartheid, which literally means "apartness." The Boers wanted to keep their race pure, untainted with black blood (eclipse Uranus/ MC square Virgo Asc). Apartheid was antithetical in a world that was moving towards racial and cultural acceptance and tolerance.

4. Birth of Republic of South Africa: 31 May 1961, 00:00, Pretoria.

In 1961, under pressure from British Commonwealth leaders to remove its Apartheid policy, South Africa separated from the Commonwealth to become a Republic.

The Republic of South Africa was born on 31 May 1961 at 00:00 hours.

• The Apartheid regime became a pariah state and gradually it was ostracized around the world. This is reflected in the chart by Pluto on the 7H cusp of international relations, square the Sun.

• Pressure from the world against its racist policies gradually ground the regime down (Pluto square the Sun).

One way this was done was through Rugby Union, which the nation loved. The Moon rules the 5H of sport and recreation. It is exalted in the 10H, in a grand-trine with Mars (sports rivalry), and Venus (love).

There was a fierce rivalry between nations and particularly between New Zealand and South Africa. 'Halt All Racist Tours' was established in New Zealand in 1969 to oppose continued tours to and from South Africa (Neptune square Mars, representing the protests by foreign idealists).

Commonwealth governments agreed to "discourage" contact, but rogue tours proceeded anyway. Rugby NZ sent an All Blacks rugby team to South Africa in 1970 with Maoris, because South Africa allowed them to enter as 'honorary whites.' This caused an uproar amongst some in NZ, but many rugby-mad fans did not care. Apartheid South Africa's last foreign tour was to New Zealand in 1981. It was met with mass protests that disrupted matches and caused fights to break out between locals. But the resistance stopped the tours.

• The state finally buckled to world pressure towards the end of the 20th Century by calling for a Democratic election. South Africa is represented by the Sun at the bottom of the chart conjunct powerful military star *Aldebaran* (8 Gemini). The rest of the world is represented by the more powerful military star - *Antares* (the 'Heart of the Scorpion'), at 9 Sagittarius, on the MC. In battles, *Antares* warriors usually beat those of *Aldebaran*.

5. End of Apartheid: 1994.

The Apartheid regime in South Africa legally came to an end in April 1994, when a new Mandela-inspired constitution came into effect.

Solar eclipse for end of Apartheid: 13 Nov 1993, 23:34, Pretoria: around S.Africa natal.

• The evolutionary pattern shaping events is Saturn square Pluto that causes major structural changes to the foundations of a nation. The eclipse Sun and Moon hit Pluto, reinforcing and accelerating their evolutionary work.

• A second pattern - Uranus conjunct Neptune, shattered the political delusions and fanaticisms of the previous order (in the 11H). Working together with Saturn and Pluto, these forces enabled ideals more in with the Aquarian Age principles of universal brotherliness to emerge.

• Eclipse Pluto on the MC, opposite the Sun, represented the death of the Apartheid regime.

• Saturn is in Aquarius that enshrines human rights and greater freedoms, conjunct *Deneb Algedi* (23 Aquarius). This star is also called "The Judicial Point of the Goat." This can be interpreted as "important legal changes to the nation's foundations, to include greater human-rights freedoms."

• The Saturn-Pluto conjunction in 2019-2020 completed this cycle. From the heights and expectations of a Mandela Presidency, the cycle ended on a low with previous President Zuma, appearing in court on charges of fraud, corruption, and racketeering. Hopefully the new 33-year deconstruct-reconstruct cycle will improve the political moral atmosphere.

6. Birth of Mandela Republic of South Africa: 27 Apr 1994, 00:00, Pretoria.

Under constant pressure, the end of Apartheid was initiated by the white government who made overtures to Africans. A key moment of this accommodation occurred when Nelson Mandela was released from jail, on 11 Feb 1990.

A new multiracial constitution came into effect on 27 April 1994 at 00:00 hours; marking the birth moment of the new nation. New and free South Africa was born with celebrations across the world. However, many white people were dismayed and left Africa, emigrating to other parts of the world.

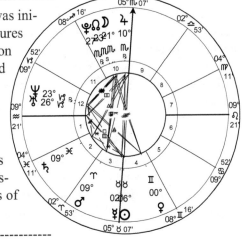

Nelson Mandela, 18 July 1918, 14:54, Mvezo, SA.

• Nelson Mandela, born a Xhosa in the Thembu royal family in Mvezo, led his people to freedom. Spiritually advanced, he was a gift to the nation. The Sabian Symbol for his Asc degree (24 Sagittarius), is "A blue 'bird' alights upon a little cottage. A blessing." Some speculate that he was born specifically to release black people from cruelty inflicted by white races.

   Born a fighter, he became an anti-apartheid revolutionary in the African National Congress.

• On the Asc are 2 stars located on the stinger of the Scorpion - *Lesath* and *Shaula* (23 Sagittarius). Vedics called them the "Two Releasers that brought relief from lingering disease." [1] This relates the stars to the healing power of Scorpio. Ruler Pluto, is a deity with the attributes of the serpent - a healer and giver of health, spiritual and physical. Mandela was gifted with the power to eliminate from the nation the poison of separateness and hate so that a healing process could begin. He started the process but it still has a long way to go.

7. The Republic of South Africa and Covid-19.

Lunar eclipse for Covid-19: 16 Jul 2019, 23:38, Pretoria; around S.Africa natal.

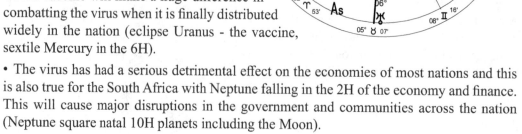

• Aware that its healthcare system had shortcomings, the government imposed a strict lockdown early. But as it began to ease restrictions numbers climbed. In spite of this, by 2021 - compared to other nations, it was doing relatively well. Almost 30 thousand people had died and 1.1 million were infected. South Africa was ranked 36th in the world for deaths per capita.

• But with the main eclipse planets falling across the 6th - 12th health houses and new more contagious variants appearing; it is likely that cases will surge in 2021. The Covid vaccine will make a huge difference in combatting the virus when it is finally distributed widely in the nation (eclipse Uranus - the vaccine, sextile Mercury in the 6H).

• The virus has had a serious detrimental effect on the economies of most nations and this is also true for the South Africa with Neptune falling in the 2H of the economy and finance. This will cause major disruptions in the government and communities across the nation (Neptune square natal 10H planets including the Moon).

---

1 Hinckley Allen, Richard; Star Names, 370.

• *Changes indicated by the Covid eclipse:* There is serious and disruptive trouble ahead (eclipse Mars square Uranus conjunct the angles of the chart and natal Sun). Rivalries between tribal groups and political factions will be fought out in the coming 33-year cycle. Hopefully in parliament rather than physical battles (eclipse Moon, Saturn, Pluto 12H).

8. The Spiritual Destiny of South Africa.

The personality of South Africa is ruled by Sagittarius.

• Since 1994, South Africa has been expressing through a Taurus Sun, giving a measure of stability. But the Sun's location on the IC cusp, opposite Jupiter on the MC; indicates the reality of the situation in South Africa at ground level - a new cycle in the struggle for national power and control is underway.

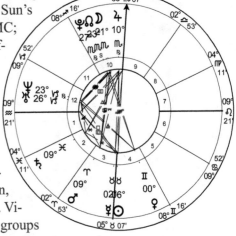

South Africa 1994 natal

• *Problem*: Sagittarius rules the 11H of politics, and ruler Jupiter dominates from the top of the chart. Ambitious people are being attracted to politics for the power and wealth it can bring (Jupiter trine Saturn in 2H of money). This poses grave risks for the fledging democratic nation, which is young in its psychological development. Vicious and brutal battles for power amongst tribal groups have been breaking across communities (Moon conjunct Pluto 10H, sesquiquadrate Mars in Aries 3H).

• Three planets that connect the 3rd and 10th houses are important for South Africa's destiny. These are Jupiter, because it is the soul ruler of Aquarius and of the nation's Sagittarius personality; and Mars and Mercury that rule Aries. This makes the field of communications a contest area between the soul and personality, for control of the nation. Whoever controls the narrative in the community, controls power.

The soul of South Africa is ruled by Aries.

• With beneficial Jupiter dominating the chart from the MC, there is a blessing and protection over the nation and people. From out of the conflict, long term, Jupiter will bring economic prosperity and stability (trine Saturn 2H, opposite Sun). The Sabian Symbol for Jupiter's degree is, "A drowning man is being rescued." [1] This is a promising omen. No matter what vicissitudes the nation goes through, it will survive. The nation will be rescued - just as Mandela came to the rescue in the 20th Century.

Jupiter is aligned with two beautiful stars in the Southern Cross (*Crux*) constellation - *Acrux* and *Mimosa* (11-12 Scorpio), the two brightest stars in the Cross. Although *Crux* can bring great suffering, this is part of the process to develop wisdom and insight.

• The Aries soul gifts the nation with will and power (Ray 1), and the power to organise and make things happen (Ray 7). Mandela drew on these forces to magically [2] give birth to the new South Africa. He epitomised the spirit of the advanced Aries soul:

---

1 Jones, Dr. Marc Edmund. Sabian Symbols, 191.

2 "Magic" is also an attribute of Ray 7.

Experience leads to rulership and in Aries, the man (nation) of power who has controlled his mind and has learned to act with love; has earned the right to guide the affairs of the world. South Africa's spiritual keynote is: "I come forth and from the plane of mind, I rule." [1]

• Since 1994, South Africa's Aries soul has been expressing through an Aquarius ascendant. This is fortunate because it will help future leaders develop and express intelligent control. Such people will bring in needed social reforms and guide the nation into the right and higher direction as Mandela did. Then South Africa can help other African nations do the same.

1   Bailey, Alice A. Esoteric Astrology, 108.

Spain

Spain's personality is ruled by Capricorn, its soul by Sagittarius. [1]

The psychology of Spain is masculine, mental, governing and empire-building - in the 17th to 19th centuries Spain established many colonies around the world. During this period, Capricorn ambition, severity and a lack of compassion dominated the nation's expression. But Spain is maturing spiritually and due to the influence of its Sagittarius soul, the people are becoming more liberal and philosophical.

1. Birth of the Kingdom of Spain: 19 January 1479, 12:00, Madrid.

Prince Ferdinand of Aragon and Princess Isabella of Castille united two Spanish crowns when they married in 1469. They assumed the Kingdom of Spain throne when Juan II died on 19 January 1479. This is the date set for the chart. 12-noon is used for the time.

• The noon chart places Jupiter in Taurus just above the ascendant, and this period of Spain's history was very prosperous and over-saw its expansion into colonies around the world.

• But this era of Spanish rule also gave birth to one of the most infamous periods in Catholic Church and Spanish history - the Spanish Inquisition.

2. Birth of the Spanish Inquisition: 1 Nov 1478, 12:00, Madrid.

The Catholic Church controlled Spain. On 1 November 1478, Pope Sixtus IV issued a papal bull, authorizing Catholic Monarchs to establish the Spanish Inquisition. This was the first major task confronting the new rulers, Ferdinand and Isabella. The Inquisition was created to maintain Catholic control in Europe, to be a watchdog and executioner for the Church and Pope. A judicial institution, it used brutal methods to uncover "heresy."

• The chart is dominated by planets in the death sign Scorpio, and appropriately, ruler Mars is in Capricorn in the 12H of hidden things. Torture in dungeons and other secret places was the method used to extract confessions from "heretics". People were murdered (Moon trine Pluto in the 8H of death). The institution was evil and did very bad things (the Sun - the Inquisition, aligned with the very evil and bloody star *Algol,* at 18 Taurus).

1 Bailey, Alice A. The Destiny of the Nations, 67.

Tomás de Torquemada, 14 Oct 1420, 12:00, Leon, Spain.

• Dominican friar Torquemada's name has become synonymous with the Inquisition's brutality. During his tenure, thousands were burnt at the stake. *(The birth time is unknown so a 12pm, 0 Aries rising chart is used).*

• He was the first Grand Inquisitor. Saturn in Virgo, is on the star *Nodus I* (25 Virgo), a star Arabs said was a hyena or wolf, lying in wait for the Camel's Foal (flushing out heretics).

Nodus is in Draco the Dragon who guarded the golden apples in the Garden of the Hesperides (according to one myth). Torquemada's job (6H) was to be a watchdog for his church.

• Torquemada was famous for his religious zeal and fanaticism (Pluto square Mars in Pisces). Pluto is on the star *Tejat Posterior* (27 Gemini), in the right heel of the Twin, representing how the Church placed its booted foot on the neck of the suffering masses.

By the 15th and 16th Centuries, inbreeding between the royal houses had rendered Spanish nobility physically and mentally weakened. Charles II (a Habsburg), who died childless in 1700, named Phillip, Duke of Anjou, heir to the crown. Phillip was of the French Bourbon Dynasty. He assumed the throne as King Phillip V in 1724 and was the first Spanish Bourbon. The current royals stem from his line.

----

3. Spain and the Spanish Flu, 1918.

Blood Moon eclipse for Flu: 15 Jul 1916, 04:40, Madrid; around Kingdom of Spain natal.

• Spain remained neutral during WWI and prospered as it exported supplies to both sides of the conflict. However, it did not escape the Spanish Flu, which from 1916 had been circulating amongst soldiers in Europe.

The virus entered Spain later, probably brought in by migrant workers from France, the virus' centre. The first public news of the epidemic in Europe appeared in a Spanish newspaper on 22 May 1918, which reported a strange influenza-like illness had been circulating. Because the flu was first publicly reported in Spain, it was dubbed the "Spanish Flu." The name stuck.

• The virus took a massive toll. Firstly, eclipse Neptune that represents the virus is on the 2 Leo epidemic degree, conjunct Spain's IC. Hitting an angle - especially the 4th that represents the people of the land was ominous. Secondly, eclipse Venus that rules the 6H of health, is conjunct Pluto the Lord of Death. 260,000 people died from the virus.

4. Birth of Spain's 2nd Republic: 14 Apr 1931, 12:45, Madrid.

By the mid-19th Century, republicans were agitating for change and they briefly controlled the nation - this was the 1st Spanish Republic (1873-1874).

Then the Bourbon's returned to the throne. But anti-royal sentiment rose again in the early 20th Century and an election victory led to the birth of the 2nd Spanish Republic (1931-39).

The 2nd Republic was proclaimed on 14 April 1931. 12-noon is used for the chart.

This democratically elected government was in power when the Civil War broke out. Thousands of people in the world who were deeply offended by the brazen power-grab of nationalists - a violation of democratic principles; came to Spain and fought on the side of the Republicans.

5. The Spanish Civil War: 1936–39.

Blood Moon eclipse for Civil War: 8 Jan 1936, 18:13, Madrid; around Spain 2nd Republic natal.

• The Spanish Civil War was triggered on 17 July 1936 by a nationalist alliance of monarchists, conservatives and Catholics, who wanted to overthrow the democratically elected republic (eclipse Uranus 10H, square natal Mars on Asc). Elevated Uranus favoured the revolutionaries.

• The war was bloody and ferocious (eclipse Moon hits the natal Jupiter-Pluto conjunction, forming a t-square with natal Uranus, eclipse Uranus square natal Mars on Asc). The many executions, murders, and assassinations on both sides reflected the great passions and hatreds involved (eclipse Pluto and Asc conjunct natal Mars 8H).

• Around 500,000 people died, which does not include those who died from malnutrition, starvation, and war-engendered disease (eclipse Moon conjunct Pluto, Sun in 6H of Health).

• Barcelona, the heart of Republican (Catalonian) resistance, fell in January 1939, and Madrid surrendered that March, effectively ending the conflict.

6. Birth of the Franco Republic: 1 Apr 1939, 12:00, Madrid

General; Francisco Franco (1892-1975), the leader of the nationalists, declared victory over the government on 1 April 1939, the day when Madrid finally fell and Republican resistance ended. A 12-noon time is used for the chart.

• Franco ruled Spain as a military dictator until his death in 1975 (military Aries planets dominate the chart from the 10H). He persecuted political opponents and repressed the culture and language of Spain's Basque and Catalan regions (Sun in Aries square Mars in Capricorn; Pluto on Asc, inconjunct Venus, ruler 4H of the people).

• Franco's government did not participate in WWII. However, Franco's sympathies clearly lay with Nazi Germany and Fascist Italy, who had given his regime support in the Civil War.

7. Birth of Democratic Spain: 22 November 1975, 12:45, Madrid.

Franco had vowed to restore the monarchy, and in 1969 picked Prince Juan Carlos, the grandson of King Alfonso XIII, as the next king.

On 22 November 1975 at 12:45, Juan Carlos (a Bourbon), was crowned King. The current chart for Spain originates from that date. A new constitution was adopted, transforming Spain into a parliamentary democracy under a constitutional or parliamentary monarchy.

The first post Franco elections were held in June 1977.

• The chart is beneficial for the nation's spiritual development because it has Neptune in Sagittarius, which is located in the 10H of power. Sagittarius rules the nation's soul.

• The chart is also helpful for the spiritualisation of the nation's values, with Neptune ruling the 2H of values and trine Jupiter in that house. It is also useful for the transformation of the nation so that it becomes fairer and more balanced in its policies (Neptune sextile Venus-Pluto 8H; Jupiter opposite Venus).

• However, Saturn which rules the nation's Capricorn personality is strong on an angle - the 7H cusp. This suggests conservative elements in the country can be influenced by zealous nationalistic activity in other nations. This would be detrimental to the direction in which the soul of Spain wishes to take the country (Saturn opposite the Asc).

8. Spain and Covid-19.

Lunar eclipse for Covid-19: 16 Jul 2019, 23:39, Madrid; around Spain Democracy natal

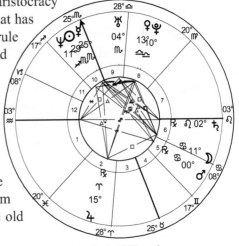

• The Spanish government instigated lock-downs early - in March 2020, but these were eased mid-year and further attempts to contain the spreading virus were spasmodic or inadequate. Consequently, Spain was hard hit and by 2021 there were 58 thousand dead and almost 2 million infected. This in a nation of 47 million people. [1]

• *Changes indicated by the Covid eclipse:* Spain's 1975 chart links the nation's karma to rampant diseases. Natal Saturn, Lord of Karma, is on the 2 Leo epidemic point, in the 6H of health. The eclipse Moon - and Saturn and Pluto that destroy old toxins, are in the 12H that is linked to unfinished business from the past.

These factors can be interpreted as an opportunity for the nation to pay back karmic debts from the past, through the pain and suffering caused by an epidemic such as Covid. What could the nature of this karma be? Saturn is also a symbol of the "Grand Inquisitor", which we can relate to the evil done by the Spanish Inquisition in the Middle Ages under Grand Inquisitor Tomas Torquemada.

9. The Spiritual Destiny of Spain.

The personality of Spain is ruled by Capricorn and Ray 7 of Ceremony, Order & Magic.

Spain was ruled for centuries by a dominant aristocracy and a politically-minded church. The problem that has come down to the present, is that the method of rule was arrogant and cruel (Capricorn personality) and fanatical and brutal (6th ray influence).

• In the 1479 national chart for Spain, Mars was in Pisces opposite Saturn, symbolising the fanaticism and harshness of the church and monarchy at that time.

The current 1975 chart also holds seeds of fanaticism with Sun in Scorpio, conjunct Neptune and inconjunct Mars. This poses a major problem for Spain, because it seems to still be using the old ways to sort out its internal problems.

Spain, 1975 natal

• The attempt to force standardization on the people by autocratic means is causing ongoing civil unrest. Basque

1   13 Jan 2021: the 12th ranked nation in the world for deaths per capita.

and Catalan troubles continue. And they will continue for as long as the old retrogressive attitudes for rigid dominance and control continue (Moon in Cancer that rules "forms," square Pluto 8H). The nation's soul is fighting to free the people from unnecessary physical controls and such conflicts will continue until its leaders start responding to the liberalising energies of the Aquarian Age. Covid and its after-effects will bring matters to a head.

• Positively, the 7th Ray that conditions the outer form of the nation has given the people of the nation great physical beauty and grace. This is also demonstrated in Spain's architecture, which is filled with magical-type buildings that blend Muslim and Christian design.

The soul of Spain is ruled by Sagittarius and Ray 6 of Idealism and Devotion.

• Since 1975, Spain's 6th ray, Sagittarius soul, has been expressing through an Aquarius ascendant. This has brought the full force of the incoming progressive energies to bear on crystallisations in the nation, accelerating the necessary freeing process. Sagittarius of all signs cannot abide any form of restriction. Embedded in the heart of every Spanish citizen is the urge to fly free. However, until the nation is fully integrated with national goals that are widely accepted, there will be future clashes.

> In Sagittarius, the arrow of the mind is projected unerringly towards the goal. Spain's spiritual keynote is: "I see the goal. I reach that goal and then I see another." [1]

Spain's spiritual motto is, "I disperse the clouds." [2]

• Ruled as it is by the magical 7th and the devotional 6th rays, the high spiritual goal for Spain is to give birth to a form of universal worship whose innovative rituals have a major spiritualising impact on the consciousness of those who practice them.

• This innovative change will arise from the people, from rituals practiced in certain regions, churches or groups across Spain (Uranus 9H trine the Moon in Cancer).

> "I disperse the clouds," is indicative of the magical work for which Spain will eventually be responsible [which concerns] the magical work of the Church of the future. [3]

In the context of this section, "dispersing the clouds" can be interpreted as the creation and discovery of spiritual practices that use music, sound, colour and invocation to reveal the nature of the soul; that will help people make conscious contact with their souls. This magical work which the Church of Spain is destined to initiate in the future, will accelerate humanity's spiritual evolution.

1 Bailey, Alice A. Esoteric Astrology, 654.
2 Bailey, Alice A. The Destiny of the Nations, 50.
3 Bailey, Alice A. The Destiny of the Nations, 62.

Sweden

Scandinavia-Sweden's personality is ruled by Cancer, its soul by Libra. [1]

Cancer is a water sign, representing the strong emotional and protective traits that characterise the people of the four Scandinavian nations. This was demonstrated by the clannish ties of the Vikings. Cancer is also a sign with strong links to the past and in particular, the gods and goddesses of Norse mythology. Christianity overtook the old religion when King Olof Skutkonung (995-1022) was converted in the early 11th century. This was a major step and hypothetically, Sweden's soul was influential during that stage.

Since those early days, the people have gradually been making the transition from Cancer emotionalism to mental alertness and balance that distinguishes Libra. It is the sign that represents justice and equality. In the future, as these four nations mature spiritually, and start to express Libra's force more effectively, they will stand closely together to ensure that all members in the family of man will be treated fairly and equally.

1. The Carolean Death March: 1719.

Weather events often reflect what is happening in humanity. During the 17th century, after winning wars against its neighbours, Sweden emerged as super-power that controlled the Baltic region. But it all ended in the early 18th century, when a coalition - led by Russia, defeated Sweden. Then a final humiliation occurred when its 1718 campaign in southern Norway also failed. The Carolean Death March occurred then. This disaster in nature symbolised Sweden's ultimate defeat as a super-power in the Baltic region.

Blood Moon eclipse for Death March: 9 Sep 1718, 21:05, Stockholm.

• After its defeat in Norway, Sweden's 6,000 remaining troops were ordered home. The route their leader chose was across the Tydal mountain range, a daunting task because the men were exhausted, poorly clothed and short of provisions. On the morning of 12 January 1719, they set out for the Swedish village of Handol - a distance of 55 kilometres. But that afternoon a violent blizzard struck. The storm was still raging on 14 January as the troops began arriving at Handol. About 3,000 men froze to death in the mountains, another 700 died later and 600 were crippled.

• The eclipse stellium is in the 5H, which rules speculation. The troop commander - Lieutenant-general Armfeldt, took a gamble when he chose the shorter but more dangerous route home. But it was ill-fated (eclipse Sun and Moon hit Pluto, the Lord of Death; the Sun is conjunct *Denebola* - 18 Virgo, a star that brings misfortune from the elements of nature). Additionally, Pluto and the Sun are semi-square Saturn in the 6H, which rules the army. Saturn is also the Lord of Winter, and in combination with air sign Libra (icy wind) and Pluto; represents the killer, blizzard storm.

---

1   Bailey, Alice A. The Destiny of the Nations, 68.

2. Birth of Constitutional Sweden: 7 Dec 1865, 15:30, Stockholm.

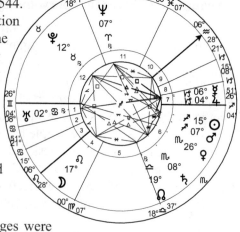

Sweden had been a hereditary monarchy since 1544. But in the 19th Century, as the industrial Revolution continued to free people from their servitude to the aristocracy, people became more active in their calls for democracy.

Heedful of this cry, on 7 Dec 1865, at around 3:30 pm, the nobility voted away their ruling privileges and Sweden became a Constitutional Monarchy with a parliamentary system.

The birth chart set up for that date is still used today as the national chart.

• The nobles who made the constitutional changes were progressive and ahead of their time. This quality was also growing in the national psyche, a progressive advancement represented in the chart by Uranus. It rules the 10H cusp of the house of governments and kings. Uranus is also rising in the 1H of the nation, in Cancer that rules public opinion and the people generally.

• Uranus opposes Mercury, indicating the growing mental acuity of the nation, a consequence of contact with foreign nations and cultures (Mercury conjunct Jupiter).

3. Sweden in World War I and the Spanish Flu.

Blood Moon eclipse for WWI: 15 Sep 1913, 13:46, Stockholm; around Sweden natal.

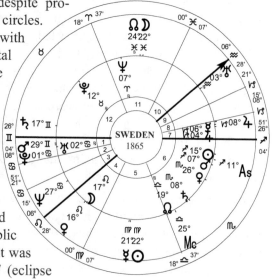

• Sweden declared neutrality in WWI, despite pro-German sentiment in royal and political circles. Moral issues aside, it was a lucky move with the eclipse Mars and Pluto falling in the natal 1H - on Uranus. If it had gone to war, there would have been massive casualties - both in lives lost and injuries to the nation's infrastructure (Moon, ruler 2H of business square Mars).

• Sweden continued to trade with Germany, especially iron ore that was needed for armaments. Consequently, Allied nations blockaded its ports, resulting in food shortages and this led to local riots. Public anger brought down the government, and it was replaced with a more liberal one in 1917 (eclipse Uranus on the MC).

• The eclipse t-square fell in the 1st (Mars, Pluto), 5th (Sun, Mercury), and 11th (the Moon) houses; indicating public, social and political disruption.

Lunar eclipse for Spanish Flu: 15 Jul 1916, 06:40, Stockholm; around Sweden natal.

• The Spanish flu reached Sweden in June 1918, creeping into army camps in remote Ostersund. From there it spread across the rest of the country like wild-fire, infecting one-third of the nation. (Eclipse Neptune is on the epidemic degree of 2 Leo, conjunct the 4H cusp of the people, trine Mars in the 6H. Mars rules soldiers). Sweden's population at the time was around 5.8 million.

Some 37,500 people died (Neptune square Saturn in the 6H which rules the 8H of death).

• The pandemic revealed disparities in health care. Victims were primarily the poor and impoverished who could not afford adequate healthcare. Consequently, Sweden introduced a welfare-system that takes care of such people. Concern and care for minority groups, for the poor and disadvantaged are hallmarks of a spiritually advanced nation.

4. Sweden in World War II.

Blood Moon eclipse for WWII: 3 May 1939, 16:17, Stockholm; around Sweden natal.

• Once again, Sweden remained neutral. It was allowed to do so by Hitler as long as it kept sending iron ore to Germany, which was required for Nazi weapon production. Sweden cooperated with the Nazis in a variety of ways, for instance, permitting the use of its rail system to transport soldiers on their way to attack the Soviet Union and Norway (eclipse Sun is trine the 7H of open enemies' planets, Mercury and Jupiter).

• As a consequence, the Allies blockaded Swedish ports and attacked its shipping (eclipse Saturn in Aries square Mars in the 9H of shipping).

• However, Sweden acted covertly (eclipse Sun-Uranus in 12H). It secretly allied with the Allies, supplying them with military intelligence, sheltered thousands of Jews fleeing from Nazi persecution and actively participated with the Allies in the last years of the war (natal Sun trine eclipse Mercury, in 11H of friends).

5. Boxing Day Earthquake and Tsunami in South East Asia, 26 Dec 2004.

This event was chosen because it is one of the worst natural disasters in recent years. It is placed here because Banda Aceh Indonesia, where the earthquake occurred, is not featured in this book. However, 543 Swedish nationals were killed and about 20,000 were in the region when the tsunami hit on 26 December, 05:07 local time (10:07 in Banda Aceh).

Blood Moon eclipse for Earth-quake and Tsunami, 28 Oct 2004,
local time 05:07 in Stockholm; around Sweden natal.

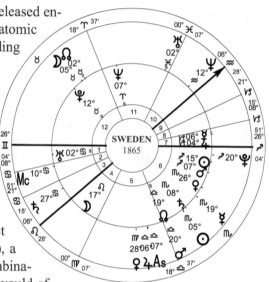

• The earthquake (9 on the Richter scale) released energy equivalent to 23,000 Hiroshima-type atomic bombs. Then tsunamis swept over surrounding countries killing about 230,000 people.

• Neptune rules the oceans and all extreme ocean weather events. Eclipse Neptune was conjunct *Armus* (13 Aquarius), a star in Capricornus that warns of major sea storms.[1] It dominates Sweden's natal chart from the MC; forming a grand-cross with the eclipse Moon and Sun and with the natal Moon in the 4H.

• Eclipse Pluto, Lord of Death, was conjunct a chart angle and *Maasym* (20 Sagittarius), a star in the Hercules constellation. The combination warned of a coming mega-event that would affect large portions of mankind. [2]

6. Sweden and Covid-19.

Lunar eclipse for Covid-19: 16 Jul 2019, 23:39,
Stockholm; around Sweden natal.

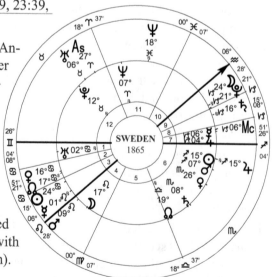

• In 2020, Sweden's chief epidemiologist, Anders Tegnell, floated the idea that a higher death rate among older people might be acceptable if it led to faster herd immunity. [3]

The government acted on this. Instead of locking down, it chose to keep most schools and businesses open, bartering lives against commercial and international trade interests (eclipse Moon and Sun span 3rd - 9th houses).

By 6 January 2021, Sweden was ranked 23rd in the world for deaths per capita, with 9,262 thousand dead (population 10 million).

---

1 Noonan, George; Fixed Stars and Judicial Astrology, 51.
2 Noonan, George; Fixed Stars and Judicial Astrology, 15.
3 https://www.abc.net.au/news/2020-08-20/sweden

• With the virus accelerating, finally, some containment measures were put in place. But, with the malevolent group of stars *Praesepe* and the *Aselli* (7 Leo) on Sweden's IC - triggered by eclipse Mercury and Mars; it was too little too late. Ironically, Sweden's economy suffered just as badly as nations who were more vigilant in trying to contain the disease.

• *Problems and changes indicated by the Covid eclipse.* The natal Moon in Leo rules the nation's 2H of money. Its square to Pluto in Taurus, indicates that those who manipulate the countries affairs for profit and gain (such as Anders Tegnell), need to be confronted and stopped. But the major problem concerns big-business interests and their agents who operate from behind the scenes (Pluto in the 12H of hidden things). These forces are trying to take the country in a direction that runs counter to the moral and ethical interests of the nation. With eclipse Uranus falling on natal Pluto, such dealings will begin to be exposed and dealt with in the coming cycle.

• Another problem concerns the rise in nationalist and popularist politics. This is the negative side of protective Cancer. Retrogressive voices in the nation have set out to convince people that recent immigration has brought crime, has lowered the social safety net and is detrimental to the national culture and traditions. (The eclipse Sun and Moon in the 3rd - 9th communication and idealism houses). Some people are susceptible and are responding. The more advanced members of the community need to counterbalance the negative messages coming from these groups. With Gemini rising in Sweden's chart, taking control of the narrative in the country is vital to ensure the nation is not driven off-course.

7. The Spiritual Destiny of Sweden.

The personality of Sweden is ruled by Cancer.

• All 4 Scandinavian countries are ruled by Cancer on the personality level. It is interesting, that the other three - Denmark, Iceland and Norway, all have Gemini Suns. Only Sweden is different. It has a Sagittarius Sun and Gemini rising. This sets it apart from the others. This difference can be gauged in the way the Covid crisis was approached. Sweden is a risk-taker and looks further ahead than the other more thoughtful three (Gemini).

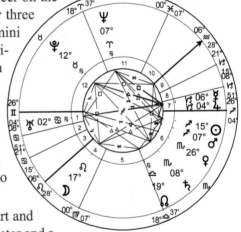

Sweden 1865 natal

• Positively, Sweden is an adventurous and confident nation composed of people who love to travel to all corners of the earth.

• Neptune is the most elevated planet in the chart and reveals an aspirational side to the Swedish character and a desire to do the right thing (it is in a wide grand-trine with the Sun and Moon). Politicians demonstrating this aspiration (Neptune 11H), have helped guide the nation to where it is today. One such politician was Prime Minister Olof Palme who was shot and killed in 1986. No one has been convicted for the murder. However, in 1996, a former South African police officer, gave evidence to the Supreme Court in Pretoria, alleging that Palme was killed because he "opposed the apartheid regime and Sweden made substantial contributions to the ANC". Whether this is correct or not, sacrificing one's life for a higher cause is in Sweden's chart (Neptune in Aries square Jupiter).

The soul of Sweden is ruled by Libra.

• Sweden is a spiritually advanced nation and because it is ruled in its soul by Libra, fairness and equality are important values influencing the nation. Consequently, the nation has become ethnically and religiously homogeneous, has an advanced welfare state and a standard of living and life expectancy that rank among the highest in the world.

• The most important planet in the chart for Sweden's spiritual growth is Uranus, which energises the nation's soul. Rising near the Asc, it keeps the nation moving towards the Aquarian Age. Retrograde at Sweden's birth, Uranus turned direct in the late 1950s and the nation has been more outwardly proactive since then. Uranus' goal is to accelerate the psychological and spiritual advancement of the people (Uranus in Cancer 1H), so that the nation is expressive of the Aquarian Age principles of universal brotherhood.

• Two stars conjunct Uranus are helping Sweden achieve this goal - *Propus* and *Dirah* (2 and 3 degrees in the Gemini constellation). *Dirah* gives power and protection and through Sweden, the power to protect nations in need. *Propus* gives the power to express ideas in reasonable and acceptable ways. The constellation Gemini endows the nation with "an agreeable life, harmonious melodies and unfading youth". [1] Wonderful gifts for Sweden's world role.

• Acting as an arbiter of peace in the world is the higher task all Scandinavian countries are called on to play because of their shared Libra-soul rulership. Their collective higher goal is to become a reconciliating force in world affairs.

> Sweden's spiritual keynote is: "I choose the way which leads between the two great lines of force." [2]

---

1   Manilius, Marcus; Astronomica, 235.
2   Bailey, Alice A. Esoteric Astrology, 654.

Switzerland

Switzerland's personality is ruled by Aquarius, its soul by Aries. [1]

In the past, Switzerland demonstrated the remoteness and isolationist tendencies that are often associated with Aquarius, that of "living in a glass tower." But it is an integrated nation and evidence that the higher qualities of Aquarius are also influencing can be seen in the proliferation of human rights organisations within its borders. With leadership sign Aries ruling its soul, and the increasing spiritual influence of its centre, Geneva; the nation will come increasingly to the fore to lead the way in protecting the rights and freedoms of the world's citizens.

1. Landslide on Pleurs, Switzerland, 4 September 1618.

Mountainous Switzerland is a natural region for landslides and avalanches and there have been numerous through the ages. This one at the village of Pleurs was hugely destructive.

Total Solar eclipse for Landslide: 21 Jul 1618, 20:15, Pleurs, 46N20, 9E25.

• Saturn that rules mountains is on the IC, representing the foundations of the mountain that had become unstable through careless mining (the eclipse in the 6H of work). Saturn also rules mining. Heavy rain exacerbated the weaknesses (Saturn square Jupiter in Pisces).

• The landslide occurred at midnight, burying the entire village and killing an estimated 1000 to 2500 people. (Saturn is conjunct *Aldebaran* {4 Gemini} and opposite *Antares* {4 Sagittarius}, stars that bring malefic and evil calamities when afflicted. Here is a local account:

> Pleurs laid under a steep rock wall that was torn apart by a mighty subterranean force and thrown on the city, the greatest part of it buried and destroyed with all churches, houses and palaces. Pleurs was beaten into the earth. [2]

When it happened, violent Mars was conjunct the eclipse Sun and Moon. Pleurs was left as it was. Nothing remained - only a church bell was found. The area is now used for pasture and agriculture. In the aftermath, stricter controls over mining methods were introduced.

Perhaps the landslide symbolised what would have happened to Switzerland if it had fought in the Thirty Years War (1618-1648), which began as a religious dispute but ended up as a fight for control of central Europe. It remained neutral and benefitted at the Treaty of Westphalia in 1648, when the Swiss Confederacy gained legal independence from the Holy Roman Empire. This set it up positively for economic prosperity in the 17th and 18th Centuries. Additionally, its population grew as Protestants fled there for sanctuary from retributive Catholics, reinforcing its growing reputation as a tolerant and neutral nation.

---

1 Bailey, Alice A. The Destiny of the Nations, 67.
2 Eberhard Werner Happel in his "Relationes curiosae, oder Denckwürdigkeiten der Welt", published in a first edition with various volumes in the years 1683 to 1689

2. Birth of Constitutional Switzerland: 12 Sep 1848, 12:55, Bern.

In 1845, cantons united and on 12 September 1848, a federal constitution was signed. The current national chart stems from then. Campion gives a time of 11:12, [1] which gives Switzerland a Scorpio Asc. However, 12:55 is given by Astro Databank as an alternative, "because people testified that a few minutes before the vote was finished, the 1 pm bells began to toll." [2] This latter time is used in this book.

• Aspirational and spiritual Sagittarius is a better fit for the Asc than war-like Scorpio. Aries, the sign that rules Switzerland's soul, governs the 4H. Located there are Uranus and Pluto, portending the location of humanitarian organisations to Switzerland with the aim of helping the suffering masses.

3. The Red Cross: 9 February, 1863.

Blood Moon eclipse for the Red Cross: 6 Dec 1862, 08:02, Geneva.

• The organisation was born from suffering, which a Blood Moon often signifies. Swiss national Henry Dunant, witnessed the suffering caused by the lack of medical support for injured soldiers in the Battle of Solferino on 24 June 1859. It inspired him to found the Red Cross, whose purpose was to provide assistance to victims of disasters, armed conflicts and health crises. Since then, it has helped millions in the world.

• The eclipse chart is amazing. The main configuration is a Mystic Rectangle. On one side is Jupiter trine Moon-Uranus; on the other Mars trine Sun-Venus. These planets link to form the other two sides of the rectangle.

A Mystic Rectangle is associated with "good works"; constructing something positive and beneficial for the greater good (the trines and sextiles), from challenges, difficulties and tragedies (the oppositions).

• The eclipse portended the birth of a visionary organisation (Sagittarius planets and north-node conjunct the Asc), born to help suffering souls (Sagittarius planets opposite the Moon in the 6H of health); people who are victims of war (Mars at the bottom point of the rectangle, in military Aries), of revolution (Moon conjunct Uranus), and of other natural and human-caused catastrophes.

1   Campion, Nicholas. The Book of World Horoscopes, 309.
2   https://www.astro.com/astro-databank/Nation:_Switzerland_1848

Natal chart for the Red Cross: 9 Feb 1863, 12:00, Geneva.

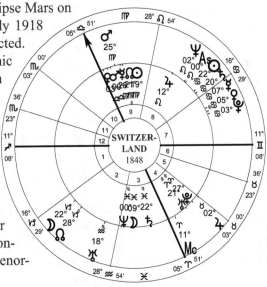

• The Red Cross is an international. humanitarian organisa-tion (Sun trine Jupiter, trine Uranus). Its purpose is to provide compassionate care (Neptune) in disasters or times of war (Aries).

• The Red Cross is truly an agent of the Aquarian Age with humanitarian Uranus on the ascendant of this 12-noon chart; trine the Sun in Aquarius.

   Uranus is conjunct military star *Rigel* (15 Gemini), in the Orion constellation. It is one of the brightest stars in the night sky. *Rigel* repre-sents the bloodshed and sickness that war brings, but also honourable actions in war that is distinc-tive of this humanitarian organisation.

• The benevolent and caring nature of the organisation is indicated by the Aquarius Sun trine Jupiter and the Moon in peace-loving Libra.

4. Switzerland in the World Wars and Spanish Flu.

Switzerland remained neutral during both World Wars. What saved it in WWI was its moun-tainous topography (unsuited for tanks), its well-organised army, making concessions to Germany and showing that its neutrality could be useful in terms of its humanitarian en-deavours. For example, it took in thousands of wounded soldiers from both sides. Additional-ly, Swiss banking prospered - most useful for the Nazi's who used Switzerland as a major hub for the sale and transfer of looted art during WWII.

Lunar eclipse for Spanish Flu: 15 Jul 1916, 05:40, Bern; around Switzerland natal.

• The Spanish Flu had a violent impact (eclipse Mars on the natal 9H stellium). It first appeared July 1918 and more than 50% of the nation was infected. Over 24,000 died. This makes the pandemic the most serious demographic catastrophe in modern Swiss history.

a. The eclipse stellium, Saturn to Neptune, falls in the natal 8H of trauma and death, square Uranus-Pluto 4H.

b. Eclipse Pluto, Lord of Death, squares natal Venus, ruler of the 6H of health.

c. Eclipse Neptune that rules viruses, and is on the 2 Leo, Sabian Symbol degree for pandemics; is square eclipse Jupiter that con-juncts Pluto - making the disease's impact enor-mous and catastrophic.

Blood Moon eclipse for WWII: 3 May 1939, 16:16, Bern; around Switzerland natal.

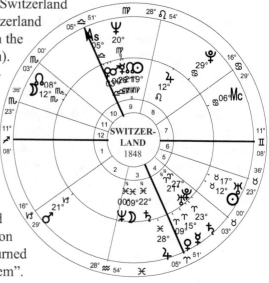

• There were many Nazi sympathisers in Switzerland and the Swiss Nazi party tried to get Switzerland to unify with Germany (Mars, ruler 11H, in the 2H of values, on *Sulaphat*, 21 Capricorn). This star is in Lyra, whose symbol (an eagle carrying a lyre), is very similar to that of the Nazis (eagle carrying a swastika). The move failed because of the nation's sense of national identity and tradition of democracy and civil liberties (eclipse Sun-Uranus trine natal Sun).

• Altruism did not entirely guide Switzerland's policies. Swiss banking profited and although 27,000 Jews fleeing Nazi persecution were permitted entry, almost as many were turned away, because of "an inability to support them".

5. Switzerland and Covid-19.

Lunar eclipse for Covid-19: 16 Jul 2019, 23:39, Bern; around Switzerland natal.

• Initially, the government resisted stern measures to contain the virus. Some suggest its leaders thought the country could remain above the troubles of Covid, as it had in the past remained above the worst effects of the World Wars.

Its agenda was to get the economy up and running (eclipse Saturn ruling the 2H and located there; opposite the Sun). Swiss Finance Minister Ueli Maurer is recorded as saying, "We can't afford a second lockdown. We don't have the money for it. A new lockdown would risk sacrificing the economy and public finances on the altar of health." [1]

• Like the Netherlands, Sweden and many other nations in the world, Switzerland bartered the nation's health against the economy. Maurer's remark, "the altar of health," revealed his condescension towards the sacredness of human life and efforts made to preserve it.

This was a dangerous attitude with the eclipse Sun falling in the 8H of death. Better advice would have come from an astrologer. Consequently, by 2021, there were over 7.7 thousand dead (in a population of 8.5 million), and it ranked 20th in the world for deaths per capita. With new waves of the virus driven by mutant strains accelerating in 2021, there would be a heavy toll to pay by the time it is all over.

1 https://foreignpolicy.com/2020/11/10/coronavirus-switzerland-is-choosing-austerity-over-life/

6. The Spiritual Destiny of Switzerland.

The personality of Switzerland is ruled by Aquarius; and the 2nd Ray that flows through Geneva.

• Aquarius rules Switzerland's personality. In the past, its detached and remote qualities were seen in the nation's efforts to remain disconnected from the troubles of the world. Positively, Aquarius has gifted the nation with the ability to form friendships and mutually beneficial political alliances. This has helped it to obtain and keep its neutral status.

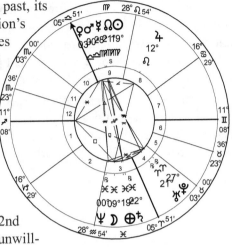

Switzerland 1848 natal

• Since 1848, Switzerland's personality has been expressing through a precise and meticulous Virgo Sun. This has been widely demonstrated through, for example, precise Swiss watch-making and engineering.

The down-side of Virgo and Pisces and the 2nd Ray that flows through both signs, is greed. An unwillingness to disturb one's prosperity and comfort even if others suffer (Pisces Moon). For example, in the mid-20th Century, some Swiss Banks were allegedly havens for criminal fortunes and money-laundering. This was considered okay at that time because business-men considered themselves exempt from moral and ethical scrutiny.

Counterbalancing Virgo greed is the Earth, the esoteric ruler of Sagittarius, located exactly opposite the Sun at 19 Pisces. The Earth is in universal Pisces conjunct responsible Saturn, in the 3H. This can be interpreted as giving responsible and caring service to Switzerland's neighbourhood of nations. Its community of cantons is a model for its relationships with the world community.

• *Problem*: there is another crisis looming. Switzerland has not remained immune to the rise of populist "me-first" politics sweeping the world. This self-interest has been exploited by far-right politics - "The Swiss People's party." It has become a force in Switzerland (Moon semi-square Uranus in the 4H of home). The battle for the soul of the nation continues.

The soul of Switzerland is ruled by Aries; and by the 1st Ray of Will and Power that flows through Geneva.

• Switzerland is destined to be a world-leader (Aries and the 1st ray), in spreading human rights values (Aquarius) and fusing world nations together in love and peace. Geneva, and therefore Switzerland's spiritual motto is: "I seek to fuse, to blend and serve." [1]

> The force which the centre at Geneva is expressing is that of the second Ray of Love-Wisdom, with its major emphasis at this time upon the quality of inclusiveness. It is concerned with the "binding together in brotherly love" and with the expression of the nature of service. [2]

• Since 1848, Switzerland's Aries soul has been expressing through Sagittarius, which promotes new ventures and projects that have a moral and spiritual basis.

---

1   Bailey, Alice A. *The Destiny of the Nations*, 58.
2   Bailey, Alice A. *The Destiny of the Nations*, 96.

So, it is not surprising that shortly after this rebirth, the Red Cross was founded (in 1863). This was followed by a proliferation of humanitarian organisations being stationed there. This is evidence of the spiritual maturity of the nation as a whole. Goodwill organisations are comfortable in Switzerland's purer atmosphere.

In this regard, it is very interesting that Uranus is aligned with a famous ship-wreck star *Baten Kaitos*. It is a topaz yellow star in the belly of the Sea Monster, Cetus; "a stormy star, known for shipwrecks and drowning." [1] The star defines more clearly, Switzerland's service role in the world - to be a peaceful and protective haven for troubled souls fleeing "ship-wreck" type situations in other parts of the world.

• Switzerland is in the process of becoming the spiritual heart of the planet. In a fashion similar to how the physical heart pumps life-giving blood around the body to nourish all cells; Switzerland - through its humanitarian organisations, is sending out love and practical support to all the needy in the world.

---

1   Rosenberg, Diana K. Interview with Edith Hathaway, 22 July 2010.

Turkey

Turkey's personality is ruled by Scorpio, its soul by Cancer. [1]

Turkey has long been warlike in its history, unsurprisingly so with Scorpio ruling its personality. Its leaders are highly protective and defensive of the nation and more so in recent years as the Cancer soul influence starts to take effect. But this is still functioning at the personality level. When higher Cancer begins to influence, Turkey's eventual role is to be defensive for the well-being of the world, to nurture humanity.

1. Birth of the Ottoman Empire: 29 May 1453, 12:00, Constantinople.

The Ottoman Empire and dynasty (1300–1923) was founded by Osman I, a nomadic Turkmen chief, in about 1300. It became a super-power, reaching its height on 29 May 1453, when it captured Constantinople under the leadership of Mehmet II. The chart is set for this date with a 12-noon time.

• Constantinople was the seat of the Byzantine, East Roman Empire. By capturing the city with all its symbolic historical might and power, Mehmet viewed himself as the "Caesar of Rome", the inheritor of the Roman Empire with all the status this brought with it. Taking the city allowed the Ottoman's to move into Eastern Europe.

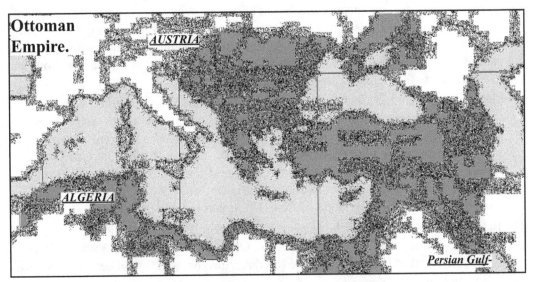

Ottoman Empire.

AUSTRIA

ALGERIA

Persian Gulf

At its peak, the Ottoman Empire (the dark-shaded areas), reached as far north as Austria, east as far as the Persian Gulf, west to Algeria, and as far south as Yemen (off the map).

---

1 Bailey, Alice A. The Destiny of the Nations, 68.

2. Famine in Anatolia (Turkey): 1873-1874.

<u>Blood Moon eclipse for the Famine: 12 May 1873, 13:14, Istanbul.</u>

Plagues and drought were a constant threat and in 1873 Turkey had a devastating famine.

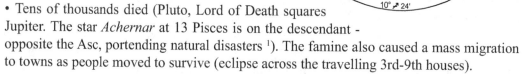

• Saturn, rules agriculture and is the Lord of Winter. It is in a grand-cross that symbolises great trouble to come. First came drought (Saturn opposite Uranus in fiery Leo), which destroyed crops (Pluto square Jupiter in Leo. Jupiter rules the 4H: village life, the weather and crops).

• After the crops failed, there was a freezing winter (Saturn afflicted, Moon on the star *Agena* at 22 Scorpio, "death by coldness"). Isolated communities could not move to save themselves (Jupiter in 12H of isolation). People began to starve.

• Tens of thousands died (Pluto, Lord of Death squares Jupiter. The star *Achernar* at 13 Pisces is on the descendant - opposite the Asc, portending natural disasters [1]). The famine also caused a mass migration to towns as people moved to survive (eclipse across the travelling 3rd-9th houses).

• The famine was a symbol of the Empire, which had become old, dry and decrepit. The evolutionary pattern was Uranus opposite Saturn - the shattering of rigid structures. Although the Balkan Wars were decades away, it was a forecast of what was to come.

3. The Balkan Wars (1912-1913).

By the 1600s, the power of European nations was on the ascent. In comparison, the Ottoman Empire was in decline - economically and militarily. Weak and still medieval in many ways, it began to lose its lands in a series of wars. Concerned, in 1908, young Turk reformers staged a revolt and began to flex their muscles in the region. This alarmed neighbouring nations. But it also provided them with an opportunity to gain independence from the Empire. This led to the Balkan Wars, of which there were two.

The first war (October 1912 to May 1913). The Balkan League (Serbia, Bulgaria, Greece and Montenegro), attacked and defeated the Ottoman Turks. It was a vicious and brutal clash. Most of the Ottoman territories west of Istanbul were taken. As a consequence of the victory, Albania became an independent nation, Crete was united with Greece, and the rest of the conquered territories were parcelled out between the victorious aggressors. But Bulgaria was unhappy with its share and it started the 2nd Balkan War (June - July 1913). It was quickly defeated.

The Balkan hostilities resulted in huge casualties. Death toll estimates are: Bulgaria 65,000; Greece 9,500; Montenegro 3,000; Serbia 36,000; Ottomans 125,000 dead. Additionally, it is estimated that a total of 1.5 million Muslim civilians died or were forcibly exiled as a result of the Balkan Wars.

1 Brady, Bernadette. Fixed Stars, 142.

Lunar eclipse for Balkan Wars: 26 Sep 1912, 13:08, Istanbul; around Ottoman Empire natal.

• The war eclipse was terrible for the Empire. The eclipse Sun and Moon were in a t-square with Pluto, dominating the Empire from the 10H.

• Uranus, representing the new and vigorous younger nations was challenging the weakened Islamic caliphate (opposite Neptune). The opposition started forming in 1903, making six exact oppositions from 1905 to 1910. Preceded by skirmishes, when the war proper started in 1912, these planets came close to forming another opposition before finally separating. The die was cast

• The enemy was fast, aggressive and bloodthirsty (Moon in Aries, 7H. The young-wolves attacked, severely wounding the weary old buck. The "sick old man of Europe" as it was derisively called, began a terminal decline.

• The Moon is conjunct the star *Deneb Kaitos* (1 Aries), a star in the Sea Monster, *Cetus*. Afflicted, it brings out the worst in war - "harsh, cruel and vindictive actions." [1] There were many reports of atrocities being committed.

Redrawn Map after the Balkan Wars.

The map shows the Balkan States (in bold type) and the approximate national boundaries formed from the old Ottoman Empire.

---

1 Rigor, Joseph; The Power of Fixed Stars, 47.

4. Turkey in World War I.

Blood Moon eclipse for WWI: 15 Sep 1913, 14:46, Istanbul;
around Ottoman Empire natal.

• WWI, which was ignited by the Balkan hostilities, finished off the Ottoman Empire. Its leaders made the fateful decision to align with Germany.

• This war eclipse was similar to that for the Balkan's War, which was a bad omen for the Empire. The eclipse Sun and Moon in a t-square with destructive Pluto and brutal Mars; dominate the Empire's nation (1H), its rulers (10) and its defences (7H).

• Eclipse Saturn on the natal MC and Sun, represents the rigidity of the Empire. Under the stress of war, the Empire broke apart.

• In the aftermath of the Great War, the Allied powers stripped all Arab provinces from the Ottoman Empire, giving independence to Armenia and Kurdistan. Small states invaded Turkey   , wanting to grab any last remnants. But the great war-leader Mustafa Kemal, rallied resistance and drove them out, including the residue of British, French and Italian troops.

Mustafa Kemal: 4 Jan 1881, 06:00, Salonika, Greece. [1]

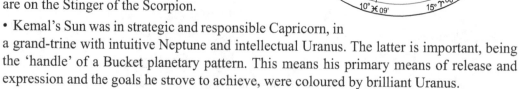

Kemal has a Scorpio-eagle look, with strong bones, piercing eyes, eyebrows that sweep up at the ends and a hawkish nose. On the Asc, that represents how one looks, is Mars that rules Scorpio and two stars in the Scorpius constellation - *Lesath* and *Shaula* (22-23 Sagittarius). Not only does he have a Scorpio appearance, he had the character of a great Scorpio military war-leader. Renowned for bravery, for his astute political and military manoeuvres, he struck his opponents with lethal skill where they were most weak. *Lesath* and *Shaula* are on the Stinger of the Scorpion.

• Kemal's Sun was in strategic and responsible Capricorn, in a grand-trine with intuitive Neptune and intellectual Uranus. The latter is important, being the 'handle' of a Bucket planetary pattern. This means his primary means of release and expression and the goals he strove to achieve, were coloured by brilliant Uranus.

---

1   Kemal's birth details are disputed. Astro.com gives the birth date as 4 January 1881, citing information "based on archive files from the Headquarters of Ataturk's Mausoleum." The 6 am birth time comes form "The historian Cemal Kutay.. 6 am given by close friends of Ataturk." The chart using this data suits the war-leader.

• Kemal was a nation builder, a social reformer and a progressive humanitarian, which is evident in the country's 1921 constitution that he helped to write. It included the words:

> To safeguard the prosperity and material and spiritual well-being of the Republic of Turkey, a democracy based on freedom. [1]

This titan amongst men was later honoured with the title Ataturk, or "Father of the Turks".

5. Birth of the Republic of Turkey: 29 Oct 1923, 20:30, Ankara.

Kemal Ataturk served as Prime Minister of the Grand National assembly from 1920 to 1921; and became the 1st President of Turkey on the day the Republic of Turkey was declared

----

The Republic of Turkey was born on 29 October 1923, with the declaration made at 20:30. This chart is used today.

• Pluto rising: represents the traumatic circumstances from which the nation was reborn and the intense manner in which it now approaches life.

• Moon in the 12H: psychologically, a period of introspection, time out for rehabilitation and healing.

• Uranus on the MC: the nation was reborn with a new generation of leaders to take the nation into the modern age.

6. Turkey and Covid-19.

Lunar eclipse for Covid-19: 16 Jul 2019, 23:38, Ankara; around Turkey natal.

• Initially, Turkey appeared to be handling Covid well. But by the end of 2020, its serious effects could no longer be hidden. There were over 21 thousand dead and 2.2 million infected (eclipse Jupiter, ruler 6H of health, is in the 6th, square Neptune that rules viruses).

Still, Turkey has a large population with 82 million people. By 2021 it was doing reasonably well in world deaths by capita, ranking 49th. [2] But, with the ruler of Covid - Neptune, conjunct the MC, there was no room for complacency. 2021 brought in new variant strains of the disease.

• *Changes indicated by the Covid eclipse:* with most eclipse planets falling in the 1st and 7th houses, the way Turkey handles internal affairs

1 Excerpt from the Constitution of the Republic of Turkey.
2 13 Jan 2021: the 49th ranked nation in the world for deaths per capita.

and its foreign relations are targeted for change. Autocratic leaders such as Tayyip Erdogan (President of Turkey in 2021), are often in peril after such a catastrophe. If he does not handle Covid well it is likely his leadership will be challenged (Neptune on MC square Jupiter 6H). However, he still retains popularity with large sections of the community (eclipse Sun and Moon in easy aspect to Neptune and the MC). Eclipse Neptune on the MC indicates the nation continues to be strongly influenced by its religion and religious leaders.

• Potentially, eclipse Neptune also indicates the gradual dissolving of Erdogan's power from 2019 onwards and a redefinition of the role that religion plays in government. Neptune is first and foremost a transformational planet, whose role is to keep humanity moving forwards. It just works more subtly than Uranus and Pluto. Definite change *is* portended with its conjunction with natal Uranus. Hopefully, Ataturk's model for a democratic nation will start to regain ground in the coming 33-year cycle.

7. The Spiritual Destiny of Turkey.

The personality of Turkey is ruled by Scorpio.

• Turkey is a Cancer-Scorpio country and its current chart has the Asc in Cancer and Sun in Scorpio. Given time, this will be spiritually beneficial.

But in the early 21st Century, it is clear that the personality of the nation is dominant again. The defensive and aggressive traits of lower Cancer and Scorpio have come to the fore. Democracy and civil rights have deteriorated while at the same time, an aggressive foreign policy has been pursued. Women's rights have gone backwards. President Erdogan and those who think like him, are trying to force women back into a more restrictive Muslim model (negative Pluto conjunct the Cancer ascendant).

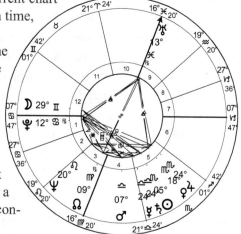

Turkey 1923 natal

• All these negative expressions are fed by the force which the Moon in the 12H represents. These are the attitudes and ideas of many in the community who want to take the nation back to its old Ottoman, Islam, conservative traditions (Moon, trine Saturn, sextile Neptune). Such people are trying to halt progressive cultural changes (5H of culture emphasis). Trying to go back to the past, against the flow of evolution, which is heading into the Aquarian Age of liberal freedoms, is a recipe for death.

• Highlighting this message is the Moon's location on *Menkalinan* (29 Gemini), a star in the constellation Auriga, the Charioteer, which (negatively aspected) is associated with savage and harsh tempests in nature and wars that bring ruin and violent death.

> The Charioteer lifts his team from the ocean where icy Boreas lashes with his bitter blasts, holds in check the 4 mouths curbed with foam-flecked bits the spirited steeds outstrip the winds. [1]

---

1 Manilius, Marcus; Astronomica, 305-309

The soul of Turkey is ruled by Cancer.

• Turkey's soul is ruled by Cancer and its higher contribution to the world is to become a nurturing mother, protector and defender of the needs and freedoms of all people. But first it has to bring its own house into order by instituting liberal freedoms.

Traditional Turkish culture is patriarchal and very family oriented. Family is the main social structure in the nation. Under modernization, this model has been changing. Now there is more egalitarianism in gender roles and young people are more independent. The development of a family model that suits the needs of all citizens in the country is Turkey's higher goal.

Then Turkey must take steps to help its neighbours do the same, "develop a family model that suits the needs of all citizens in the country." Particularly the Balkan nations (Neptune in 3H), a karmic requirement since the Ottoman Empire ruled this region for centuries and many of its policies were repressive.

However, this "model" of the ideal family must be shaped by spiritually advanced leaders in the nation, and be based on Aquarian values of universal brotherliness. This will build a lighted "family" house that all nations in eastern Europe are comfortable with.

> The objective of the Cancer experience and the purpose for which incarnation has been taken is: "I build a lighted house and therein dwell." [1] This is Turkey's spiritual keynote.

• Neptune is located on two stars in the Leo constellation (*Algenubi* and *Ras Elased Borealis*, at 20 Leo). In its lowest expression, Leo is cruel, brutish and destructive and this chart indicates that these traits are present in Turkey and they need to be dissolved and refined. At its highest, Neptune in Leo is the spiritual warrior-king with a huge heart and tremendous courage; fighting to the death to protect his tribe - in this case, the family of man. This is Turkey's spiritual future.

---

1   Bailey, Alice A. *Esoteric Astrology*, 654.

United Kingdom

The United Kingdom's personality is ruled by Taurus, its soul by Gemini. [1]

The United Kingdom [2] has had a profound effect upon the world in terms of its culture and human-rights principles that have been adopted by most nations. It has been stubborn and staunch in acquiring its material aims and is still a force to be reckoned with economically (Taurus). But as other nations rise in power and its Gemini soul increases its influence, it is changing. From its material Taurus past, the United Kingdom (UK) is transitioning into the role of being a wise, elder statesman, guiding the world's people into right ways of living through the wisdom of its thoughts and words.

1. Norman Invasion 1066, and the Magna Carta, 1215.

The origins of the UK can be traced to the time of the Anglo-Saxon king Athelstan, who in the 10th century united with Celtic kingdoms and became ruler. Edward the Confessor, was the last Anglo-Saxon king. The Norman invasion was triggered when he named Harold II as his successor. This infuriated William the Conqueror (Edward's cousin), because Edward had promised him the throne in 1051. William invaded England on 28 Sep 1066 and Harold was killed at the Battle of Hastings on 14 October. William was the first Norman King of England, reigning until his death in 1087.

Solar eclipse for the Invasion and Battle of Hastings: 22 Sep 1066, 05:51, Hastings.

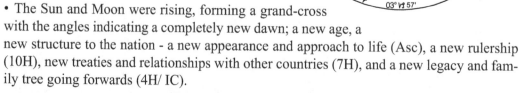

• The eclipse was an annular solar eclipse, where the Moon covers the face of the Sun except for a corona of fire around its perimeter. It is a portrayal in nature of the events to follow. The Sun represents the king - the Moon covering its face symbolises the death of one king, and the crown of fire, the rising or birth of a new one.

• Venus, the dawn star, dominates the chart. It rules the ascendant, the eclipse and the 9H of foreigners with Taurus on that cusp. Located on the Asc, it symbolises a foreigner assuming the seat of influence - after a fight with its current occupant (square MC).

• The Sun and Moon were rising, forming a grand-cross with the angles indicating a completely new dawn; a new age, a new structure to the nation - a new appearance and approach to life (Asc), a new rulership (10H), new treaties and relationships with other countries (7H), and a new legacy and family tree going forwards (4H/ IC).

• William was crowned King William I in December 1066. All monarchs since then are in some way considered to be descendants of William. He brought extensive political, administrative and social changes to the British Isles.

---

1 Bailey, Alice A. The Destiny of the Nations, 67.
2 Great Britain is a geographic term referring to the island, while the United Kingdom includes England, Wales, Scotland and northern Ireland.

Solar eclipse chart for the Magna Carta: 31 Mar, 1215, 21:54, Runnymede, Eng.

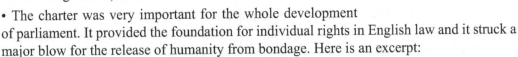

King John reined from 1199 to 1216. He was the notorious and greedy King John in the Robin Hood story. There seems to be truth in the tale because English Barons forced John under fear of death, to sign (place his seal upon), the Magna Carta, on 15 June 1215. The charter bound King John and future kings (Leo, the Sun) to the rule of law (Sun semi-square Jupiter, which rules law and the charter negotiations and document signing).

• The charter is considered to be one of the most influential legal documents in British history. (Eclipse Pluto was in Leo in the 9H, trine the Sun. Major Pluto aspects signify massive changes with far-reaching effects).

• The charter was very important for the whole development of parliament. It provided the foundation for individual rights in English law and it struck a major blow for the release of humanity from bondage. Here is an excerpt:

> No free man shall be seized or imprisoned, or stripped of his rights or possessions, or outlawed or exiled, or deprived of his standing in any other way, nor will we proceed with force against him, or send others to do so, except by the lawful judgement of his equals or by the law of the land.

• The IC represents the legacy of the charter. Three stars in the constellation Pegasus are located there. Pegasus is the Winged Horse who was born from the blood of Medusa when Perseus cut off her head - symbolically, cutting off the king's power. Pegasus flew to heaven, an analogy for the elevated effect the charter would have on future generations.

2. Birth of the Commonwealth of England: 27 March, 12:00, 1649, London.

Parliamentarians (Roundheads) led by Oliver Cromwell fought Royalists in the English Civil War (1642 to 1651); over issues of governance and religion. The Roundheads won, executed the king (Charles I), abolished the monarchy and founded a republic - the Commonwealth of England on the 27th March in 1649. It was short-lived, ending in 1660 (Sun in Aries square Uranus).

During the period of the republic, Cromwell ruled as Lord Protector. Within 2 years of his death in 1658, the monarchy was restored with the consent of Parliament. The civil wars effectively set England and Scotland on course towards a parliamentary-monarchy form of government.

3. Birth of England - King Charles II: 29 May 1660, 12:00, London.

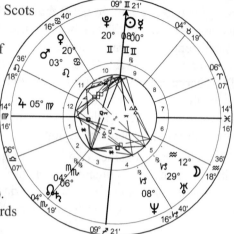

When Oliver Cromwell executed Charles I, the Scots proclaimed his son Charles, King of Scotland.

However, Charles' reign as King Charles II of England, only began when he entered London. This was on 29 May 1660 around noon. [1] The people were jubilant with this change of leadership.

• After the austerity and heaviness of Oliver Cromwell (Taurus Sun), Londoners welcomed the lighter and brighter Charles (Gemini Sun). Cromwell was a Puritan who was intolerant towards Catholicism.

• Charles is considered to be one of the most popular English monarchs (Sun trine Moon) and was called the "Merry Monarch." A Gemini Sun person, he was attuned to the nation's Gemini soul and the importance of education. He was a patron of education and founded a number of schools. His greatest test came a few years later when the plague hit and then the great fire.

4. The Great Plague of London, 1665-66.

Lunar eclipse for the Great Plague, 31 Jan 1665, 06:18, London;
around England (Charles II) natal.

Rats carried the fleas that caused the bubonic plague. (Virgo - rising in the natal chart, rules small rodents). The earliest infections appeared in spring (March-May) of 1665. The death rate rose during summer, peaking in September when 7,165 Londoners died in one week. Overall, it killed an estimated 100,000 in 18 months - almost a quarter of London's population. Here is how its effects were described by two eyewitness observers.

(i). Some were immediately overwhelmed: violent fevers, vomitings, insufferable headaches, pains in the back, ravings and ragings with those pains. Others with swellings and tumours in the neck or groin, or armpits, which till they could be broke put them into insufferable agonies and torment. Others were silently infected. [2]

---

1 Campion gave the date as 19 May 1660 (page 341). However, Britannica records the date as the 29th May. https://kids.britannica.com/kids/article/Charles-II/476238. Charles was born 29 May and he entered London on his 30th birthday.
2 Daniel Defoe (1660-1731), 18th century account of the plague in, A Journal of the Plague Year

(ii). Every day sadder and sadder news of its increase. In the City died this week 7,496; and of them 6,102 of the plague. But it is feared that the true number of the dead this week is near 10,000 – partly from the poor that cannot be taken notice of through the greatness of the number. [1]

• The evolutionary pattern shaping events is a separating Saturn-Pluto opposition. The conjunction 15-16 years previously, marked the birth of the English Republic under Oliver Cromwell. He lasted until the first Saturn-Pluto quarter.

• Charles II's return in 1660 coincided with London's explosion as an international metropolis. From its port, ships came and went to all parts of the globe. One or more brought in the plague (Venus in Pisces, ruler of the 9H of shipping, with Taurus on the cusp).

• The virulence of the disease and the toll it took on the local population is represented by eclipse Mars and Uranus on the cusp of the nation's 6H of health (Uranus rules the 6H with Aquarius on the cusp). Mars rules the 8H of death and its trine to the Lord of Death Pluto, portends the deadly toll the disease would take on the health of the city.

• Open drains were breeding grounds for germs. As a consequence of the disease, the city was re-structured, with improved sanitation and sewerage disposal (eclipse Pluto opposite Saturn).

5. The Great London Fire: 2 September 1666.

Solar eclipse for the Great Fire: 2 Jul 1666, 07:46, around England (Charles II) natal.

• Fire is the greatest purifying agent and it burnt out the residue of the plague. The eclipse chart warned of the danger of a massive fire.

The eclipse Asc is in fiery Leo, conjunct the star *Adhafera* (23 Leo) - "liquid fire." The fire reached a very high temperature with combustible fuel added to the blaze. Opposite *Adhafera*, was Uranus, adding its electrical and highly incendiary force.

Additionally, eclipse Sun-Moon are conjunct the great star *Sirius* (9 Cancer). One of this star's names is 'Scorching'.

• The fire started in a baker's shop. Eclipse Sun-Moon are in Cancer that rules bakers (domestic trades), square eclipse Mars. About 4/5 of the city was destroyed.

• After the purification of the fire, the city was transformed (eclipse Mercury, ruler of the Asc, conjunct natal Pluto 10H). In an attempt to avoid a future plague, living conditions and sanitation improvements were made (eclipse Sun-Moon sextile natal Asc, eclipse Uranus 6H trine natal Sun, MC, Pluto). The city was restructured (eclipse Sun-Moon trine natal Saturn). Streets were widened, open sewers were abolished and the capital became a healthier and more attractive environment in which to live.

---

1   Samuel Pepys was the UK's most famous diarist from the period. He was a navy administrator and civil servant.

Just 22 years after these catastrophes another upheaval took place. When James II assumed the throne in 1685, his overt Roman Catholicism alienated Protestants. Fearing a revival of Catholic control, William of Orange (later William III of England), was asked by rebels to take control of the nation. He did and the Glorious Revolution (1688-1689), a mostly bloodless revolt, occurred.

6. Birth of Great Britain: 12 May 1707, 00:00, Westminster.

William was succeeded to the throne by Queen Anne, who was on the throne when the Treaty of Union was signed, creating the new state of Great Britain - the merged parliaments of England and Scotland. This happened on 12 May 1707.

• But further trouble was ahead (Mars on an angle). In 1745, 'Bonnie Prince Charlie', the grandson of James II, gathered an army in Scotland and marched south to claim the English throne as Charles III. His forces were defeated at Culloden, ending the Jacobite revolt of 1745-1746. Charles spent the rest of his life hiding in Europe. Later, in 1775, Britain went to war against rebels in its Americas colonies. The rebels won and the colonies declared their independence.

• In this incarnation period, the Industrial Age began around 1760 (Capricorn rising),

7. Birth of the United Kingdom: 1 January 1801, 00:00, Westminster.

Then in 1801 the major rebirth that still exists today, took place. This occurred when the United Kingdom was formed, a merging of England, Wales, Scotland and Ireland. Although Ireland left the union in 1921, this natal chart is still used today for the United Kingdom.

• The chart is dominated by Uranus rising and Saturn moving into opposition with Pluto. Old structures were being shattered and tremendous changes were taking place.

• The conjunction of Saturn and Pluto 15 years before saw the United States War of Independence, convicts being shipped to Australia and pressure to abolish the slave trade.

The next 100 plus years (3 Saturn-Pluto cycles), were strife-filled. Nations fought to expand their borders and control the world's resources. Britain fought Napoleon (1793-1815), and the Crimean war against Russia (1853 to 1856). Then came the UK's greatest fights for survival - the World Wars in the early 20th Century.

8. The United Kingdom in World War I and the Spanish Flu.

In the troubled period of the early 20th Century, the UK was swept up in the events following the assassination of Austria's Duke Ferdinand. It declared war on Germany on 4 August 1914, drawing in simultaneously, Commonwealth countries.

Blood Moon eclipse for WWI: 15 Sep 1913, 12:45, London; around UK natal.

• War-planets Mars-Pluto on the MC, portended that the UK would go to war, and it would shatter the nation (Mars-Pluto form a grand-cross on the angles, igniting the natal Uranus-Sun square).

• Eclipse Mars is on the star *Menkalinan* (29 Gemini), warning of ruin and violent death. This star is in the constellation Auriga, the Charioteer, a parallel symbol to the Biblical Four Horsemen of the Apocalypse that portends a major war.

Almost a million British died - over 19,000 on the first day of the Battle of the Somme (1916). This battle has a prominent place in British history, representing the dire cost involved in settling international disputes by war. But that was the way it was then. The toll that the machine-gun and other modern weapons took, the brutality and carnage; this caused some to call WWI the "War to end all wars!" Yet 19 years later, a greater conflagration took place - WWII.

• The 1919 'Treaty of Versailles', signed at the end of WWI, imposed penalties on Germany, which fuelled poisonous nationalist sentiment and led to the rise of Adolf Hitler. In the meantime, another more insidious battle was waging - the flu epidemic.

Lunar eclipse for the Spanish Flu: 15 Jul 1916, 05:40 London; around UK natal.

• The virus dominated the world, including the UK, which the stellium in Cancer around the MC depicts. It was spread by troops returning from the war.

• The UK is susceptible to viral pandemics. Natal Jupiter which makes everything so much bigger than normal, is on 2-degrees Leo, the Sabian Symbol epidemic degree; and Neptune that represents viruses rules the UK 6H of health.

• Eclipse Neptune, hit Jupiter and the epidemic degree. The flu flooded seamlessly through the nation. A quarter of the British population were affected and 228,000 died.

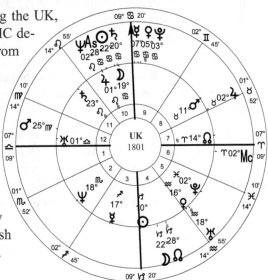

9. The United Kingdom in World War II.

Blood Moon eclipse for WWII: 3 May 1939, 16:15, London; around UK natal.

• On 3 September 1939, at 10:15, Prime Minister Neville Chamberlain announced "This country is at war with Germany." Troops were drawn from ordinary households across the Commonwealth. The Sabian Symbol for the eclipse Asc (30 Virgo), is "An emergency call frees householders from routine duty. Rising to the occasion."

• The causal WWII eclipse t-square - Pluto-Mars-Saturn, fell in houses 7, 10 and 4. They represented the enemy (7), the government who made the decision to go to war (10); and the people who would fight the war and be killed in it (Mars in 4).

Mars also rules the 7H of open enemies. Germany was a formidable, well-organised and equipped killing-machine.

• Hitler and Goebbels versus Churchill and Roosevelt; it is possible they were reincarnations of ancient gladiators from an ancient war fought aeons ago in Atlantis; [1] returning millenniums later to complete that unfinished battle. The millions who sacrificed their lives to fight the Nazi evil is immeasurable. The meaning of the Sabian Symbol for the eclipse IC (30 Sag) is, "Effective and spectacular sacrifice of self in service to the race".

Winston Churchill: 30 Nov 1874, 01:30, Woodstock, Eng.

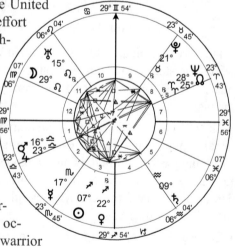

• Winston Churchill is the hero of WWII. Before United States entry, he took up the fight and held the effort together in the dark days when defeat loomed. Without him - and those he inspired to fight; we may now have Nazi over-lords.

• The angles of Churchill's chart (and stars on them), are identical within a few minutes to the angles in the eclipse chart that warned the war was coming. He was born to fight it.

• He was a 1st ray soul, a man forged from spiritual steel. His superb leadership skills (Ray 1), speaking skills (Virgo Ascendant, Mercury in Scorpio), and an ability to inspire people to rise to the occasion (Sun in Sagittarius); held the line until his warrior brother Roosevelt, came to his and the world's assistance.

1 Bailey, Alice A. Initiation, Human and Solar, 35.

After the tremendous challenges in the 18th, 19th and early 20th Centuries; the UK was battered, its military forces were diminished and it was broke. Russia and the United States who had ramped up their industries to feed their war efforts became the new super-powers militarily and economically. The UK could no longer compete.

10. United Kingdom, Brexit and Covid-19.

Outer chart: lunar eclipse for Covid-19: 16 Jul 2019, 22:39, London;
Middle chart: solar arc directions for 16 July; inner chart: UK natal.

• Natal Jupiter parked on the epidemic degree of 2 Leo, renders the UK very susceptible to epidemics. A reason for this is because its leaders can make crucial mistakes through over-confidence. As did Boris Johnson who did not lock down the nation early enough because of a belief that herd immunity would develop and this would protect the public.

• The eclipse hit natal Jupiter, exploding the virus' toxicity. Additionally, Neptune that rules viruses was in the 6H of health in a t-square with Jupiter, Mars, Mercury in the 3H; and solar-arc Neptune in the 9H.

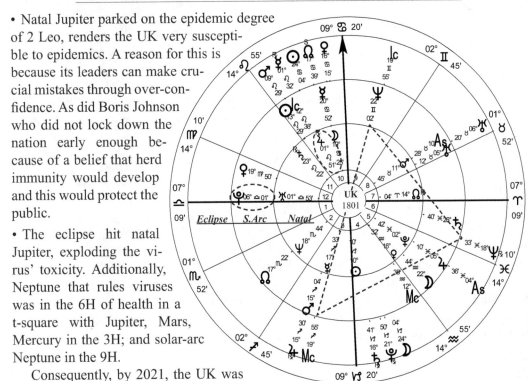

Consequently, by 2021, the UK was one of the worst affected nations [1] with over 75 thousand dead and 2.93 million infected. This in a nation of 67 million. By 2021 containment measures were in place, but the virus had bolted and everything after that was an attempt to clean up the mess.

• Another reason the virus has been so virulent is Brexit. Years of stress and arguing about leaving the EU, lowered vitality, rendering people susceptible to infection. With the Brexit vote, the UK took control of its destiny and is now going through a rebirth (solar-arc Pluto crossing the Asc). There is further disruption ahead and "deaths" (the Commonwealth disintegrating?), with solar-arc Pluto moving into and through the 1H.

• *Changes indicated by the Covid eclipse:* The IC, the legacy point of the eclipse chart, is in the 9H on *Hoedus II* (20 Gemini), a star in the Charioteer. This constellation brings major winds and storms (Brexit, Covid). Long term, the competitive spirit of this great nation will be unleashed, giving it an opportunity to fly to greater successes - the Charioteer winning the race. Additionally, (with the IC in Gemini that rules UK's soul, conjunct solar-arc Neptune), this period will have a spiritually transformative effect on the nation long-term.

1   13 Jan 2021: the 7th ranked nation in the world for deaths per capita.

11. The Spiritual Destiny of the United Kingdom.

The personality of the UK is ruled by Taurus and Ray 1 of Will & Power

• England has demonstrated to the world its stubborn, bullish and aggressive personality; its mental, political, nation and empire-building power (Taurus personality, 1st ray influence, Capricorn Sun on the IC and Uranus rising square MC).

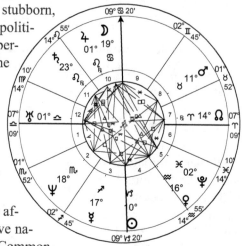

United Kingdom 1801

• Mars in Taurus symbolises the vicious bulldog with a bite to match its bark. Its sextile to the MC and trine to the Sun, indicates the inherent strength in the nation, its endurance and fighting power - qualities that can be called upon whenever troubles arise.

• Uranus rising dominates the Asc, and therefore affects all the angles. This indicates the progressive nature of Britain and some of the more advanced Commonwealth nations, and their ability to continually go through internal renewals in order to adapt to the changing world.

• Since 1801, the UK's wealth-minded Taurus personality has been working through an ambitious Capricorn Sun. In its early years, the nation took full advantage of the business opportunities presented by the Industrial Revolution and Capitalism. London has become the World's Financial Hub. It is the highest net exporter of financial services. The Sun trine Mars in the 8H of business and corporate money, confirms this; conjunct the IC, this prosperity will endure. Along with this, the Moon in Taurus indicates the nation's limiting pattern is a too strong attachment to materialism, comfort and unbridled greed.

The soul of the UK is ruled by Gemini and Ray 2 of Love & Wisdom.

• The United Kingdom is old and experienced and is one of the most spiritually advanced nations in the world. This does not discount the fact that there are disruptions at the physical and personality levels because of the influx of people continuously moving into the country. It is a magnet for refugees and asylum seekers because of its human-rights record. It continues to grow as a nation and to recognise what works for the good of its people and what does not.

> The United Kingdom's spiritual keynote is: "I recognise my other self (what is old and does not work) and in the waning of that self I grow and glow." [1]

The UK has a spiritually enlightened soul that is intelligent, group-conscious and inclusive: [2] its symbol is the three feathers, representing the three aspects of Spirit, Soul and Body. Somewhere in the early to Middle Ages it was given the task of guiding humanity's spiritual (not religious) development, at the heart of which was to implement Aquarian Age values

---

1   Bailey, Alice A. Esoteric Astrology, 654
2   In esoteric terms, it is the "Custodian of the wisdom aspect of the second ray force for the Aryan race. Bailey, Alice A. Esoteric Psychology I, 387.

such as human-rights, fairness and justice. This was notably seen in the Magna Carta, which enshrined values that all developed nations in the world now have as the basis upon which they run their societies. This was a tremendously profound and wonderful evolutionary and spiritual gift that England gave to the world.

In this sense, the UK is an agent of the Aquarian Age (Uranus conjunct the Asc, sextile Jupiter, the esoteric ruler of Aquarius. Venus, the esoteric ruler of Gemini, is in Aquarius).

• Though it is no longer the most powerful nation on earth in material terms, it is the heart of the voice of reason and wisdom and will continue to wield considerable moral weight and be a steadying influence in the world for many centuries.

The UK's spiritual motto is, "I serve." [1]

Very simply, the UK's higher task is to serve the people of the world.

---

1   Bailey, Alice A. The Destiny of the Nations, 50.

United States of America.

The United States personality is ruled by Gemini, its soul by Aquarius. [1]

Native American Indians and Inuit are the indigenous people of the United States (US). Gemini - the social and travelling sign brought millions of immigrants to the continent. This has slowed down the integration of the personality of the nation. Each time a great number of people arrive, such as at the end of the World Wars; another period of absorption has to take place. In time, as its deeply entrenched materialism is overcome - and with Aquarius ruling its soul; this great nation is destined to lead the way into the Aquarian Age.

1. Christopher Columbus discovers the Americas: 12 October 1492.

Italian explorer Christopher Columbus (1451-1506) landed in the Bahamas and never set foot on United States soil. However, his four trips led to the widespread knowledge of the "New World," and the other explorers and settlers arrived shortly after.

Lunar eclipse for Columbus Bahamas landing: 5 Oct 1492, 17:39, Nassau, Bahamas.

• Columbus landed in the Bahamas on 12 October 1492. The eclipse Moon is rising (discovery of a new land), on the pioneering and explorative Aries Asc.

• Aries represents migration as well as large scale aggression, military actions and barbaric raiding, correctly portending what was to follow as the invaders moved in. The eclipse is powerful, lying on the angles of the chart and in a t-square with Uranus, the Awakener. In a sense, the birth of a new nation.

• Columbus is represented by Neptune in the 9H in Sagittarius - sailing across the oceans on a voyage of discovery.

• All 16th and 17th Century European settlements were challenged by disease, hunger, danger from local Indians and from rival European nations (Sun in 6H of health, conjunct 7H cusp of open enemies; challenged Moon rules the 4H of the land, indigenous people and attempts to settle).

• The evolutionary pattern that was shaping events was a Saturn to Pluto square, indicating destruction of the old and the building new and futuristic (Aquarius) structures. Their conjunction occurred in 1482, around the time that Columbus began seeking patronage for his explorations. The square aspect was just separating when Columbus landed in the Bahamas.

The first permanent English settlement attempt was at Jamestown, Virginia in 1606. Later, the Mayflower pilgrims arrived in Plymouth Bay in 1620. As the numbers of settlers grew, conflict arose with Indians who fought to protect their lands and people from the more ruthless amongst the newcomers. But they were defeated by the sheer numbers coming in who believed they had a right to take the land.

1 Bailey, Alice A. The Destiny of the Nations, 67.

2. The American War of Independence, 1775-1783.

Lunar eclipse for the Boston Tea Party, 30 Sep 1773, 13:16, Boston;
around the Kingdom of Great Britain 1707 natal.

• The colonials wanted to be free of punitive British controls and taxes (evolutionary pattern dominating the event, Neptune conjunct Saturn - the desire to be free of rigid controls).

• The 'Boston Tea Party' happened on 16 Dec 1773, when rebels threw British tea into the sea to protest taxes (eclipse stellium falls in 8H of death and taxes). It ignited the trouble. The British mobilised and marched. On 16 April 1775, Paul Revere rode to Concord to warn the British were coming, a deed immortalised by poet Henry Longfellow. The closing verse is:

In darkness and peril and need, the people
will waken and listen to hear, the hurrying
hoof-beats of that steed, and the midnight message
of Paul Revere.

• In the later years of the war, other countries that held grudges against Britain joined the colonials - notably France. After George Washington's victory at Yorktown in 1781, Britain's defeat was inevitable. This was portended in the chart by eclipse Pluto on Britain's Asc. It symbolised cutting the umbilical cord to the Mother-land. There were almost 24,000 US casualties from various causes. Britain's were much higher, around 50,000.

3. Birth of the United States Republic: 4 Jul 1776, 17:10, Philadelphia, PA.

On 4 July 1776, delegates from the 13 colonies adopted the Declaration of Independence. Since then, July 4th has been celebrated as the birth of American independence. The chart from that date is still currently used today.

• The 17:10 Sibley chart giving a 12 Sagittarius Asc is used in this book. Justifying that time is the fact that on the day of the 9/11 terrorist attack, transit Pluto that rules terrorism, was exactly conjunct the Asc.

• Uranus on the DC angle represents the revolutionary fervour that preceded the declaration, and that the desire for independence was the way to go (Uranus sextile north-node).

4. The American Civil War, 1861 - 1865.

Millions of slaves had been brought from Africa to work cotton plantations. They were bought, sold, mated and traded like cattle. This inhuman treatment ignited the war.

Lunar eclipse for the Civil War: 1 Aug 1860, 12:24, Washington: around US natal.

• When Lincoln was elected President on 4 March 1961 on an anti-slavery platform, southern states seceded. This triggered the war. The US was going through its first Uranus return, an appropriate time for a revolution.

• Slavery was the issue. Eclipse Pluto was conjunct *Achird* (8 Taurus), a star in Cassiopeia, that represents bondage and slavery. The Moon and Sun were t-square Pluto and *Achird*.

• The main part of the war was brutal (eclipse Sun in 8H of death; Mars conjunct natal Pluto). In the aftermath, much of the South was left in ruins. An estimated 750,000 soldiers died and millions more were injured.

• The war ended in 1865, and on 6 December 1865, the 13th amendment to the US Constitution abolishing slavery was ratified. But it is not over for some. According to historian David Blight, it left "a culture of death and mourning." Many Southerners are stuck in the past. Brandishing the Confederate flag, stewing in their bitterness, such people continue to oppose the country's changing moral character and racial demographics. Much of this underlies modern-day racism in the US.

Abraham Lincoln, 12 Feb 1809, 06:54, Hodgenville, Kentucky.

• Great souls appear at the founding of a nation and Lincoln was such a man. With Aquarius governing his Sun and Asc, his task was to establish in the US nation, the Aquarian Age principles of universal brotherhood, justice and fairness. The legal abolishing of slavery was his great accomplishment, along with the preservation of the Union and vindication of democracy.

When the South seceded, Lincoln said: "Secession would destroy the only democracy in existence and prove for all time - to both future Americans and the world - that a government of the people could not survive."

• On his MC was great the military star *Antares* (7 Sagittarius), conjunct inclusive Neptune and stable Saturn. Against all odds, he won the battle, restructuring the nation upon a healthier psychological, moral and spiritual basis.

5. The US in World War I and the Spanish Flu.

Blood Moon eclipse for WWI: 15 Sep 1913, 07:48, Washington; around US natal.

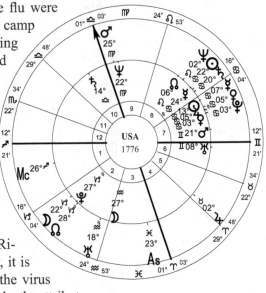

• The war eclipse hit the angles of the US chart, making it inevitable that it would become heavily involved. When Germany began torpedoing its passenger and merchant ships, President Woodrow Wilson declared war on 6 April 1917 (war planets Pluto and Mars are in the 7H of open enemies.

Boosted by the presence of millions of American soldiers and supplies, the Allies pushed back the Germans on the Western Front and on the morning of 11 November 1918, Germany surrendered. The US suffered over 116,000 military deaths and 200,000 wounded.

• WWI marked the end of an era and rise of the US to become a global super-power. The eclipse Sun on the MC, trine natal Pluto in the 2H of business, sextile natal Mercury in the 8H of international finance; prophesied this mega-rise of fortunes.

Lunar eclipse for Spanish Flu: 14 Jul 1916, 22:40, Fort Riley; around United States natal.

• In the US, the first recorded cases of the flu were in March 1918 at Fort Riley, a US Army camp in Kansas. However, it had been circulating amongst soldiers in Europe since 1916 and its appearance at an army camp suggests it was brought home by a soldier returning from the war-zone (eclipse Mars in the 9H conjunct natal Neptune).

• It was clear in the astrology that the outbreak in the US was going to be virulent (the eclipse Sun and Neptune that represents the virus, are in the 8H of death, opposite Pluto).

• About a third of the 15,000 people at Fort Riley became infected, and 800 died. Overall, it is reported that more US soldiers died from the virus than were killed in the war, and many of the deaths attributed to WWI were related flu deaths. Overall, 63,114 of its people died from disease - largely due to the epidemic, while 53,402 died in combat.

• The terrible virulence of the virus is explained by the eclipse Sun and Moon aligning with the powerful 1st magnitude star *Pollux* (22 Cancer), in the 8H of death. One of this star's names is "The Heartless Judge." When afflicted, it brings calamities, virulent diseases that cause extreme sickness, fevers and death.

6. The Great Depression, 1929-1939.

The Great Depression was the worst economic downturn in the history of the industrialized world, lasting from the stock market crash of 24 October 1929 to 1939.

Total Solar eclipse for Crash:
9 May 1929, 02:07, New York.

• The eclipse is in Taurus, the greedy sign. It rules most of the US 5H of speculation, the stock exchange and share market. The eclipse stellium falls in the US 5H (see the chart below).

• Venus is the lord of the eclipse (as ruler of Taurus). Ruling money and business, in the eclipse chart it rules the 8H of international finance. The destruction of the stock-market, the crashing economy and repercussions on international finance are shown by its square to Pluto in the 5H. Pluto is the natural ruler of the 8H.

• The consequential depression is shown by dominant Saturn at the top of the chart.

Total Solar eclipse for Crash: 9 May 1929, 02:07, New York (outer circle);
around Solar-Arc Directions (middle circle), and the US natal (inner circle.

• With shares over-valued (Mars, ruling the 5H; eclipse stellium in a grand-cross with eclipse Neptune, solar-arc Mars and Neptune); the stock market crashed (eclipse Saturn opposite natal Mars). The nation and the world went into a deep depression (Saturn in the US 1H).

• Republican President Herbert Hoover refused to help on the principle that the government should not intervene in the economy or provide economic relief for people. His decision killed off his Presidency and people died.

• Franklin Roosevelt became President in 1932. His 'New Deal' public work projects and financial regulations reformed Wall Street and brought relief. He saved the day. The nation came out of the depression into a hopeful new reality and sense of self (directed Sun moving from the 12H into the 1H).

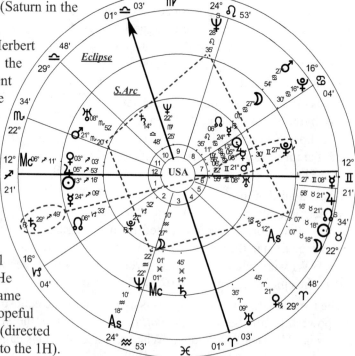

7. The US in World War II.

Blood Moon eclipse for WWII: 3 May 1939, 10:16, Washington; around US natal.

In the early years of the war, Roosevelt covertly give support to the UK.

• Then Pearl Harbour happened on 7 Dec 1941. It was a sneak attack (eclipse Pluto that rules the covert 12H, falls in the US 8H of death and destruction). The US declared war on 8 Dec 1941 and set about rapidly equipping a vast military force and providing material aid for its allies (Mars in 2H of business and money, opposite Pluto). Industry boomed and there were progressive cultural changes made (Sun-Uranus in 5H). The need for workers removed discrimination in the labour market for Negroes, women and other minority groups who filled positions previously held by white men.

• The toll was high (Pluto in 8H), with 416,800 US military deaths. By now, the US was truly the global super-power (eclipse Jupiter, planet of magnificence and expansion, is conjunct the IC of the US chart, indicating the prosperous legacy that was to follow the war.

Franklin Delano Roosevelt, 30 Jan 1882, 20:35, Hyde Park, NY.

• Roosevelt was born into a privileged family. He was inspired to run for office by his distant cousin "Uncle" Teddy Roosevelt, becoming a NY State Senator in 1910. In August of 1921, he was suddenly paralysed in both legs due to polio. This potential was in his chart with Neptune (the polio virus), conjunct Jupiter (mobility). Neptune co-ruled the 6H of health with Pisces sharing the 6H cusp.

• Roosevelt continued his career in politics. In 1932, he campaigned for president on a promise that his government would be responsible for the welfare of the people (Moon in 10H sextile Saturn). He was elected and served from 1933 to 1945. He fought for the workers of America (Mars 10H trine Mercury in the 6H of the working classes).

His enduring legacy was to steer the US admirably through the Great Depression and WWII, and to shape the image of the President as the caretaker of the American people.

• Roosevelt was an Aquarian Age man (Sun in Aquarius), a social reformer, with a discerning and uncanny ability to find the best solutions to help and heal the nation (Uranus on Virgo Asc).

8. Attack on the World Trade Centre and Invasion of Iraq: 2001.

Lunar eclipse for 9/11: 5 Jul 2001, 11:04, NY; around the US.

On 11 September 2001, two passenger planes hi-jacked by Al-Qaeda terrorists, crashed into the World Trade Center in New York, killing almost 3,000 people (eclipse Mars-Pluto on the US Asc, opposite Saturn and natal Mars and Uranus).

• By 2018, nearly 10,000 people who were in the area were diagnosed with cancer and more than 2,000 deaths have been attributed to 9/11 illnesses. (Eclipse Venus is in the 6H of health on the *Pleiades* stars (0 Gemini), that portends suffering through fires and sickness).

• President George Bush used the catastrophe to invade Iraq (20 March 2003), incorrectly inferring it was behind 9/11. It destroyed Iraq and led to instability in the region. Some observers believe it increased Islamic extremism and their attacks on the West.

The legacy of 9/11 was further death and destruction that has continued into the 21st Century and is not over yet. (Eclipse Mars-Pluto, as well as being conjunct the US Asc, are on the eclipse IC at 16 Sagittarius, indicating the legacy that was to follow this event).

9. Covid-19, Racism, and the Trump influence.

Lunar eclipse for Covid-19: 16 Jul 2019, 17:38, Washington; around USA natal.

• Covid's destructive path has been greater in the US than in any other country. It was always going to be difficult to contain. The country is vast with thousands coming through its international airports every day.

But President Trump's mishandling of the crisis, trying to save the economy rather than people, casting off the problem to state governors to handle rather than manage a central, federal approach; made things very much worse than they needed to be.

• By 2021, the USA was the hardest hit nation in the world - 364 thousand dead and 21.5 million infected (eclipse stellium in 8H of death). This in a nation of 328 million people. In fairness, it is much harder to contain pandemics in large nations with dense populations and vast borders to control. By January 2021, the US was the 11th ranked nation in the world for deaths per capita.

9a. The Murder of George Floyd on 25 May 2020.

Lunar eclipse for the murder of George Floyd: 10 Jan 2020, 13:21,
Minneapolis: around US natal chart.

• George Floyd was a 46-year-old black man and US citizen. On 25 May 2020 he was publicly murdered (Mars conjunct Asc). A white police officer knelt on his neck for 9 minutes while he was handcuffed and lying face down in the street. He begged for his life, saying "I can't breathe" and calling out for his mother. Racism goes back to the founding of the country. The only thing different this time was that the execution was filmed. It caused world-wide protests against institutionalised racism.

• This violence happened on a Saturn-Pluto conjunction. Consequently, it began a 33-year process that will see the purging of racist attitudes and practices in political and law and order departments. Changes in law will be made to solidify this process (Jupiter in Capricorn opposite natal Sun, trine Uranus).

• The legacy of the eclipse is indicated by the star *Talitha* (3 Leo), on the IC of the eclipse chart. In the Bible (Mark 5: 22-23), we read that Talitha was dying and Jesus healed her and raised her up. This is a metaphor for the healing and raising up of African Americans

9b. The influence of Donald Trump on America.

Donald Trump natal chart: 14 Jun 1946, 10:54, Queens, NY; around US natal.

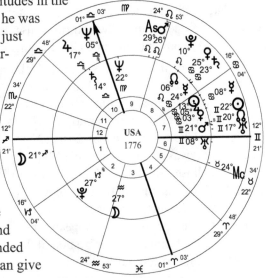

Trump paid the price for his perceived ineptitudes in the November 2020 Presidential election, when he was overwhelmingly voted out of office after just one term. Many of his detractors say he tarnished the office of the President with lies, corruption and by embracing the White Supremacy movement.

Unable to accept that he lost the 2020 election, he cried "foul", repeatedly told the American people the election was stolen. Millions blindly accepted what he said, rather than face the reality of for instance, two recounts of the Georgia vote overseen by a Republican Governor, and multi-courtcases that dismissed his unfounded claims. Why is this? As always, astrology can give insight and an answer.

• Firstly, Trump dominated the emotions of the American people - at least those driven by their desires, wants and wishes (his Sun-Uranus conjuncts the US Mars and his Moon is rising in the 1H opposite). Mars is a symbol for the solar plexus chakra, which is the seat of emotionalism in the body. Trump was able to electrify with excitement, those who were susceptible to his message and whose sense of discrimination and common sense were not strong enough to overcome his charismatic power. This excludes all those intelligent people who supported him for other personal or cynical reasons.

• Secondly, Trump's natal Neptune dominates the US MC. Neptune throws glamour over people, rendering them susceptible to illusion and being taken in by charlatans and liars. This is a reason why millions blindly accepted whatever he said and who looked to him as a sort of messiah to alleviate their troubles.

• Thirdly, when he ran for office in 2016, transit Neptune was moving over the US progressed Sun. It was just moving on at the time of the 2020 election, allowing enough people to break free of Trump's spell to help vote him out of office.

• Trump is a representative of the Leo Age of, "it is all about me!" He has Leo rising in his chart. He carried this into his politics with the theme of "Put America first," then into the handling of Covid-19. When the virus began killing Americans in their thousands, he encouraged people to be selfish and to put themselves first. He mocked those who encouraged people to be responsible and to look after vulnerable Americans by for example, wearing masks. But the age of the Leo autocrat has passed. Not only are we moving into the Aquarian Age, but in 2018 *Regulus* the star of "kings", moved into modest and serving Virgo. People are demanding more accountability from their leaders and higher moral standards.

• Evolution is leaving dictators like Trump behind. Rapidly becoming relics of the past, their days are numbered as our solar system continues to move into the Aquarian Age of collective responsibility.

9c. Attack on the Capitol, 6 January 2021.

Total Solar eclipse for Attack: 14 Dec 2020, 11:17, Washington: around US natal.

• The Saturn-Pluto pattern was still in effect, enclosing between their destructive and transformational forces, Jupiter, which rules moral, beliefs, religion and important Supreme Court changes.

• Observers say that Trump's repeated claim that the election was stolen and that patriotic Americans had to do something about it led directly to this attack on the capitol.

This is borne out by the star *Ensis* (23 Gemini), that was aligned with natal Mars and the eclipse Sun and Moon. *Ensis* means 'sword.' The mob at the capitol was Trump's sword, which he incited because of his loss at the ballot box. It appeared he wanted them to bring down the bastion of democracy so that he could rule the nation. *Ensis* portends arrogance, violence, rape and danger of treachery.

10. The Spiritual Destiny of the US.

The   of the US is ruled by Gemini
and Ray 6 of Devotion & Idealism.

• Generally, the US is quite a conservative and devout nation. Research in 2020 found about 3/4 of the population have a religious or spiritual affiliation. But Neptune (in the 9H) is seriously afflicted in Virgo, and religious and ideological conflicts have created divisions in the nation, which are being fought out to this day (Neptune square Mars).

• The Gemini personality has contributed to this chaos. It has weakened the integrative work that is necessary to produce a strong nation, by bringing to the fore too many selfish voices, with too much to say, so there are too many competing ideologies.

• The major conflict is between isolationists (Moon in Aquarius), who reject the multi-cultural and inclusive policies of the great presidents Lincoln and Roosevelt (sesquiquadrate Saturn in 10H, exalted in the sign of justice and balance, Libra).

The soul of the US is ruled by Aquarius
and Ray 2 of Love & Wisdom.

The US is playing a vital political role in the world today, because it is there that Democracy is being fought out. Democracy is defined as "government by the people through elected representatives." However, the eastern Master Djwhal Khul said:

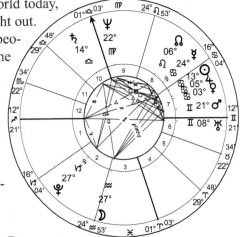

USA 1776 natal

> True Democracy is as yet unknown; it awaits the time when an educated and enlightened public opinion will bring it to power. *The battle of Democracy will be fought out in the United States.* There the people at present vote and organise their government on a personality basis and not from any spiritual or intelligent conviction. [1]

• The struggle in the US is happening in all other Democracy's to some degree or another, the result of a collective striving to become an "educated and enlightened public".

The US spiritual motto is, "I light the Way." [2]

• America's mission in the world is to "Light the Way." That is, lead the way into the Aquarian Age of universal sharing and brotherliness. If this is its mission, we can understand why the USA, the richest and most prosperous nation on the planet, is being tested so rigorously from the angle of greed.

Unregulated Capitalism is the means through which greed flourishes. It places wealth and power in the hands of privileged elites and widens the gap between the wealthy and poor. By this definition, the US is one of the greediest nations on earth. A report in 2019 stated that "the wealthiest 10% of American households control nearly 75% of household

1 Bailey, Alice A. The Rays and Initiations, 746.
2 Bailey, Alice A. The Destiny of the Nations, 50.

net worth." [1] Greed is responsible for much suffering on earth. This attitude runs counter to Aquarian Age principles and gradually, as more citizens guide their actions by a sense of inclusive unity and love, avaricious leaders will no longer be represented in the halls of power.

• The US chart has only one planet in Aquarius, the sign ruling the soul of America - the Moon at 27 Aquarius. It was interpreted in the US personality section negatively. But the purified Moon also rules Aquarius [2] at its highest spiritual and global (Hierarchy) level. From this angle, the Moon represents the pure universal-sharing forces of Aquarius issuing forth – through America.

• When it sorts out its issues, the United States will fulfill its task to "light the Way." This task is symbolised by *Enif* (29 Aquarius), a triple star, yellow and blue, on the nose of the Winged Horse, Pegasus (conjunct the Moon). The champion Perseus rode Pegasus, who could see where he was going because of the light of the star. This is a symbol for the US leading and lighting the way for all other nations, into the Aquarian Age.

The 20th Century symbol of the US, as the champion of humanity, courageously defending the rights of the citizens of the world, suffered a blow in the early 21st Century under the Trump administration. But Pegasus, the flying-horse is waiting, and when the right rider (President), mounts him, once again the world's champion will ride forth, to be followed by his or her successors

THE END.

---

1   www.usatoday.com Grant Suneson and Samuel Stebbins, 28 May 2019.
2   Bailey, Alice A. Esoteric Astrology, 68.

A final quote:

In the Aquarian Age, as a result of the existing combination of ray influences, humanity enters into an expansion of consciousness which will reveal to him group relations instead of his individual and self-centred personal relations. Aquarius is to be found in the upper half of the zodiacal circle and is exactly opposite to Leo which is found in the lower half. Leo is the sign of individual unfoldment and of the self as self-assertive. This highly individualised sign consummates in Aquarius wherein the individual finds full expression through the medium of the group, passing from service to himself and expression of himself as a personality to service of the group... Humanity has reached a stage where the sense of individuality is rapidly emerging. In every field of human expression, men and women are becoming definitely self-assertive. The Old Commentary refers symbolically to this in the following words:

> "The Lion begins to roar. He rushes forth and, in his urge to live, he wields destruction. And then again he roars and — rushing to the stream of life — drinks deep. Then, having drunk, the magic of the waters works. He stands transformed. The Lion disappears and he who bears the water pot stands forth and starts upon his mission."

Those with vision can see this happening upon every side today. The water-carrier (another name for the world server) is starting upon his self-appointed task. Hence the anchoring upon earth of the New Group of World Servers, whose representatives are found in every land and in every great city. This has taken place without exception in every land and they express many points of view; their field of service is widely differing and their techniques so diverse that in some cases comprehension is not easy to the smaller minded person. But, they all carry the pitcher containing the water of life upon their shoulder, reverting to the language of symbolism, and they all emit the light in some degree throughout their environment.

Bailey, Alice. A. Destiny of the Nations, pages 145 and 146.

Bibliography

Allen, Richard Hinckley. *Star Names*. LSC Communications, 2019.

Bailey, Alice. A. *Destiny of the Nations*. Lucis Press, London, third printing 1968.

Bailey, Alice. A. *Esoteric Astrology*. Lucis Press, London, eighteenth printing 2016.

Bailey, Alice. A. *Esoteric Healing*. Lucis Press, London, eighth printing 1977.

Bailey, Alice. A. *Esoteric Psychology I*. Lucis Press, London, ninth printing 1979

Bailey, Alice. A. *Esoteric Psychology II*. Lucis Press, London, eighth printing 1981.

Bailey, Alice. A. *Externalisation of the Hierarchy*. Lucis Press, London, seventh printing 1982.

Bailey, Alice. A. *Initiation, Human and Solar*. Lucis Press, London, sixth edition 1951.

Bailey, Alice. A. *Letters on Occult Meditation*. Lucis Press, London, eleventh printing 1973.

Bernhart, Arnold. Fixed Stars and Constellations. Self-published, 1989.

Brady, Bernadette. *Fixed Stars*. Samuel Weiser, Inc. 1998.

Bullinger, E. W. *The Witness of the Stars*. Martino Publishing, 2011.

Campion, Nicholas. *The Book of World Horoscopes*. Aquarian Press. 1999.

Carter, C. E. O. *Mundane Astrology*. Astrology Classics, 2004

Ebertin-Hoffman. *Fixed Stars and their Interpretation*. AFA printers, 2009.

Green, H. S. *Mundane Astrology*. Astrology Classics, 2004.

Houck, C. M. *The Celestial Scriptures*. Writer's Club Press, 2002.

Jones, Dr Marc Edmund. *The Sabian Symbols*. Aurora Press, 1993.

Manilius, Marcus. *Manilius Astronomica*. Goold translation. Harvard University Press, 1997.

Morse, Dr Eric. *The Living Stars*. Amethyst Books, 1988.

Noonan, George C. *Fixed Stars and Judicial Astrology*. AFA printers, 2009.

Oken, Alan. Complete Astrology. Bantam Books, 1988.

O'Reilly, Michael. *Political Astrology*. Wingspan Press, 2005.

Ptolemy, Claudius. *The Almagest*. Princeton University Press, 1998.

Raphael. *Mundane Astrology*. Astrology Classics, 2004.

Rigor, Joseph E. *The Power of Fixed Stars*. Astrology & Spiritual Publishers Inc. 1979.

Robson, Vivian. *Fixed Stars & Constellations in Astrology*. Astrology Classics, 2005.

Rosenberg. Diana K. *Secrets of the Ancient Skie*s, volumes 1 & 2. Libra Press, 2012

Rudhyar, Dane. *The Astrology of Personality*. Aurora Press, 1991.

Visser, Cornelius. *Cassiopeia Unveiled*. Self-published. 1996

Index

Printed in the USA
CPSIA information can be obtained
at www.ICGtesting.com
LVHW071602301123
765048LV00105B/1107